McDOUGAL LITTELL

STUDENT ATLAS OF THE WORLD

McDougal Littell

Evanston, Illinois • Boston • Dallas

ALTERNATIVE PROGRAMS DEPT.
OSCEOLA COUNTY SCHOOLS

Published by

MAPQUEST

Copyright © 2005
by MapQuest.com, Inc.
All rights reserved.
Printed in Canada

ISBN 0-618-37779-4

Acknowledgements:
"Using This Atlas", written by Elspeth Leacock.

Mexico State coat of arms on page 76, © 2003 mexican-flag.com

Photographs on pages 24–25 (Deserts, Nature, China/Tibet, Alaska, Brazil, Arctic), 26–27 (Landscapes, Nature, Australia, China/ Tibet), 59 (rivers), 60–61(nature, Landscapes, Hawaii, Caribbean), 62–63 (Arctic) Copyright © 2003 Corel corp. and their suppliers.

Photographs on pages 26–27 (Vol.16, 44, 74), 60–61 (Vol. 16, 44), 62–63 (Vol. 16, 44)
Copyright © 2003 PhotoDisc, Inc.

Photograph on page 42 (Wright brother's flight)
Copyright © 2003 NASA

Photographs on pages 58, 62–63 (Southern California)
Copyright © 2003 Digital Stock Corp.

Photograph on page 62 (Rockiespring)
Copyright © 2003 Freestockphotos.com

Photographs on pages 68–69 (Vol. 194)
Copyright © 2003 Corbis Corp.

AN ATLAS is a collection of maps that can be

used to find information about your world. The very latest data has been collected to make these maps. Hundreds of satellite images were used to map the dramatic shrinking of Earth's forests. The latest census data from each and every country was used to build a picture of Earth's current population. The most recent scientific research was used to create thematic maps of continental drift, the ocean floor, the environment and our natural resources. Look closely and you will see that the information for the maps comes from many different sources such as NASA, the U.S. Department of the Interior or the World Bank. You can use these maps to explore your world, discover connections between places, and see relationships between places and peoples.

But this atlas is more than just a wealth of information. It is fun to look at too. You will find that these maps and photographs can evoke images of far away places. They invite you to pause and to dream. With a map you can journey the world without ever getting wet, cold, tired or hungry. You can imagine great adventures and not leave the comfort of your favorite chair!

To get the most out of this atlas you need to know how to read maps. Just as you learned to read words like the ones on this page, you can learn how to read the language of maps. The map skills you need to know are:
1. locating places
2. measuring distance
3. finding direction
4. reading map symbols

Locating Places
To find places in this atlas, you can begin with the index. To find Dallas follow these steps.

1. Look up Dallas in the index at the end of this book.
2. The index tells you that Dallas is a city in Texas and that it can be found on page 50. You will also learn that Dallas is located at 32°47'N (32 degrees 47 minutes north) and 96°48'W (96 degrees 48 minutes west.)
3. Go to page 50 and find the line of latitude nearest to the number 32°N and the line of longitude nearest to the number 96°W. You will find Dallas close to where those two lines meet. You can learn more about latitude and longitude on pages 8–9.

Measuring Distance
To measure distance most maps have a distance scale. You can learn more about measuring distance on page 7.

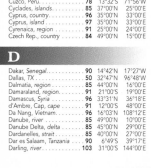
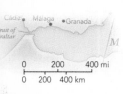

Finding Direction
To find directions use the map's compass rose. You can also use lines of latitude and longitude to find direction. Every line of longitude points north and south. Every line of latitude points east and west. You can learn more about latitude and longitude on pages 8–9.

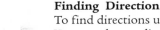

Reading Map Symbols
Every map symbol shows the location of something. It could be something as large as a continent or as small as a bird-house. A dot shows the location of a city. A blue line shows the course of a river. But map symbols are not the same on all maps. One map might show a city with a square. Map legends or keys help explain the symbols used on a map. You can find out more about legends and the map symbols used in this atlas on page 6.

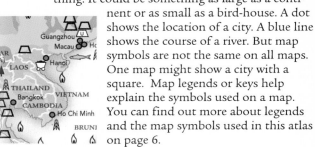

Special Features of this Atlas

This atlas has been designed and organized to be easy for you to use. Here is a "road map" to your atlas.

The Blue Tab Bar
Somewhere along the top blue tab bar of each spread you will see a darker blue tab. It tells you

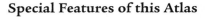

| Geographic Features | **Climate** | Land Cover |

the subject of the map or maps you are looking at. The light blue tabs tell you the subjects of the surrounding map spreads. If, for example, you are looking at the World Climate map and would like to compare it to the World Vegetation map, you can use the tabs to find that map quickly and easily.

Map Skills
Look at the blue tab bar above and you will see that you are in the map skills section. This section should be called "Read Me First" because it is here that you will find all sorts of helpful information about maps and how to read them. Even if you are a practiced map reader, read this section!

The World
In this section you will find a world political map, a world physical map, and 35 world thematic maps. The world political map shows the most up to date national boundaries. On the world physical map you can see huge deserts,

great mountain ranges, and even the sea ice that covers much of the Arctic. The thematic maps include the most up to date information on everything from the world distribution of computers and televisions to life expectancy, religion and literacy. If you want to see the ocean floor, or to find where in the world volcanoes form, this is the section to look in.

Continents

The continent units are designed to all have the same kinds of maps. This will enable you to compare and contrast one continent with another with ease and accuracy. There is a political map, a physical map, and a total of seven thematic maps per continent.

Used individually each map can provide answers to many questions. But all together, each set of maps can be used to tell a story.

Imagine a journey crossing a continent. You can see the regions visited, the mountains climbed, or the deserts crossed. You can tell if many people are passed along the way or few. You can describe the activities of the people. Will you see miners or ranchers or farmers? And you can tell about the different climates experienced along the way. All of this information and more is on the maps for every continent but Antarctica.

Environmental Issues

There is a special "Environmental Issues" feature for each continent and one for the world. To create these features the latest scientific information was gathered and organized for you. The topics cover the three major environmental issues faced by citizens today, desertification, deforestation, and acid rain.

The United States

In the section on the United States you will find a political map with two pages of political facts, a physical map with two pages of physical facts, and seven thematic map spreads.

Canada and Mexico

Canada and Mexico both have their own spreads that include a political and physical map.

Geographic Features

There are two special "Geographic Features" included in this atlas. To find out how the continents, Earth's greatest land features, have been drifting around the globe, turn to pages 22–23. To take an in depth look at fall lines, divides, and faults turn to the United States Geographic Features spread on pages 58–59.

Charts and Graphs

This atlas is filled with charts, graphs and diagrams. They are used to give more information about subjects shown on the maps. To make these charts and graphs, long lists of the most up to date data was gathered. Then all those numbers were organized into graphic displays that can be read simply and accurately.

Line graphs are used to show change in amounts over time.

Bar graphs are used to compare amounts.

Pie charts show percentages of a total.

Glossary

There are many geographic terms found on maps such as *fjord, isthmus,* or *plateau.* You can find the meaning of these and other terms in the geographic glossary located on the inside back cover.

The staff at Mapquest worked hard to make this atlas a reference book that is both full of information and fun and easy to use. We hope that you enjoy your copy.

Legend

The following symbols are used here for general reference maps. Maps with special subjects (thematic maps) have their own unique legends.

General Reference Maps

- ⊛ National capital
- ★ Other capital
- • Other city
- International boundary (political map)
- International boundary in dispute/undefined (political map)
- State or provincial boundary
- International boundary (physical map)
- International boundary in dispute (physical map)

- Nonsubject area
- ▲ Mountain peak
- ▽ Lowest point
- Perennial lake
- Intermittent lake
- Perennial river
- ≈ Falls

Physical Maps Legend

Pack ice — Ice caps
Mountains — Tundra
Oceans and seas — Forests
Arid lands — Grasslands

Projections

A globe is the most accurate picture of the Earth. Only a globe can show distance, direction, and the true shape and area of land and sea. Mapmakers struggle with how to show the round world on a flat map.

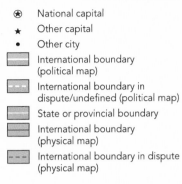

Imagine the Earth as a large balloon.

Cut it apart, and flatten it to make a map.

Mercator Projection

Gerardus Mercator, a Dutch mapmaker, wanted a map projection that showed direction and shape accurately. The problems with distortions are more obvious on this projection. You can see that the land areas are very distorted the closer to the poles that you get. So, this projection ended up greatly distorting distance and size.

To show the round Earth on flat paper, mapmakers used different **projections**, or ways of showing a round shape on a flat surface.

With every projection the shapes of places are changed somewhat. This is called distortion. To find distortion, you can compare the latitude and longitude lines of a map to those same lines on a globe.

This diagram shows how a Mercator projection distorts the sizes of places. Compare Greenland on the map and the globe.

Projections – Making the Round World Flat

Robinson Projection

Arthur Robinson, an American mapmaker, wanted to develop a map projection that "looked" right. This projection uses many distortions but none are significant. You can see this by comparing one of the large scale World maps in this atlas to a globe.

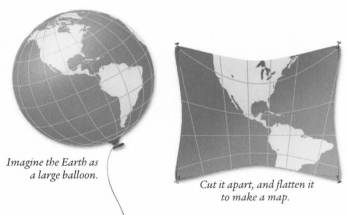

Azimuthal Projection

This is a projection used to show Antarctica and the Arctic. Azimuthal maps show direction and distance accurately, if measured from the center of the map. But, other distances, shape and size are distorted.

Map Scale

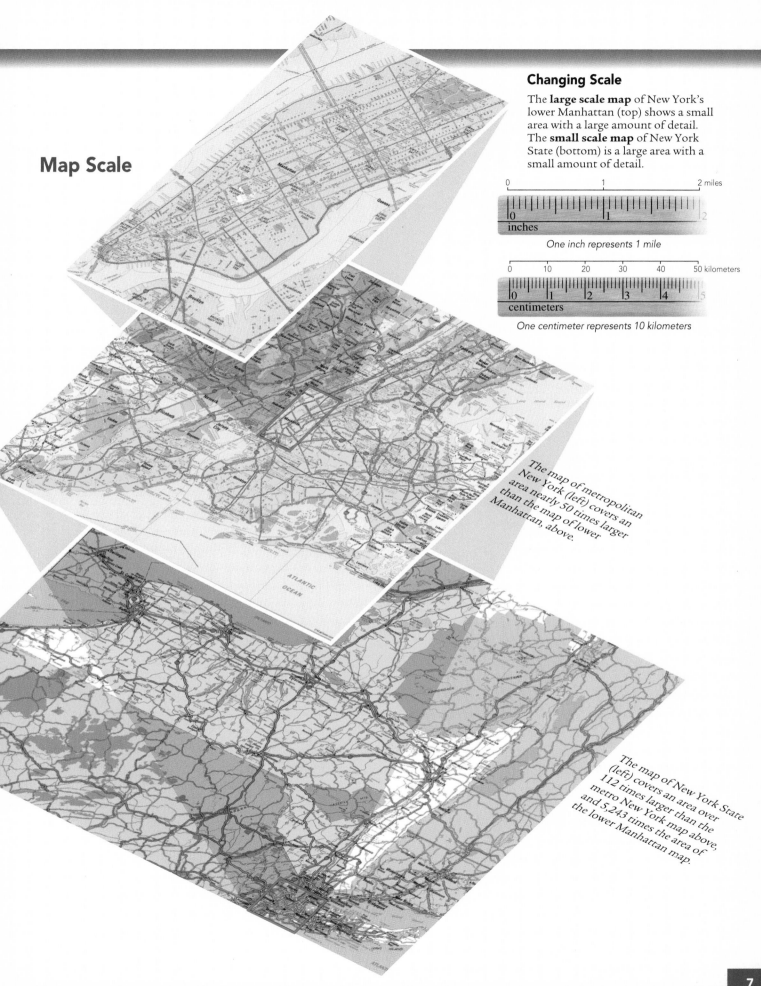

Changing Scale

The **large scale map** of New York's lower Manhattan (top) shows a small area with a large amount of detail. The **small scale map** of New York State (bottom) is a large area with a small amount of detail.

0	1	2 miles

0   1   2
inches

One inch represents 1 mile

0   10   20   30   40   50 kilometers

0   1   2   3   4   5
centimeters

One centimeter represents 10 kilometers

The map of metropolitan New York (left) covers an area nearly 50 times larger than the map of lower Manhattan, above.

The map of New York State (left) covers an area over 112 times larger than the metro New York map above, and 5,243 times the area of the lower Manhattan map.

Latitude and Longitude

Since ancient times, mapmakers, geographers, and navigators have worked to develop a system for accurately locating places on the Earth. On a sphere, such as the Earth, there are no corners or sides, no beginning or end. But since the Earth rotates on an axis, there are two fixed points: the North Pole and the South Pole. These points make a good starting place for a system of imaginary lines.

These imaginary lines form a grid over the Earth, allowing us to pinpoint the exact location of any spot on the Earth. This spherical grid is called the **graticule**. It is formed by lines called **latitude** and **longitude**.

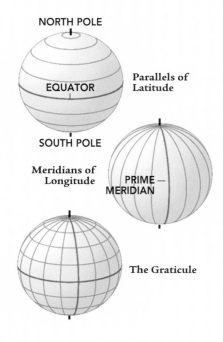

Parallels of Latitude

Meridians of Longitude

The Graticule

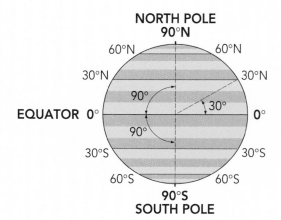

Latitude

Halfway between the poles the equator circles the globe in an east-west direction. Latitude is measured in degrees north or south of the equator, which is 0 degrees (°). Lines of latitude are called **parallels** because they circle the globe parallel to the equator. Parallels are numbered from 0° at the Equator to 90°N at the North Pole and 90°S at the South Pole.

Longitude

Running from pole to pole, lines of longitude—called **meridians**—circle the globe in a north-south direction. As in any circle or sphere, there are 360 degrees (°) of longitude. The meridians are numbered from the Prime Meridian which is labeled 0°. Meridians east or west of the Prime Meridian are labeled E or W up to 180°. The International Date Line generally follows the 180° meridian, making a few jogs to avoid cutting through land areas.

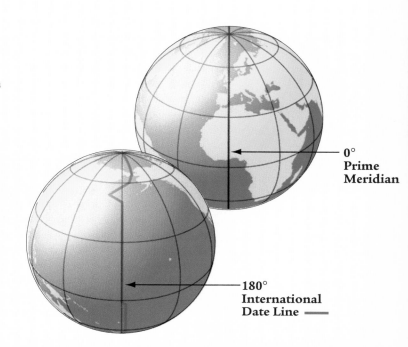

0°
Prime Meridian

180°
International Date Line

Parallels and Meridians—The Facts

Parallels
- are lines of latitude used to measure location north or south of the Equator
- are always the same distance apart (about 70 miles)
- differ in length
- The Equator, the longest parallel, is almost 25,000 miles long

Meridians
- are lines of longitude used to measure location east or west of the Prime Meridian
- meet at the poles
- are all the same length

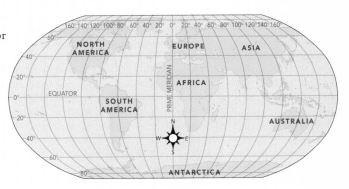

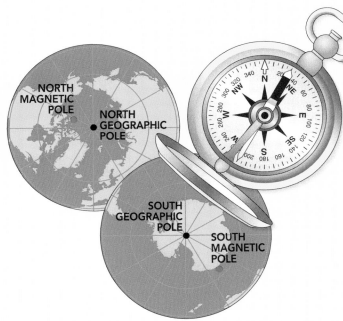

Which way north...

The geographic North and South Poles are fixed points located at each end of the Earth's axis. The Earth's magnetic fields cause the needle of a compass to point toward magnetic north, not geographic north. The north magnetic pole is located in the northern territories of Canada. The south magnetic pole is located near the coast of Antarctica. The magnetic poles are constantly moving.

Degrees, Minutes, Seconds

A degree (°) of latitude or longitude can be divided into 60 parts called minutes ('). Each minute can be divided into 60 seconds ("). The diagram at right is an example of a place located to the nearest second.

It is written as:
42° 21' 30" N   71° 03' 37" W

● This place is city center, Boston, Massachusetts.

The index at the back of this Atlas uses degrees and minutes of latitude and longitude to help you find places.

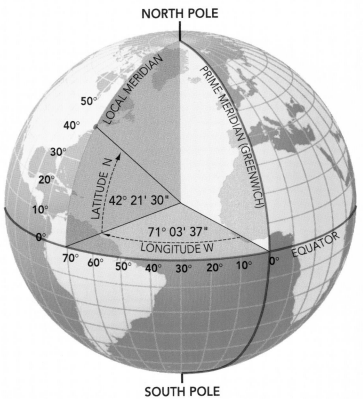

Different Kinds of Maps

Maps are special pictures of places on Earth.

All maps are alike in these important ways:
- All maps are a view from above
- All maps show selected information using symbols
- All maps are smaller than the real place on Earth that they show.

Because people want to show many different things on Earth, they create many different kinds of maps.

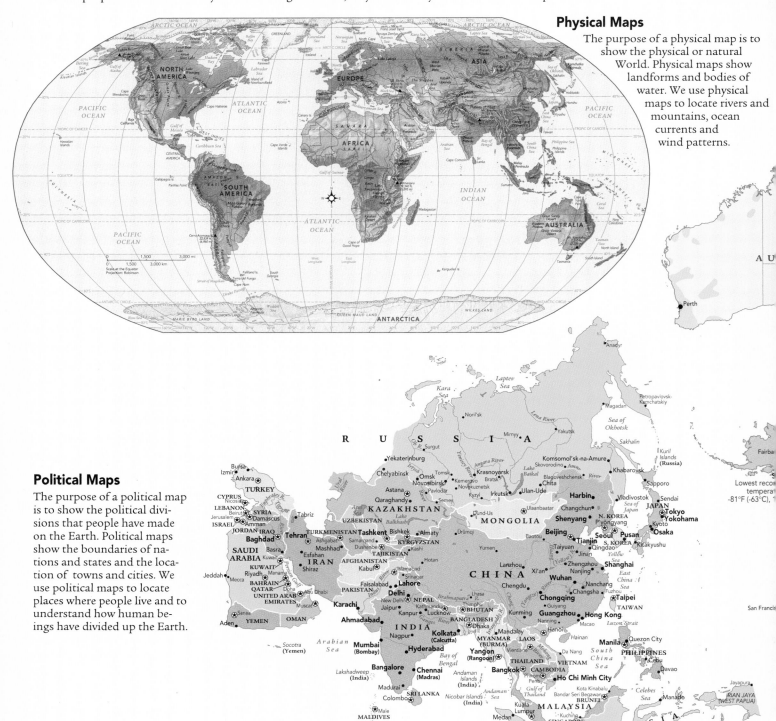

Physical Maps

The purpose of a physical map is to show the physical or natural World. Physical maps show landforms and bodies of water. We use physical maps to locate rivers and mountains, ocean currents and wind patterns.

Political Maps

The purpose of a political map is to show the political divisions that people have made on the Earth. Political maps show the boundaries of nations and states and the location of towns and cities. We use political maps to locate places where people live and to understand how human beings have divided up the Earth.

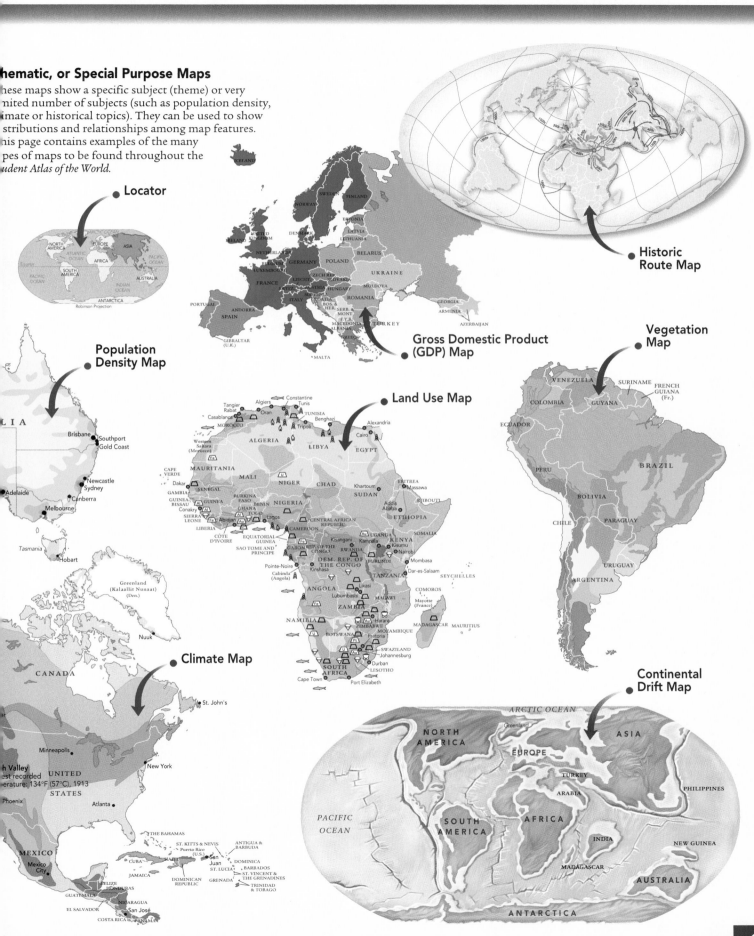

hematic, or Special Purpose Maps

hese maps show a specific subject (theme) or very
nited number of subjects (such as population density,
imate or historical topics). They can be used to show
stributions and relationships among map features.
his page contains examples of the many
pes of maps to be found throughout the
udent Atlas of the World.

Our Solar System

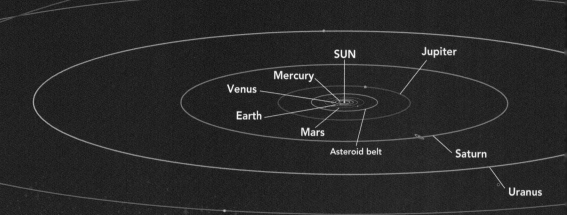

SUN
Jupiter
Mercury
Venus
Earth
Mars
Asteroid belt
Saturn
Uranus

Titan
Rhea
Tethys
Mimas
Dione
Miranda
Triton
Nereid
Pluto
Neptune
Uranus
Saturn
Jupiter
Ganymede

	Pluto	Neptune	Uranus	Saturn	Jupiter
Diameter	1,485 mi (2,390 km)	30,775 mi (49,528 km)	31,763 mi (51,118 km)	74,897 mi (120,536 km)	88,846 mi (142,984 km)
Mean distance from Sun (millions of miles/millions of km)	3,647 mi (5,870 km)	2,793 mi (4,495 km)	1,785 mi (2,873 km)	891 mi (1,434 km)	484 mi (779 km)

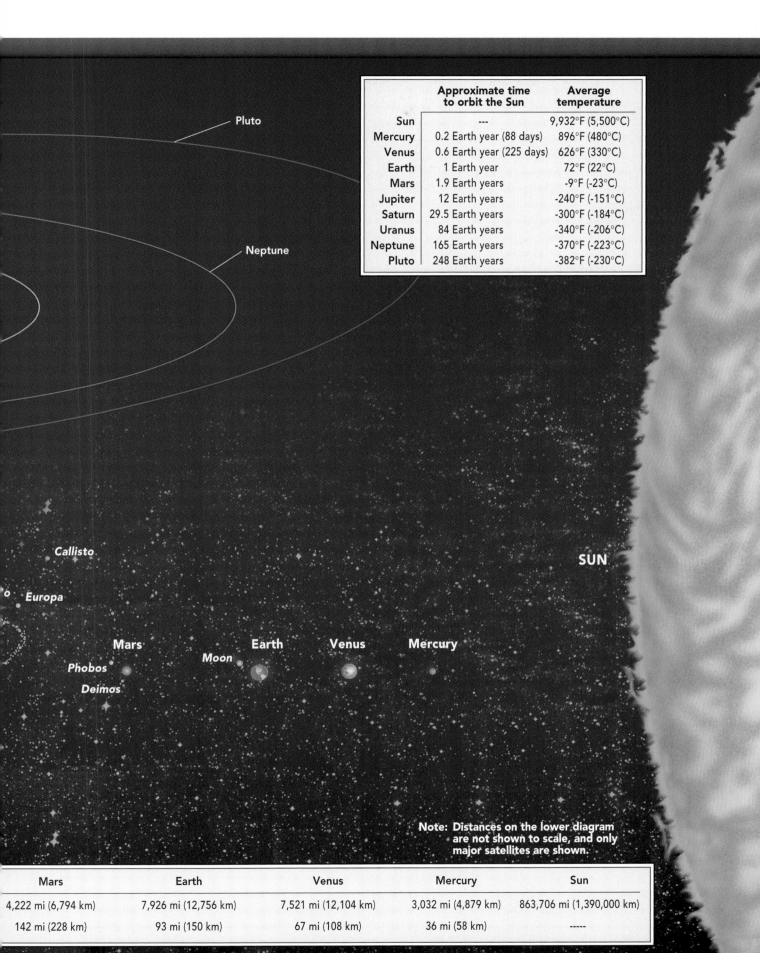

Pluto

Neptune

	Approximate time to orbit the Sun	Average temperature
Sun	---	9,932°F (5,500°C)
Mercury	0.2 Earth year (88 days)	896°F (480°C)
Venus	0.6 Earth year (225 days)	626°F (330°C)
Earth	1 Earth year	72°F (22°C)
Mars	1.9 Earth years	-9°F (-23°C)
Jupiter	12 Earth years	-240°F (-151°C)
Saturn	29.5 Earth years	-300°F (-184°C)
Uranus	84 Earth years	-340°F (-206°C)
Neptune	165 Earth years	-370°F (-223°C)
Pluto	248 Earth years	-382°F (-230°C)

Callisto

Europa

SUN

Mars   Earth   Venus   Mercury

Moon

Phobos

Deimos

Note: Distances on the lower diagram are not shown to scale, and only major satellites are shown.

Mars	Earth	Venus	Mercury	Sun
4,222 mi (6,794 km)	7,926 mi (12,756 km)	7,521 mi (12,104 km)	3,032 mi (4,879 km)	863,706 mi (1,390,000 km)
142 mi (228 km)	93 mi (150 km)	67 mi (108 km)	36 mi (58 km)	-----

Sources: JPL/NASA; World Almanac, 2002

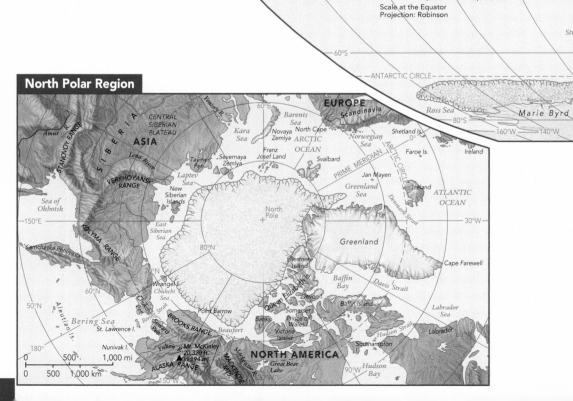

International boundary
▲ Mountain peak

ARCTIC OCEAN

160°W | 140°W | 120°W | 100°W | 80°W | 60°W

80°N

Point Barrow
Beaufort Sea
Queen Elizabeth Islands
Ellesmere Island
Greenla
Baffin Bay
Victoria Island
Baffin Island
Davis Strait

Yukon R.
Mackenzie R.
Great Bear Lake
Great Slave Lake
Hudson Bay
Cape Farewell

60°N
Bering Strait
▲ Mt. McKinley 20,320 ft (6,194 m)
ROCKY MOUNTAINS
NORTH AMERICA
Lake Winnipeg
The Great Lakes
Labrador Sea
Newfoundland

Bering Sea
Gulf of Alaska

Aleutian Islands

40°N
Cape Mendocino
GREAT BASIN
GREAT PLAINS
Missouri R.
Mississippi R.
APPALACHIAN MTS.
Cape Hatteras
ATLANTIC OCEAN
Azo

PACIFIC OCEAN

Baja California
SIERRA MADRE OCCIDENTAL
SIERRA MADRE ORIENTAL

TROPIC OF CANCER
Gulf of Mexico
Cuba
West Indies
Cape Ve Islan

20°N
Hawaiian Islands
Yucatan Pen.
Caribbean Sea

CENTRAL AMERICA
LLANOS
GUIANA HIGHLANDS

EQUATOR
0°
Galápagos Is.
AMAZON
Amazon R.
BASIN
Pariñas Point
SOUTH AMERICA

Polynesia
ANDES
MATO GROSSO PLATEAU
BRAZILIAN HIGHLANDS

20°S
TROPIC OF CAPRICORN
GRAN CHACO
Paraná R.

Pitcairn I.
Easter I.
PAMPAS

PACIFIC OCEAN
Mt. Aconcagua 22,834 ft (6,960 m)
ANDES
Patagonia

0 | 1,500 | 3,000 mi
0 | 1,500 | 3,000 km
Scale at the Equator
Projection: Robinson

40°S
Falkland Is.
South Georgia
Tierra del Fuego
Strait of Magellan
Cape Horn
Drake Passage

60°S
ANTARCTIC CIRCLE
Antarctic Peninsula
Weddell Sea

Ross Sea
80°S
Ellsworth Land
Marie Byrd Land

160°W | 140°W | 120°W | 100°W | 80°W | 60°W

North Polar Region

Amur
STANOVOY RANGE
SIBERIA
ASIA
CENTRAL SIBERIAN PLATEAU
Yenisey R.
Barents Sea
Novaya Zemlya
North Cape
EUROPE
Scandinavia
90°E
60°E

Kara Sea
Norwegian Sea
Shetland Is.

Lena River
Taymyr Pen.
Severnaya Zemlya
Franz Josef Land
Svalbard
ARCTIC OCEAN
Faroe Is.
Ireland

VERKHOYANSK RANGE
Laptev Sea
New Siberian Islands
Jan Mayen
PRIME MERIDIAN
ARCTIC CIRCLE
0°

150°E
KOLYMA RANGE
Sea of Okhotsk
East Siberian Sea
80°N
North Pole
Greenland Sea
Iceland
ATLANTIC OCEAN
30°W

Kamchatka Peninsula
Wrangel I.
Chukchi Sea
70°N
Greenland
Denmark Strait

60°N
Bering Sea
St. Lawrence I.
Nunivak I.
Seward Pen.
Bering Strait
BROOKS RANGE
Point Barrow
Beaufort Sea
Banks
Prince of Wales I.
Victoria Island
Somerset I.
Queen Elizabeth Is.
Devon I.
Ellesmere Island
Baffin Bay
Baffin Island
Cape Farewell

50°N
Aleutian Is.
180°
0 | 500 | 1,000 mi
0 | 500 | 1,000 km
Chukchi Pen.
Yukon R.
▲ Mt. McKinley 20,320 ft (6,194 m)
ALASKA RANGE
NORTH AMERICA
MACKENZIE MTS.
Great Bear Lake
90°W
Hudson Strait
Labrador
Southampton
Hudson Bay
150°W

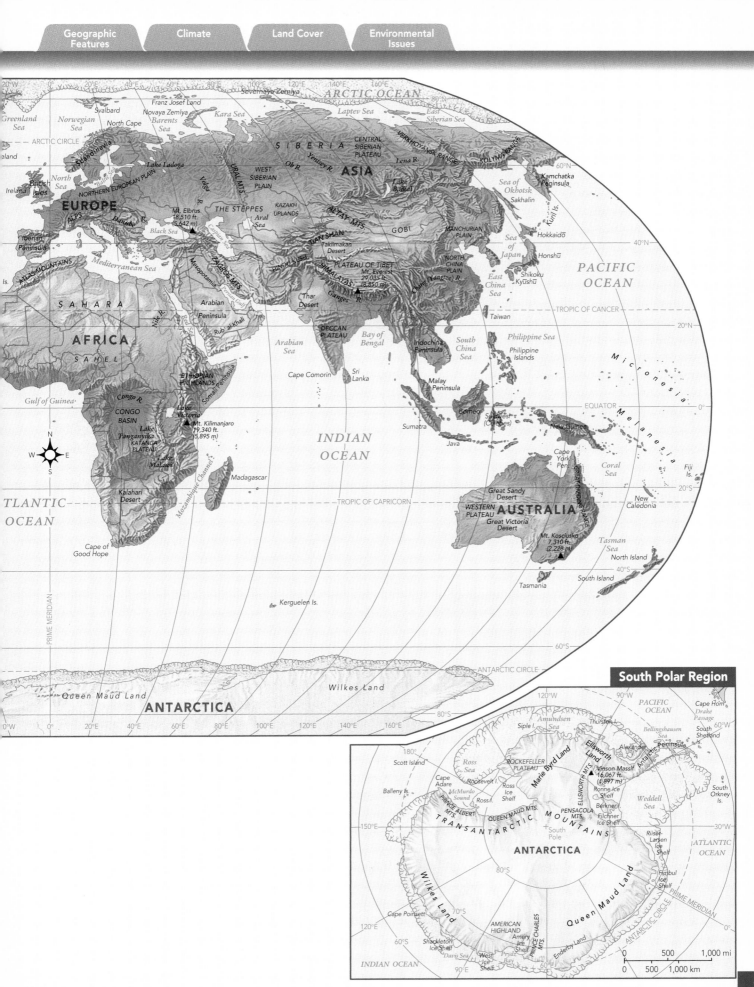

ARCTIC OCEAN

Greenland Sea
Norwegian Sea
Svalbard
Franz Josef Land
Novaya Zemlya
Severnaya Zemlya
Kara Sea
Laptev Sea
East Siberian Sea
ARCTIC CIRCLE
North Cape
Barents Sea
Scandinavia
SIBERIA
CENTRAL SIBERIAN PLATEAU
VERKHOYANSK RANGE
KOLYMA RANGE
Lake Ladoga
URAL MTS.
Ob R.
Yenisey R.
Lena R.
Kamchatka Peninsula
North Sea
British Isles
Ireland
NORTHERN EUROPEAN PLAIN
WEST SIBERIAN PLAIN
ASIA
Sea of Okhotsk
Sakhalin
Kuril Is.
EUROPE
Volga R.
THE STEPPES
KAZAKH UPLANDS
Lake Baikal
ALPS
Mt. Elbrus 18,510 ft. (5,642 m)
Aral Sea
ALTAY MTS.
GOBI
MANCHURIAN PLAIN
Hokkaidō
Danube R.
Black Sea
Caspian Sea
TIAN SHAN
Sea of Japan
Iberian Peninsula
ZAGROS MTS.
Taklimakan Desert
PLATEAU OF TIBET
NORTH CHINA PLAIN
Honshū
Kyūshū
Shikoku
PACIFIC OCEAN
Is.
ATLAS MOUNTAINS
Mediterranean Sea
HINDU KUSH
HIMALAYAS
Mt. Everest 29,035 ft. (8,850 m)
Chang (Yangtze) R.
East China Sea
SAHARA
Mesopotamia
Persian Gulf
Ganges R.
Thar Desert
Taiwan
TROPIC OF CANCER
Nile R.
Red Sea
Arabian Peninsula
DECCAN PLATEAU
Bay of Bengal
Indochina Peninsula
South China Sea
Philippine Sea
AFRICA
SAHEL
Rub' al Khali
Arabian Sea
Sri Lanka
Philippine Islands
Micronesia
Cape Comorin
Somali Peninsula
ETHIOPIAN HIGHLANDS
Malay Peninsula
Gulf of Guinea
Congo R.
Lake Victoria
Mt. Kilimanjaro 19,340 ft. (5,895 m)
Borneo
Sulawesi (Celebes)
Melanesia
CONGO BASIN
Lake Tanganyika
KATANGA PLATEAU
Lake Malawi
Sumatra
Java
New Guinea
EQUATOR
N W E S
INDIAN OCEAN
Cape York Pen.
Coral Sea
Fiji Is.
Madagascar
Mozambique Channel
Great Sandy Desert
New Caledonia
ATLANTIC OCEAN
Kalahari Desert
TROPIC OF CAPRICORN
WESTERN PLATEAU
AUSTRALIA
GREAT DIVIDING RANGE
Great Victoria Desert
Mt. Kosciusko 7,310 ft. (2,228 m)
Tasman Sea
Cape of Good Hope
North Island
Kerguelen Is.
Tasmania
South Island
PRIME MERIDIAN
ANTARCTIC CIRCLE
Queen Maud Land
Wilkes Land
ANTARCTICA

PACIFIC OCEAN
Cape Horn
Drake Passage
Amundsen Sea
Thurston I.
Bellingshausen Sea
Siple I.
Antarctic Peninsula
South Shetland Is.
Alexander I.
Ross Sea
ROCKEFELLER PLATEAU
Marie Byrd Land
Ellsworth Land
Scott Island
Roosevelt I.
ELLSWORTH MTS.
Vinson Massif 16,067 ft. (4,897 m)
Weddell Sea
South Orkney Is.
Cape Adare
McMurdo Sound
Ross I.
Ross Ice Shelf
Ronne Ice Shelf
Berkner I.
Balleny Is.
TRANSANTARCTIC
PRINCE ALBERT MTS.
Queen Maud Mts.
PENSACOLA MTS.
Filchner Ice Shelf
ATLANTIC OCEAN
South Pole
MOUNTAINS
Riiser-Larsen Ice Shelf
ANTARCTICA
Queen Maud Land
Wilkes Land
Fimbul Ice Shelf
PRIME MERIDIAN
Cape Poinsett
ANTARCTIC CIRCLE
AMERICAN HIGHLAND
Amery Ice Shelf
PRINCE CHARLES MTS.
Enderby Land
Shackleton Ice Shelf
Davis Sea
West Ice Shelf
Prydz Bay
INDIAN OCEAN

0   500   1,000 mi
0   500   1,000 km

15

80°N

160°W 140°W 120°W 100°W 80°W

Alaska (U.S.)

60°N

CANADA

NORTH AMERICA

40°N

UNITED STATES

Midway Islands (U.S.)

Area of inset

Bermuda (U.K.)

ATLANTIC OCEAN

20°N

Hawaii (U.S.)

TROPIC OF CANCER

MEXICO

PACIFIC OCEAN

0°

EQUATOR

VENEZUELA **GUYANA** **SURINAME**

French Guiana (France)

COLOMBIA

ECUADOR

Tokelau (N.Z.) **KIRIBATI**

Galápagos Islands (Ecuador)

BRAZIL

PERU **SOUTH AMERICA**

American Samoa (U.S.)
SAMOA

French Polynesia (France)

BOLIVIA

Cook Islands (N.Z.)

20°S

PARAGUAY

CHILE

TONGA *Niue (N.Z.)*

TROPIC OF CAPRICORN

Pitcairn Is. (U.K.)

Easter Island (Chile)

URUGUAY

ARGENTINA

40°S

Falkland Islands (U.K.)

PACIFIC OCEAN

South Georgia (U.K.)

60°S

ANTARCTIC CIRCLE

80°S

160°W 140°W 120°W 100°W 80°W

Central America and the Caribbean

100°W 90°W 80°W

UNITED STATES

30°N

Gulf of Mexico

ATLANTIC OCEAN

30°N 70°W

THE BAHAMAS

60°W

20°N

CUBA

Turks and Caicos Is. (U.K.)

20°N

Puerto Rico (U.S.)

Anguilla (U.K.)

MEXICO

Cayman Islands (U.K.)

HAITI **DOMINICAN REPUBLIC**

St. Martin **(Fr. and Neth.)**

BELIZE

JAMAICA

Virgin Islands (U.S. and U.K.)

ANTIGUA AND BARBUDA

Montserrat (U.K.)

Guadeloupe (Fr.)

ST. KITTS AND NEVIS **DOMINICA**

GUATEMALA **HONDURAS**

Caribbean Sea

Martinique (Fr.)

ST. LUCIA

EL SALVADOR

NICARAGUA

Aruba (Neth.)

Netherlands Antilles (Neth.)

BARBADOS

ST. VINCENT AND THE GRENADINES

10°N

Panama Canal

GRENADA

TRINIDAD AND TOBAGO

10°N

COSTA RICA

PANAMA

PACIFIC OCEAN

0 200 400 mi

0 200 400 km

Projection: Azimuthal Equal-Area

90°W 80°W 70°W 60°W

International boundary

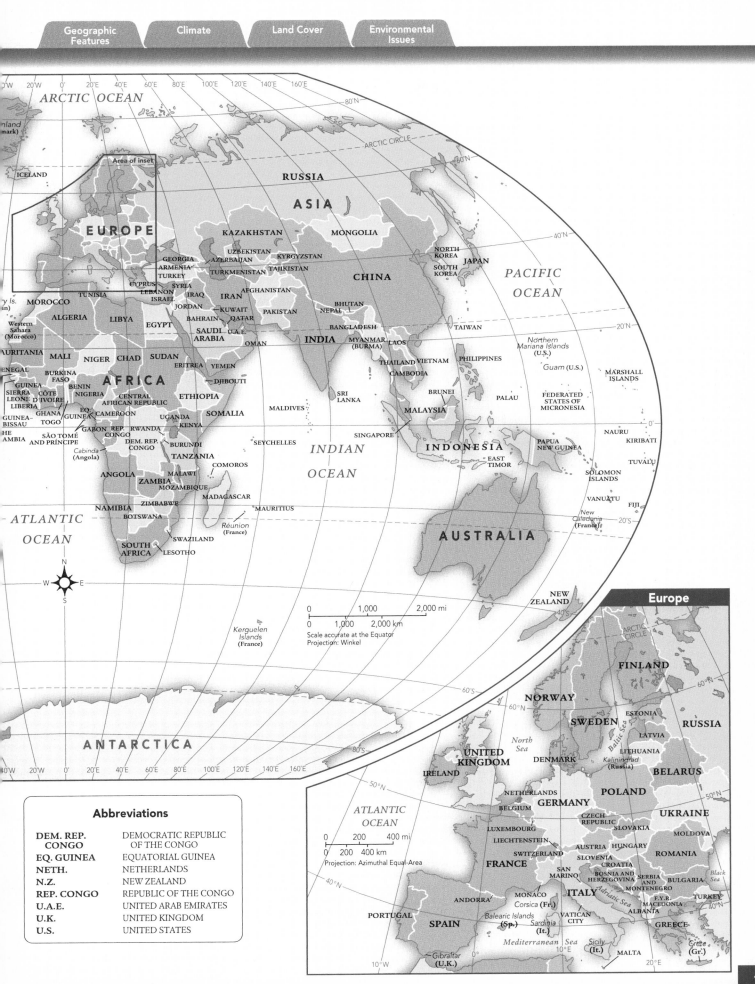

ARCTIC OCEAN

ICELAND

Area of inset

EUROPE

RUSSIA

ASIA

ARCTIC CIRCLE

KAZAKHSTAN   MONGOLIA

GEORGIA   UZBEKISTAN   KYRGYZSTAN
ARMENIA   AZERBAIJAN
TURKEY   TURKMENISTAN   TAJIKISTAN

NORTH KOREA   JAPAN
SOUTH KOREA

CHINA   PACIFIC OCEAN

CYPRUS
LEBANON   SYRIA   IRAQ   AFGHANISTAN
ISRAEL   JORDAN   PAKISTAN

TUNISIA

MOROCCO

Western Sahara (Morocco)

ALGERIA   LIBYA   EGYPT

KUWAIT
BAHRAIN   QATAR
SAUDI   U.A.E.
ARABIA   OMAN

IRAN

BHUTAN
NEPAL

BANGLADESH   MYANMAR (BURMA)   LAOS

TAIWAN

INDIA

MAURITANIA   MALI   NIGER   CHAD   SUDAN   ERITREA   YEMEN

THAILAND   VIETNAM
CAMBODIA

PHILIPPINES

Northern Mariana Islands (U.S.)

Guam (U.S.)

MARSHALL ISLANDS

SENEGAL
GUINEA
BURKINA FASO   BENIN
SIERRA LEONE   CÔTE D'IVOIRE   NIGERIA
LIBERIA

AFRICA

DJIBOUTI

CENTRAL AFRICAN REPUBLIC   ETHIOPIA

SRI LANKA

MALDIVES

BRUNEI

PALAU

FEDERATED STATES OF MICRONESIA

GUINEA-BISSAU
GHANA   EQ. GUINEA   CAMEROON
THE GAMBIA   TOGO
GABON   REP. CONGO   RWANDA
SÃO TOMÉ AND PRÍNCIPE   Cabinda (Angola)   DEM. REP. CONGO   BURUNDI

UGANDA
SOMALIA
KENYA

MALAYSIA

SINGAPORE

SEYCHELLES

INDONESIA

PAPUA NEW GUINEA

NAURU

KIRIBATI

TANZANIA   COMOROS

EAST TIMOR

SOLOMON ISLANDS

TUVALU

ANGOLA   ZAMBIA   MALAWI
MOZAMBIQUE
ZIMBABWE   MADAGASCAR

INDIAN OCEAN

VANUATU

FIJI

New Caledonia (France)

NAMIBIA   BOTSWANA

MAURITIUS

Réunion (France)

AUSTRALIA

ATLANTIC OCEAN

SOUTH AFRICA   SWAZILAND
LESOTHO

NEW ZEALAND

N
W   E
S

Kerguelen Islands (France)

0   1,000   2,000 mi
0   1,000   2,000 km
Scale accurate at the Equator
Projection: Winkel

ANTARCTICA

Europe

ARCTIC CIRCLE

FINLAND

NORWAY   SWEDEN

ESTONIA
LATVIA
LITHUANIA
Kaliningrad (Russia)

RUSSIA

BELARUS

North Sea

UNITED KINGDOM   DENMARK

IRELAND

NETHERLANDS
BELGIUM   GERMANY

POLAND

UKRAINE

ATLANTIC OCEAN

0   200   400 mi
0   200   400 km
Projection: Azimuthal Equal-Area

LUXEMBOURG
LIECHTENSTEIN
SWITZERLAND

CZECH REPUBLIC   SLOVAKIA

MOLDOVA

AUSTRIA   HUNGARY
SLOVENIA   CROATIA

ROMANIA

FRANCE

SAN MARINO

BOSNIA AND HERZEGOVINA   SERBIA AND MONTENEGRO

BULGARIA

Black Sea

ANDORRA   MONACO
Corsica (Fr.)

ITALY

VATICAN CITY

F.Y.R. MACEDONIA
ALBANIA

TURKEY

PORTUGAL   SPAIN

Balearic Islands (Sp.)   Sardinia (It.)

GREECE

Gibraltar (U.K.)

Mediterranean Sea

Sicily (It.)   MALTA

Crete (Gr.)

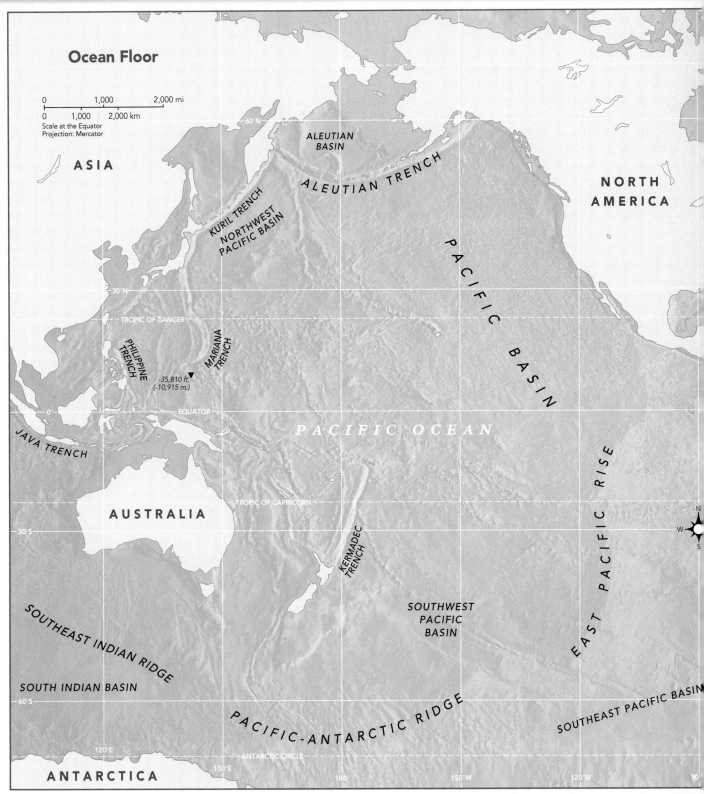

Ocean Floor

0   1,000   2,000 mi
0   1,000   2,000 km
Scale at the Equator
Projection: Mercator

ASIA

ALEUTIAN BASIN

ALEUTIAN TRENCH

NORTH AMERICA

KURIL TRENCH

NORTHWEST PACIFIC BASIN

PACIFIC BASIN

PHILIPPINE TRENCH

MARIANA TRENCH

-35,810 ft. (-10,915 m.)

JAVA TRENCH

PACIFIC OCEAN

EAST PACIFIC RISE

AUSTRALIA

KERMADEC TRENCH

SOUTHWEST PACIFIC BASIN

SOUTHEAST INDIAN RIDGE

SOUTH INDIAN BASIN

PACIFIC-ANTARCTIC RIDGE

SOUTHEAST PACIFIC BASIN

ANTARCTICA

TROPIC OF CANCER
EQUATOR
TROPIC OF CAPRICORN
ANTARCTIC CIRCLE

60°N
30°N
0°
30°S
60°S
120°E
150°E
180°
150°W
120°W
90°

Surrounding most of the continents are gently sloping areas called continental shelves, which reach depths of about 650 ft. (200 m). At the edges of the continental shelves lie steeper continental slopes leading down to the deep ocean basin, or abyss. The abyss contains many of the same features we see on land, including plains, mountains ranges (ridges), isolated mountains (known as sea mounts or guyots), and trenches. The Mid-Ocean Ridge system marks the areas where crustal plates are moving apart, and is very active geologically, as molten rock rises and erupts to create new crust. Earthquakes and volcanoes are common along many undersea trenches and ridges.

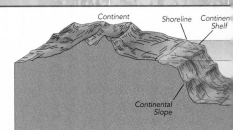

Continent | Shoreline | Continental Shelf

Continental Slope

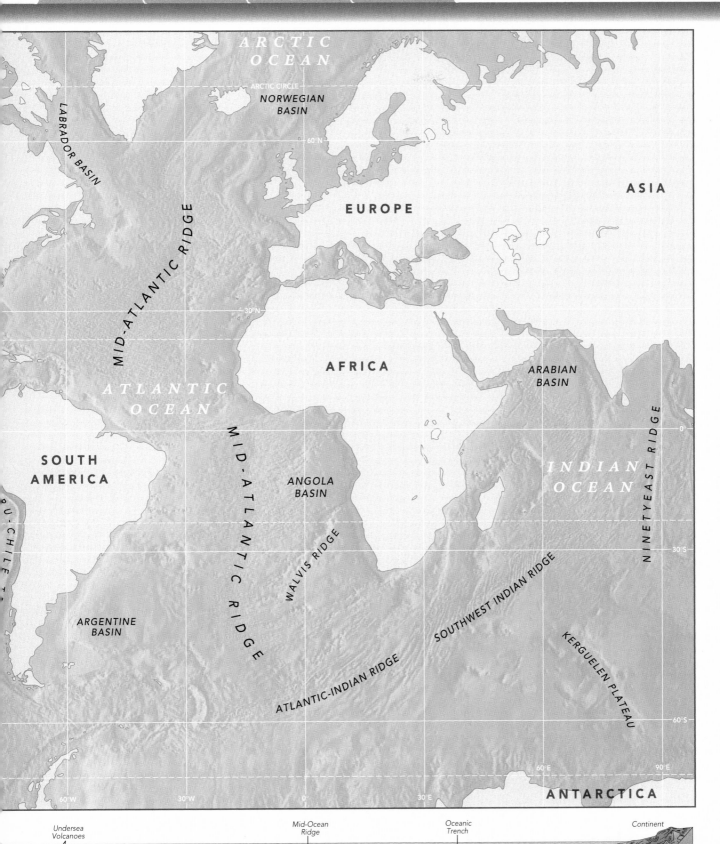

ARCTIC OCEAN

ARCTIC CIRCLE

NORWEGIAN BASIN

LABRADOR BASIN

60°N

EUROPE

ASIA

30°N

AFRICA

ARABIAN BASIN

ATLANTIC OCEAN

MID-ATLANTIC RIDGE

SOUTH AMERICA

INDIAN OCEAN

0°

ANGOLA BASIN

MID-ATLANTIC RIDGE

NINETYEAST RIDGE

WALVIS RIDGE

30°S

ARGENTINE BASIN

SOUTHWEST INDIAN RIDGE

KERGUELEN PLATEAU

PU-CHILE T

ATLANTIC-INDIAN RIDGE

60°S

60°W

30°W

0°

30°E

60°E

90°E

ANTARCTICA

Undersea Volcanoes

Mid-Ocean Ridge

Oceanic Trench

Continent

ssal in

Guyots

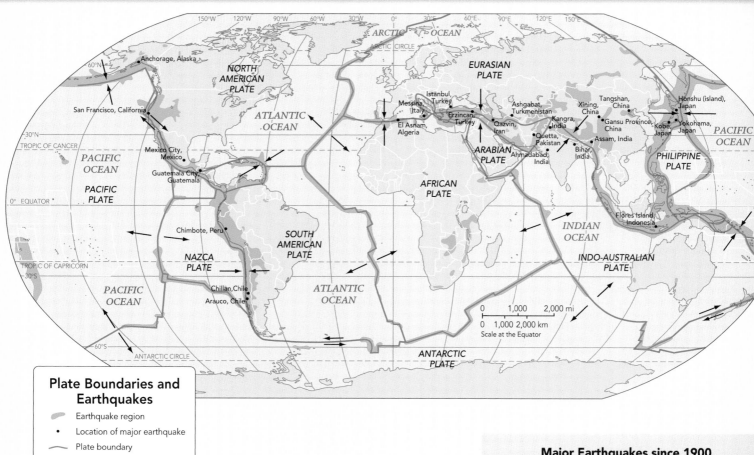

Plate Boundaries and Earthquakes

- Earthquake region
- Location of major earthquake
- Plate boundary
- Direction of plate movement

The movement of Earth's crustal plates causes the phenomena known as earthquakes. The surface of the Earth actually moves or quakes. An **earthquake** can have the destructive energy of an atomic bomb. However, thousands of earthquakes occur each day all over the world without most people realizing it.

The majority of earthquakes occur along a **fault**. A fault is usually a weak or broken area in the rocks beneath the surface of the Earth, but some, like the *San Andreas Fault* in California, can be seen on the surface. See pages 58–59 to learn more about faults.

The Richter Scale measures the energy of an earthquake. This measurement is obtained from the focus, or hypocenter, the spot where the first break in the rock layers occurs. The spot on the surface of the Earth, directly above the focus and nearest to the source of energy is called the epicenter.

Earthquake damage is caused by this energy, called seismic energy, moving through the rocks or along the surface. Many geographic factors, both physical and human, determine how much damage is done by these seismic waves of energy.

Major Earthquakes since 1900

Date	Location	Richter Scale Magnitude
April 4, 1905	Kangra, India	8.6
April 18, 1906	San Francisco, California	7.8
Dec. 28, 1908	Messina, Italy	7.5
Dec 16, 1920	Gansu Province, China	8.6
Sept. 1, 1923	Sagami Bay (near Yokohama), Japan	8.3
May 22, 1927	Xining, China	8.3
Dec. 25, 1932	Gansu Province, China	7.6
March 2, 1933	off northeast coast of Honshu, Japan	8.9
Jan. 15, 1934	Bihar, India/Nepal	8.4
May 30, 1935	Quetta, Pakistan	7.5
Jan. 25, 1939	Chillán, Chile	8.3
Dec. 26, 1939	Erzincan, Turkey	8.0
Dec. 21, 1946	Honshu, Japan	8.4
Oct. 5, 1948	Ashgabat, Turkmenistan	7.3
Aug. 15, 1950	Assam, India	8.7
May 22, 1960	Arauco, Chile	9.5
March 27, 1964	Anchorage, Alaska	9.2
May 31, 1970	Northern Peru, near Chimbote	7.8
Feb. 4, 1976	Guatemala City, Guatemala	7.5
July 28, 1976	Tangshan, China	8.0
Oct. 10, 1980	El Asnam, Algeria	7.7
Sept. 19, 1985	Mexico City, Mexico	8.1
June 20, 1990	Western Iran, near Qazvin	7.7
Dec. 12, 1992	Flores Island, Indonesia	7.5
Jan. 17, 1995	Kobe, Japan	6.9
Aug. 17, 1999	Istanbul, Turkey	7.4
Jan. 26, 2001	Ahmadabad, India	7.7

Source: National Earthquake Information Center, U.S.G.S

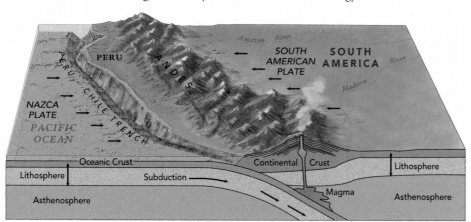

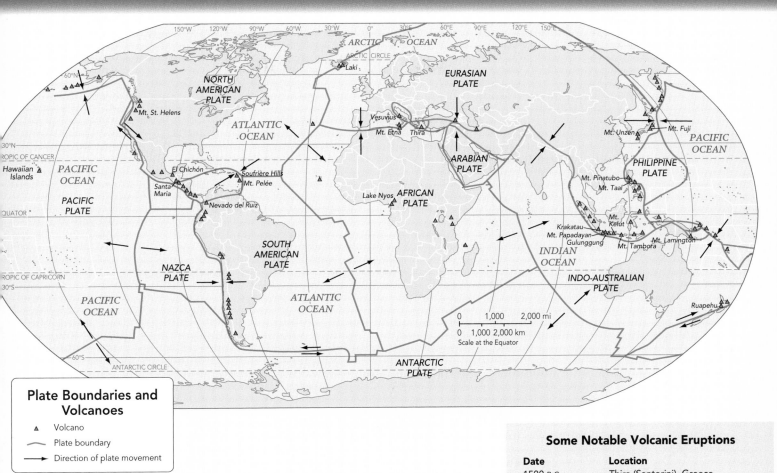

Plate Boundaries and Volcanoes

▲ Volcano

⌒ Plate boundary

→ Direction of plate movement

A **volcano** is an opening in the Earth's crust often capped by a cone-shaped hill or mountain formed from erupted lava and ash.

Volcanoes are associated with plate boundaries. Powerful forces occurring far beneath the surface at the edges of plates cause rock to melt and, at the same time, open cracks in the crust. An eruption occurs when magma (melted rock) flows, and many times explodes, through a weakness, such as a crack in the Earth's crust. Once magma is flowing on the Earth's surface it is called lava. Flowing lava can be several thousand degrees Fahrenheit.

In a few cases, volcanoes exist without being near the edge of a plate. In these cases, such as the Hawaiian Islands, a powerful and persistent flow of magma has broken through the crust.

Some Notable Volcanic Eruptions

Date	Location
1500 B.C.	Thira (Santorini), Greece
Aug. 24, A.D. 79	Vesuvius, Italy
1169	Mt. Etna, Italy
1586	Mt. Kelut, Java, Indonesia
Dec. 15, 1631	Vesuvius, Italy
March–July, 1669	Mt. Etna, Italy
Aug. 12, 1772	Mt. Papandayan, Java, Indonesia
June 8, 1783	Laki, Iceland
May 21, 1792	Mt. Unzen, Japan
Apr. 10–12, 1815	Mt. Tambora, Sumbawa, Indonesia
Oct. 8, 1822	Galunggung, Java, Indonesia
Aug. 26–28, 1883	Krakatau, Indonesia
Apr. 24, 1902	Santa Maria, Guatemala
May 8, 1902	Mt. Pelée, Martinique
Jan. 30, 1911	Mt. Taal, Philippines
May 19, 1919	Mt. Kelut, Java, Indonesia
Jan. 17–21, 1951	Mt. Lamington, New Guinea
May 18, 1980	Mt. St. Helens, United States
Mar. 28, 1982	El Chichón, Mexico
Nov. 13, 1985	Nevado del Ruiz, Colombia
Aug. 21, 1986	Lake Nyos, Cameroon
June 15, 1991	Mt. Pinatubo, Philippines
June–Sept., 1997	Soufrière Hills, Montserrat

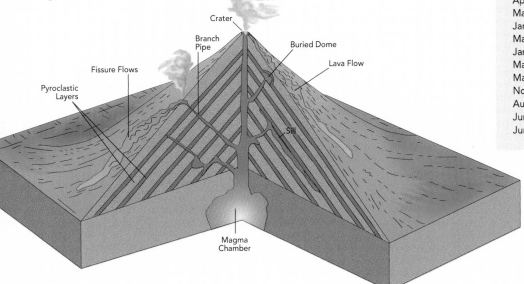

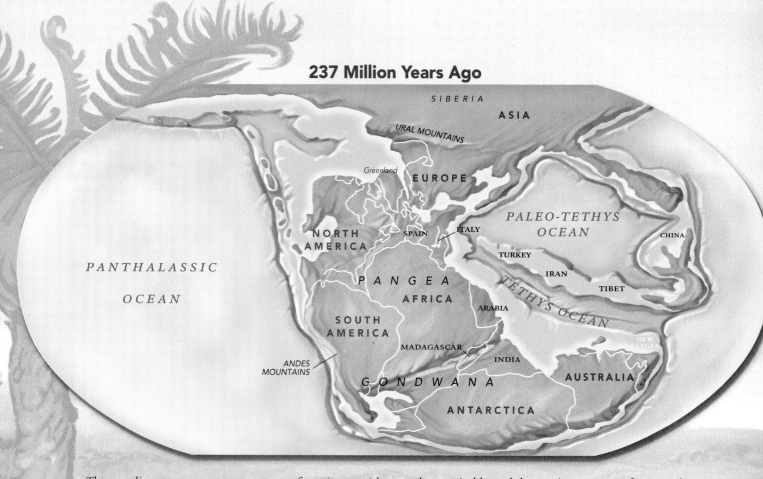

237 Million Years Ago

This peculiar—to our eyes—arrangement of continents with its unfamiliar oceans and seas, mountains and plains, and peninsulas and islands reminds us that the dinosaurs lived in a far different landscape than our own. As the last dinosaurs receded into memory, the future Atlantic Ocean and Mediterranean Sea were becoming more substantial

and recognizable, and the continents, except for Australia and Antarctica, were nearing their present latitudes. Within the last 65 million years, most continents nestled unhurriedly into their current positions. However, the Indian sub-continent "sprinted" north, crashing into Asia and bulldozing up the Himalayas, earth's loftiest mountain range.

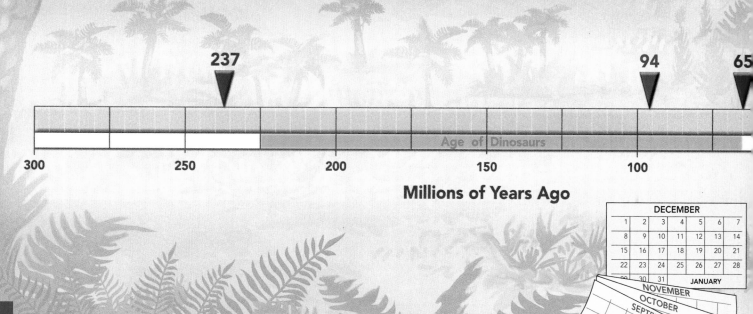

Millions of Years Ago

94 Million Years Ago

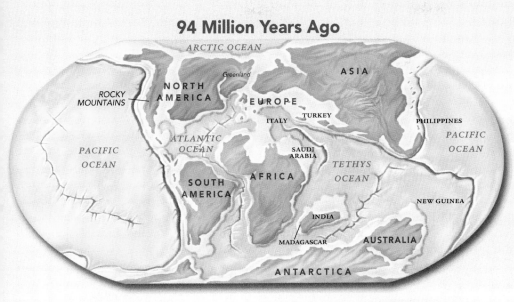

The highly controversial theory of Continental Drift was proposed in 1915 by Alfred Wegener to explain both geologic and fossil discoveries. Although supported by strong data and seemingly obvious visual evidence—most notably, the close fit of the coastlines of Africa and South America—the theory was rejected by other scientists. By the 1960s, further studies, especially those that discovered that some rocks contained a record of the alignment of the Earth's magnetic field, resurrected the theory, which was redefined under the term Plate Tectonics. Few scientists now dispute its general premise, that continental and oceanic plates move atop a layer of hot and semi-solid rock below them, although many details, particularly the causes and mechanics of the motion, are still not well understood.

65 Million Years Ago

Present day

Humans

0

If a year (365 days) represented the approximate age of the Earth (4.5 billion years), then the first map which shows the Earth 237 million years ago, would have occurred about December 13th. 94 and 65 million years ago would have occurred about December 25th and 27th respectively.

Recorded history started about 5,500 years ago: on this calendar, that would have been about 21 seconds before the New Year.

Present Day

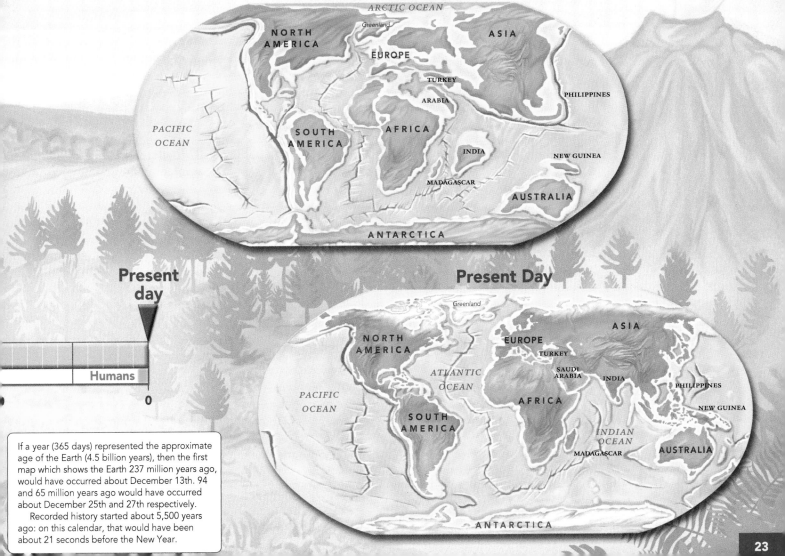

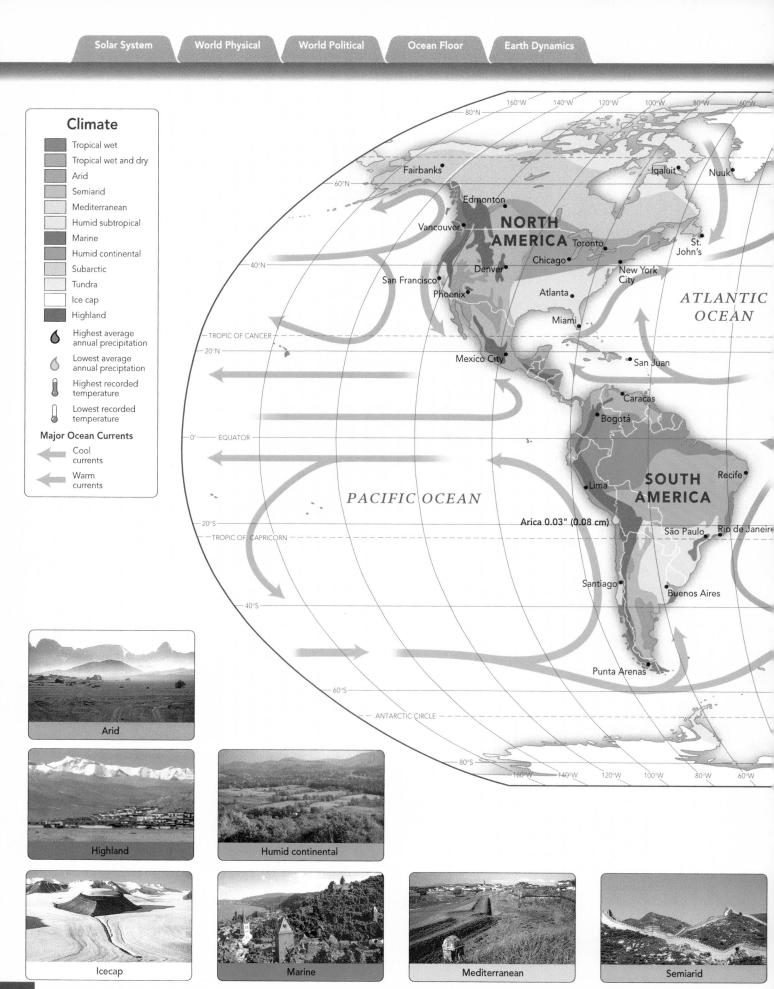

Climate

- Tropical wet
- Tropical wet and dry
- Arid
- Semiarid
- Mediterranean
- Humid subtropical
- Marine
- Humid continental
- Subarctic
- Tundra
- Ice cap
- Highland

- Highest average annual precipitation
- Lowest average annual precipitation
- Highest recorded temperature
- Lowest recorded temperature

Major Ocean Currents

- Cool currents
- Warm currents

NORTH AMERICA

SOUTH AMERICA

ATLANTIC OCEAN

PACIFIC OCEAN

Fairbanks
Edmonton
Vancouver
San Francisco
Denver
Phoenix
Toronto
Chicago
New York City
Atlanta
Miami
St. John's
Iqaluit
Nuuk
Mexico City
San Juan
Caracas
Bogotá
Lima
Recife
São Paulo
Rio de Janeiro
Santiago
Buenos Aires
Punta Arenas

Arica 0.03" (0.08 cm)

80°N
60°N
40°N
TROPIC OF CANCER
20°N
0° EQUATOR
20°S
TROPIC OF CAPRICORN
40°S
60°S
ANTARCTIC CIRCLE
80°S

160°W 140°W 120°W 100°W 80°W 60°W

Arid

Highland

Humid continental

Icecap

Marine

Mediterranean

Semiarid

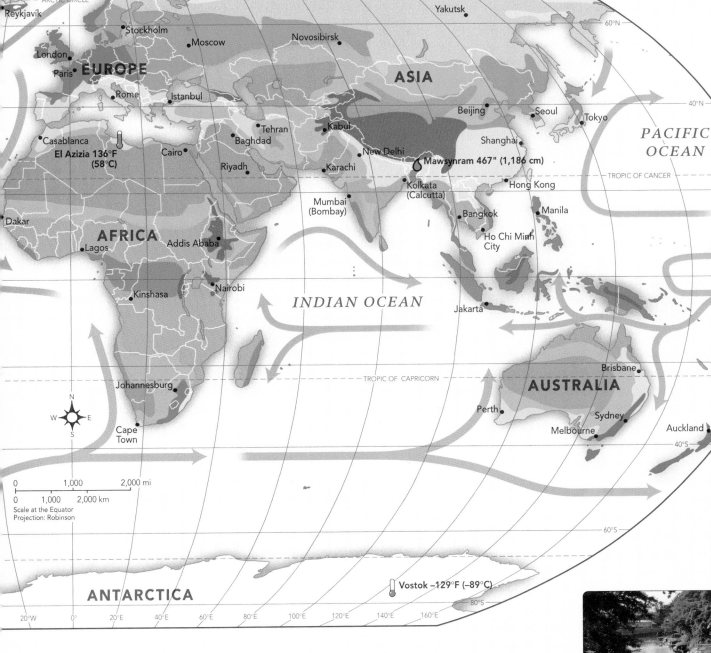

ARCTIC OCEAN

20°W 0° 20°E 40°E 60°E 80°E 100°E 120°E 140°E 160°E 80°N

Tromsø
Murmansk
ARCTIC CIRCLE
Reykjavík
Yakutsk
60°N
Stockholm
Moscow
Novosibirsk
London
Paris EUROPE
ASIA
Beijing Seoul
Rome Istanbul 40°N
Tokyo
PACIFIC OCEAN
Casablanca Tehran Kabul
Shanghai
El Azizia 136°F Baghdad New Delhi
(58°C) Cairo
Riyadh Karachi Mawsynram 467" (1,186 cm)
TROPIC OF CANCER
Kolkata Hong Kong 20°N
Dakar (Calcutta)
Mumbai Manila
AFRICA Addis Ababa (Bombay) Bangkok
Lagos Ho Chi Minh
City
0°
Kinshasa Nairobi INDIAN OCEAN
Jakarta
AUSTRALIA
20°S
Brisbane
Johannesburg TROPIC OF CAPRICORN
N Perth Sydney
W   E Melbourne Auckland
S
Cape 40°S
Town

0 1,000 2,000 mi
0 1,000 2,000 km
Scale at the Equator
Projection: Robinson

Vostok −129°F (−89°C)

ANTARCTICA

20°W 0° 20°E 40°E 60°E 80°E 100°E 120°E 140°E 160°E 80°S

60°S

Humid subtropical

Subarctic

Tropical wet

Tropical wet and dry

Tundra

Vegetation

- Unclassified highlands or ice cap
- Tundra and alpine tundra
- Coniferous forest
- Midlatitude deciduous forest
- Subtropical broadleaf evergreen forest
- Mixed forest
- Midlatitude scrubland
- Midlatitude grassland
- Desert
- Tropical seasonal and scrub
- Tropical rain forest
- Tropical savanna

NORTH AMERICA

SOUTH AMERICA

ATLANTIC OCEAN

PACIFIC OCEAN

PACIFIC OCEAN

Fairbanks
Edmonton
Vancouver
Toronto
Chicago
Denver
New York City
San Francisco
Phoenix
Atlanta
Miami
Mexico City
Iqaluit
Nuuk
St. John's
San Juan
Caracas
Bogotá
Lima
Recife
São Paulo
Rio de Janeir
Santiago
Buenos Aires
Punta Arenas

TROPIC OF CANCER
EQUATOR
TROPIC OF CAPRICORN
ANTARCTIC CIRCLE

80°N
60°N
40°N
20°N
0°
20°S
40°S
60°S
80°S

160°W | 140°W | 120°W | 100°W | 80°W | 60°W

Coniferous forest

Deciduous forest

Desert

Midlatitude scrubland

Mixed forest

Subtropical broadleaf evergreen forest

Tropical rain forest

Geographic
Features

Climate

Land Cover

Environmental
Issues

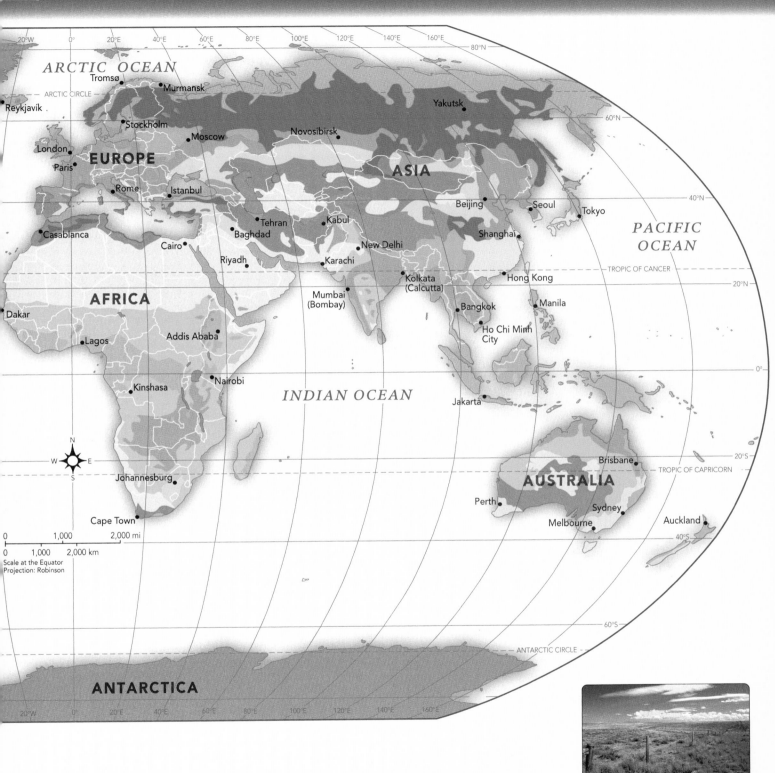

ARCTIC OCEAN

Tromsø
Murmansk
Yakutsk
Reykjavík
ARCTIC CIRCLE
Stockholm
Moscow
Novosibirsk
London
EUROPE
Paris
ASIA
Rome
Istanbul
Beijing
Seoul
Tokyo
PACIFIC
OCEAN
Tehran
Kabul
Casablanca
Baghdad
Shanghai
Cairo
New Delhi
Riyadh
Karachi
Hong Kong
TROPIC OF CANCER
AFRICA
Kolkata
(Calcutta)
Dakar
Mumbai
(Bombay)
Bangkok
Manila
Lagos
Addis Ababa
Ho Chi Minh
City
Kinshasa
Nairobi
INDIAN OCEAN
Jakarta
AUSTRALIA
Johannesburg
Brisbane
TROPIC OF CAPRICORN
Perth
Sydney
Cape Town
Melbourne
Auckland

1,000   2,000 mi
1,000   2,000 km
Scale at the Equator
Projection: Robinson

ANTARCTICA
ANTARCTIC CIRCLE

80°N
60°N
40°N
20°N
0°
20°S
40°S
60°S

20°W 0° 20°E 40°E 60°E 80°E 100°E 120°E 140°E 160°E

Midlatitude grassland

Tropical savanna

Tropical seasonal and scrub

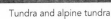

Tundra and alpine tundra

Unclassified highlands or ice cap

World Forest Cover

Forests help regulate climate by storing huge amounts of carbon dioxide, while providing habitats for countless animal and plant species. Environmentalists have voiced concern over a long-term decrease in forest cover, as forest lands have been cleared for such purposes as farming, logging, mining, and urban expansion.

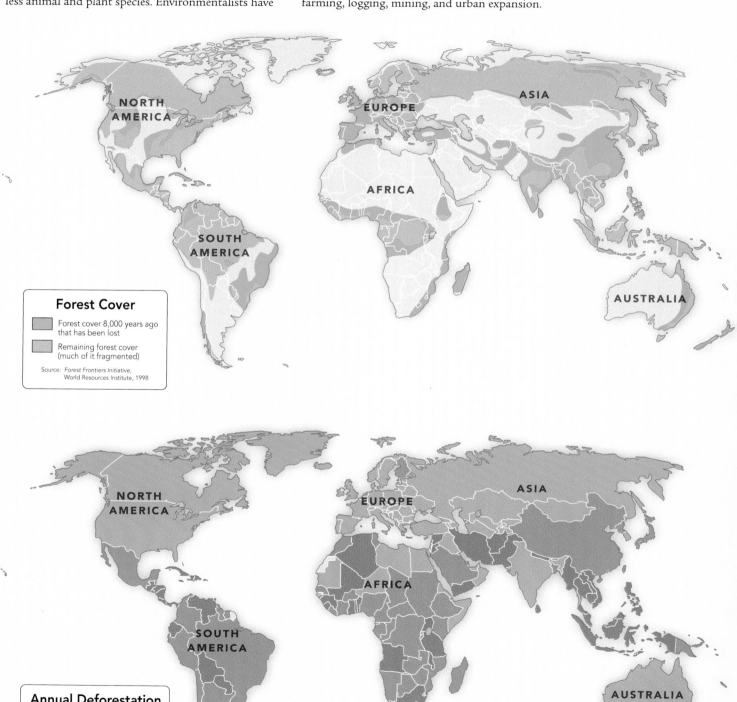

Forest Cover

Forest cover 8,000 years ago that has been lost

Remaining forest cover (much of it fragmented)

Source: *Forest Frontiers Initiative,* *World Resources Institute, 1998*

Annual Deforestation Rates

More than 0.9% deforested
0.1 to 0.9% deforested
Stable or increased forest area
No current data available

Source: World Resources Institute

Tropical Rain Forests

Tropical rain forests, found around the Earth within 10 degrees of the equator, contain more than half of all the world's plants and animal species, besides to being home to many indigenous peoples. They are vital to the balance of nature. In the past 40 years alone, about one-fifth of the acreage has been cleared for logging and other purposes. These rain forests, including the major forests pinpointed here, remain under serious threat.

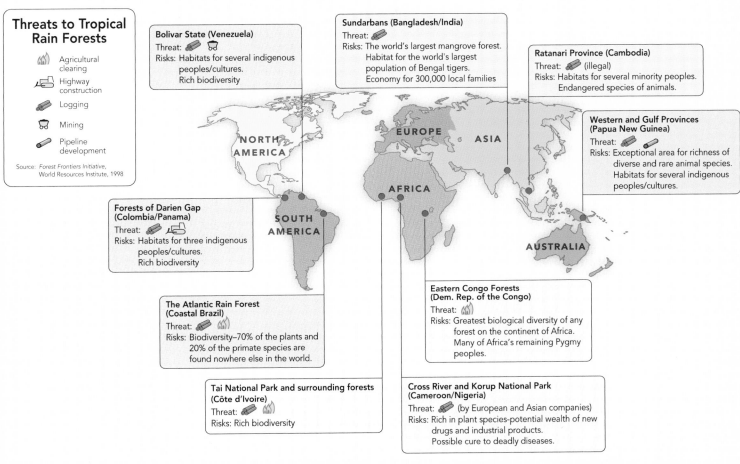

Threats to Tropical Rain Forests

- Agricultural clearing
- Highway construction
- Logging
- Mining
- Pipeline development

Source: *Forest Frontiers Initiative, World Resources Institute, 1998*

Bolivar State (Venezuela)
Threat:
Risks: Habitats for several indigenous peoples/cultures. Rich biodiversity

Sundarbans (Bangladesh/India)
Threat:
Risks: The world's largest mangrove forest. Habitat for the world's largest population of Bengal tigers. Economy for 300,000 local families

Ratanari Province (Cambodia)
Threat: (illegal)
Risks: Habitats for several minority peoples. Endangered species of animals.

Western and Gulf Provinces (Papua New Guinea)
Threat:
Risks: Exceptional area for richness of diverse and rare animal species. Habitats for several indigenous peoples/cultures.

Forests of Darien Gap (Colombia/Panama)
Threat:
Risks: Habitats for three indigenous peoples/cultures. Rich biodiversity

The Atlantic Rain Forest (Coastal Brazil)
Threat:
Risks: Biodiversity–70% of the plants and 20% of the primate species are found nowhere else in the world.

Eastern Congo Forests (Dem. Rep. of the Congo)
Threat:
Risks: Greatest biological diversity of any forest on the continent of Africa. Many of Africa's remaining Pygmy peoples.

Tai National Park and surrounding forests (Côte d'Ivoire)
Threat:
Risks: Rich biodiversity

Cross River and Korup National Park (Cameroon/Nigeria)
Threat: (by European and Asian companies)
Risks: Rich in plant species-potential wealth of new drugs and industrial products. Possible cure to deadly diseases.

According to the World Resources Institute, only about one-fifth of the Earth's forest cover of 8,000 years ago survives unfragmented, in the large unspoiled tracts it calls *frontier forests*. These forests are big enough to provide stable habitats for a rich diversity of plant and animal species.

Percentage of Frontier Forest Under Moderate or High Threat of Destruction
(through 2030)

Source: *Forest Frontiers Initiative, World Resources Institute, 1998*

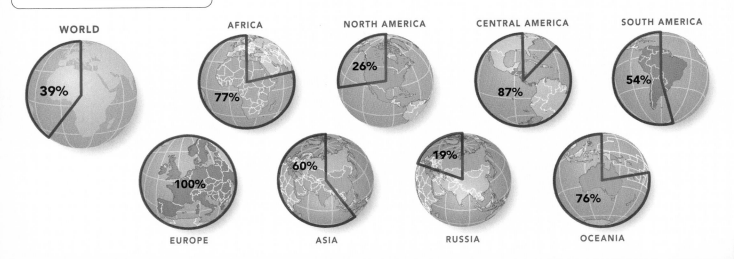

WORLD 39%

AFRICA 77%

NORTH AMERICA 26%

CENTRAL AMERICA 87%

SOUTH AMERICA 54%

EUROPE 100%

ASIA 60%

RUSSIA 19%

OCEANIA 76%

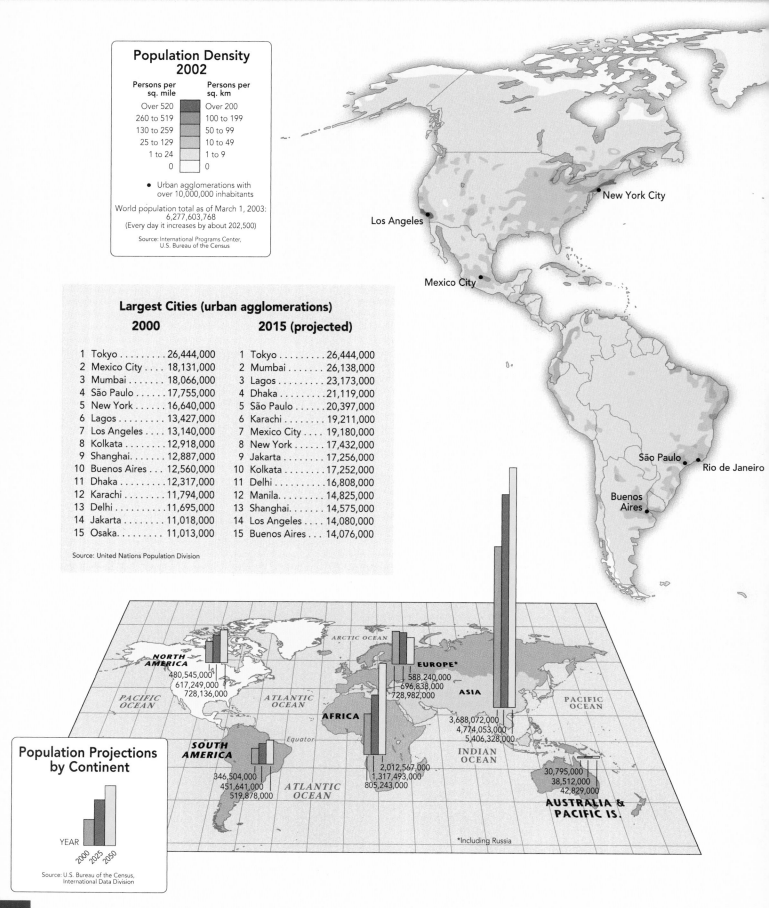

Population Density 2002

Persons per sq. mile		Persons per sq. km
Over 520		Over 200
260 to 519		100 to 199
130 to 259		50 to 99
25 to 129		10 to 49
1 to 24		1 to 9
0		0

● Urban agglomerations with over 10,000,000 inhabitants

World population total as of March 1, 2003: 6,277,603,768
(Every day it increases by about 202,500)

Source: International Programs Center, U.S. Bureau of the Census

Largest Cities (urban agglomerations)

	2000		2015 (projected)
1	Tokyo 26,444,000	1	Tokyo 26,444,000
2	Mexico City 18,131,000	2	Mumbai 26,138,000
3	Mumbai 18,066,000	3	Lagos 23,173,000
4	São Paulo 17,755,000	4	Dhaka 21,119,000
5	New York 16,640,000	5	São Paulo 20,397,000
6	Lagos 13,427,000	6	Karachi 19,211,000
7	Los Angeles 13,140,000	7	Mexico City 19,180,000
8	Kolkata 12,918,000	8	New York 17,432,000
9	Shanghai. 12,887,000	9	Jakarta 17,256,000
10	Buenos Aires . . . 12,560,000	10	Kolkata 17,252,000
11	Dhaka 12,317,000	11	Delhi 16,808,000
12	Karachi 11,794,000	12	Manila. 14,825,000
13	Delhi 11,695,000	13	Shanghai. 14,575,000
14	Jakarta 11,018,000	14	Los Angeles 14,080,000
15	Osaka. 11,013,000	15	Buenos Aires . . . 14,076,000

Source: United Nations Population Division

New York City
Los Angeles
Mexico City
São Paulo
Rio de Janeiro
Buenos Aires

NORTH AMERICA
480,545,000
617,249,000
728,136,000

EUROPE*
588,240,000
696,838,000
728,982,000

ASIA
3,688,072,000
4,774,053,000
5,406,328,000

AFRICA
2,012,567,000
1,317,493,000
805,243,000

SOUTH AMERICA
346,504,000
451,641,000
519,878,000

AUSTRALIA & PACIFIC IS.
30,795,000
38,512,000
42,829,000

ARCTIC OCEAN
PACIFIC OCEAN
ATLANTIC OCEAN
INDIAN OCEAN
Equator

*Including Russia

Population Projections by Continent

YEAR
2000 2025 2050

Source: U.S. Bureau of the Census, International Data Division

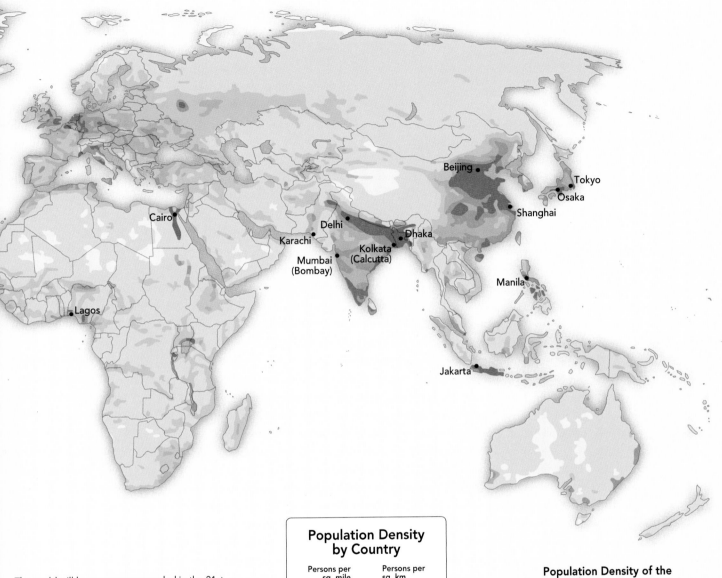

The world will become more crowded in the 21st century. In mid-2000, China already had the highest population in the world, with an estimated 1.3 billion inhabitants, one-fifth of the world total. India had reached 1 billion, while the United States had the world's third-largest population, with about 275 million, followed by Indonesia, Brazil, and Russia.

Population Density by Country

Persons per sq. mile	Persons per sq. km
1170 and over	450 and over
780 to 1169	300 to 449
390 to 779	150 to 299
195 to 389	75 to 149
65 to 194	25 to 74
Under 65	Under 25
	Other countries

Source: U.S. Bureau of the Census, U.S. Dept. of Commerce

Population Density of the Current Most Populous Countries

2000	Persons per square mile	2050 (projected)	Persons per square mile
China	330	China	360
India	800	India	1,450
United States	70	United States	100
Indonesia	290	Indonesia	450
Brazil	50	Brazil	70
Russia	20	Russia	20

2000

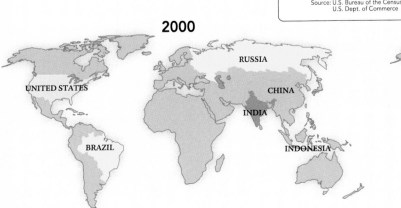

2050

Life Expectancy

Life expectancy at birth is a common measure of the number of years a person may expect to live. There are many factors, such as nutrition, sanitation, health and medical services, that contribute to helping people live longer.

As some of the above factors improve in the develop-ing countries, life expectancy there should increase. But most of sub-Saharan Africa will have less than average life expectancies.

Although it is not included here, females almost always have a longer life expectancy than males.

2000

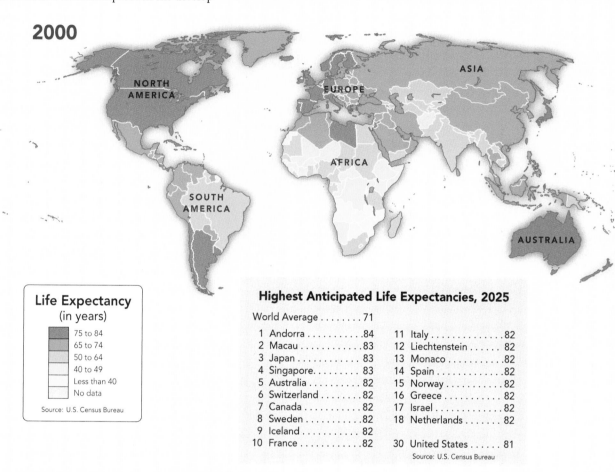

Life Expectancy
(in years)

- 75 to 84
- 65 to 74
- 50 to 64
- 40 to 49
- Less than 40
- No data

Source: U.S. Census Bureau

Highest Anticipated Life Expectancies, 2025

World Average 71

1	Andorra 84	11	Italy 82
2	Macau 83	12	Liechtenstein 82
3	Japan 83	13	Monaco 82
4	Singapore. 83	14	Spain 82
5	Australia 82	15	Norway 82
6	Switzerland 82	16	Greece 82
7	Canada 82	17	Israel 82
8	Sweden 82	18	Netherlands 82
9	Iceland 82		
10	France 82	30	United States 81

Source: U.S. Census Bureau

2025

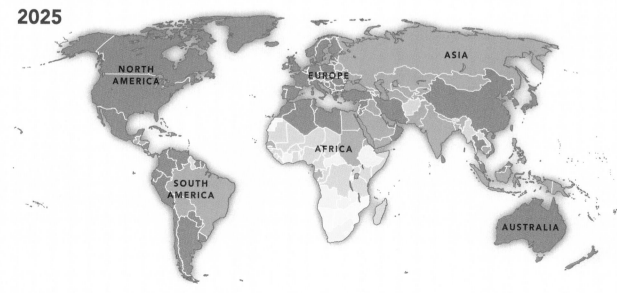

Youthful Population

A country with a youthful population often reflects a high birthrate and a short life expectancy. The youthful component of a country's population should be the healthiest and the most energetic. In countries where there is a good system of education, the standards of living can only benefit from a large, educated youthful population. Furthermore, large numbers of young workers offer a means for provid-ing financial and social support for the older members of the population. Unfortunately, a country's economic and physical resources may not be able to absorb a ballooning youthful population. A lack of opportunity in rural regions encourages migration to over-crowded cities where, in turn, a lack of jobs or space in schools leads to swelling numbers of unemployed.

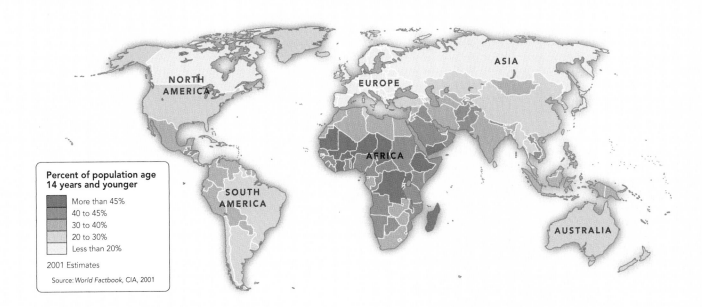

Percent of population age 14 years and younger

- More than 45%
- 40 to 45%
- 30 to 40%
- 20 to 30%
- Less than 20%

2001 Estimates

Source: *World Factbook*, CIA, 2001

Food and Nutrition

There has been a general trend towards better nutrition, but sub-Saharan Africa remains a problem area: increasing numbers of people will be suffering from undernutrition.

On a worldwide basis, the food supply seems adequate. Unfortunately the availability of food and the distribution of people don't always match up.

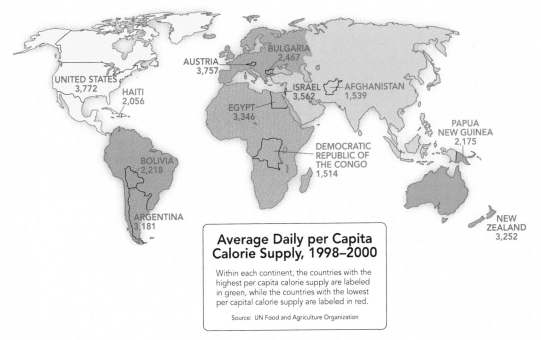

UNITED STATES
3,772

HAITI
2,056

AUSTRIA
3,757

BULGARIA
2,467

ISRAEL
3,562

AFGHANISTAN
1,539

EGYPT
3,346

DEMOCRATIC
REPUBLIC OF
THE CONGO
1,514

PAPUA
NEW GUINEA
2,175

BOLIVIA
2,218

ARGENTINA
3,181

NEW
ZEALAND
3,252

Average Daily per Capita Calorie Supply, 1998–2000

Within each continent, the countries with the highest per capita calorie supply are labeled in green, while the countries with the lowest per capital calorie supply are labeled in red.

Source: UN Food and Agriculture Organization

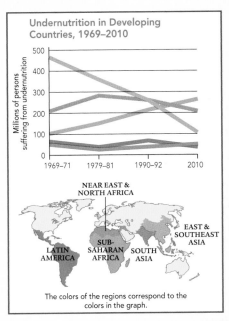

Undernutrition in Developing Countries, 1969–2010

Millions of persons suffering from undernutrition

500
400
300
200
100
0

1969–71   1979–81   1990–92   2010

NEAR EAST & NORTH AFRICA

LATIN AMERICA

SUB-SAHARAN AFRICA

SOUTH ASIA

EAST & SOUTHEAST ASIA

The colors of the regions correspond to the colors in the graph.

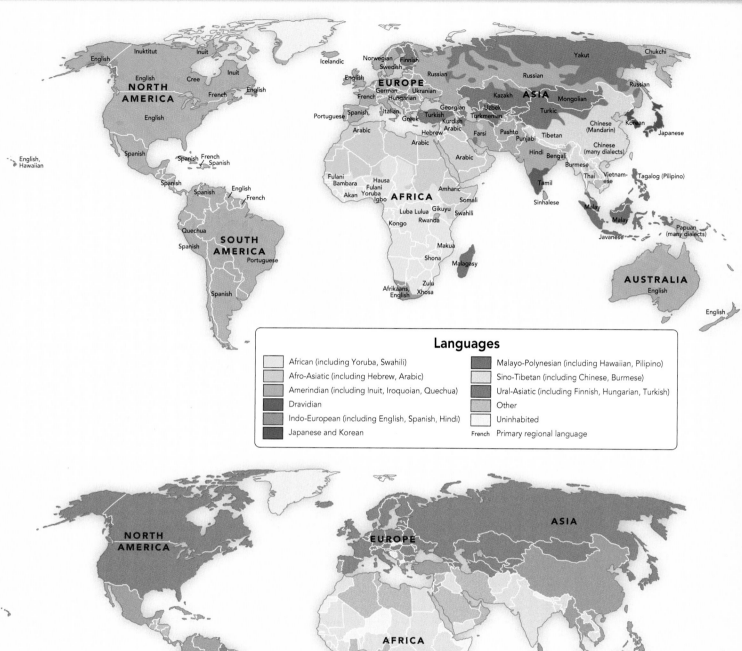

Languages

- African (including Yoruba, Swahili)
- Afro-Asiatic (including Hebrew, Arabic)
- Amerindian (including Inuit, Iroquoian, Quechua)
- Dravidian
- Indo-European (including English, Spanish, Hindi)
- Japanese and Korean
- Malayo-Polynesian (including Hawaiian, Pilipino)
- Sino-Tibetan (including Chinese, Burmese)
- Ural-Asiatic (including Finnish, Hungarian, Turkish)
- Other
- Uninhabited
- French Primary regional language

Literacy

2001 Estimates

- 97 to 100%
- 81 to 96%
- 61 to 80%
- 30 to 60%
- Less than 30%
- No current data available

World literacy rates are based on the percentage of the population who can read their native language. The data varies between the years of 1989 to 2000.

Source: *World Factbook*, CIA, 2001

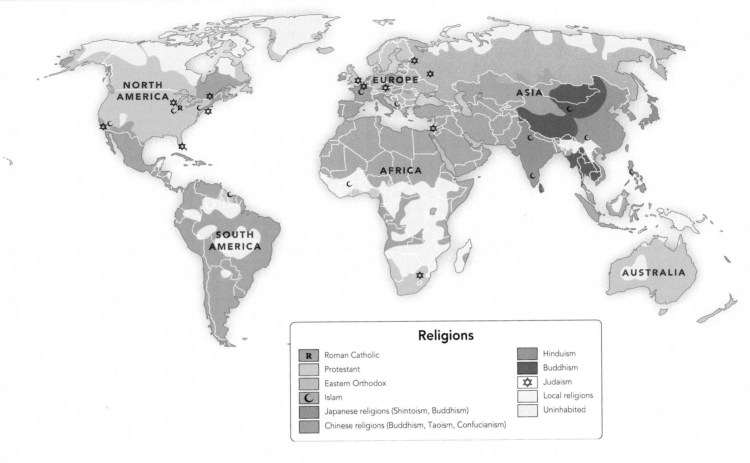

Religions

R	Roman Catholic		Hinduism
	Protestant		Buddhism
	Eastern Orthodox	✡	Judaism
☾	Islam		Local religions
	Japanese religions (Shintoism, Buddhism)		Uninhabited
	Chinese religions (Buddhism, Taoism, Confucianism)		

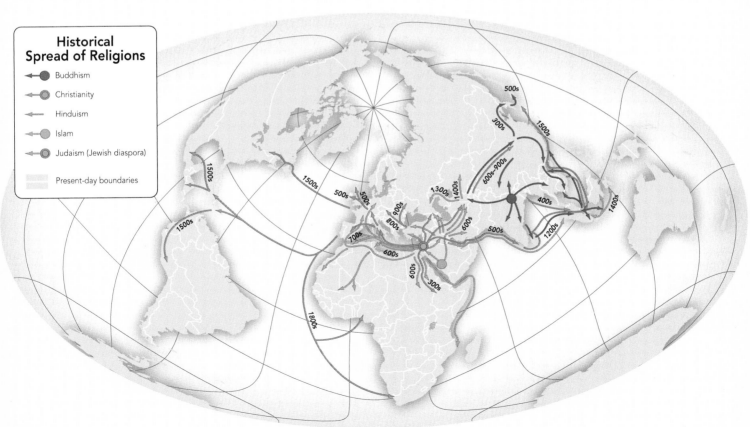

Historical Spread of Religions

- ← ● Buddhism
- ← ● Christianity
- ← Hinduism
- ← ● Islam
- ← ● Judaism (Jewish diaspora)

- Present-day boundaries

Population

Population
Issues

Languages/
Literacy/Religions

**Land Use/GDP/
Employment**

Mining/Energy

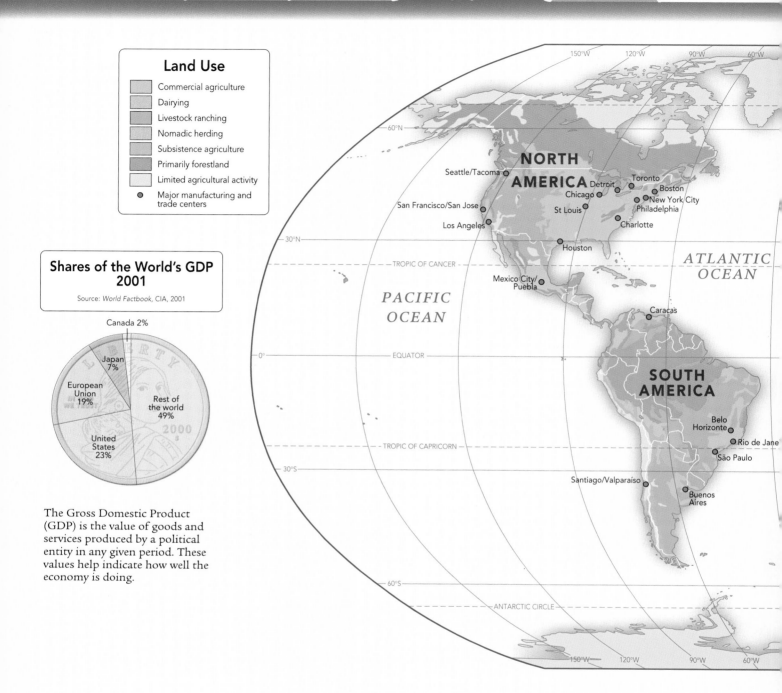

Land Use

- Commercial agriculture
- Dairying
- Livestock ranching
- Nomadic herding
- Subsistence agriculture
- Primarily forestland
- Limited agricultural activity
- ● Major manufacturing and trade centers

Shares of the World's GDP 2001

Source: *World Factbook*, CIA, 2001

Canada 2%
Japan 7%
European Union 19%
Rest of the world 49%
United States 23%

The Gross Domestic Product (GDP) is the value of goods and services produced by a political entity in any given period. These values help indicate how well the economy is doing.

Industrial Employment

- More than 40%
- 30 to 40%
- 15 to 29.9%
- Less than 15%
- No current data available

Percentage of total labor force employed in industry.

Source: *World Factbook*, CIA, 2001

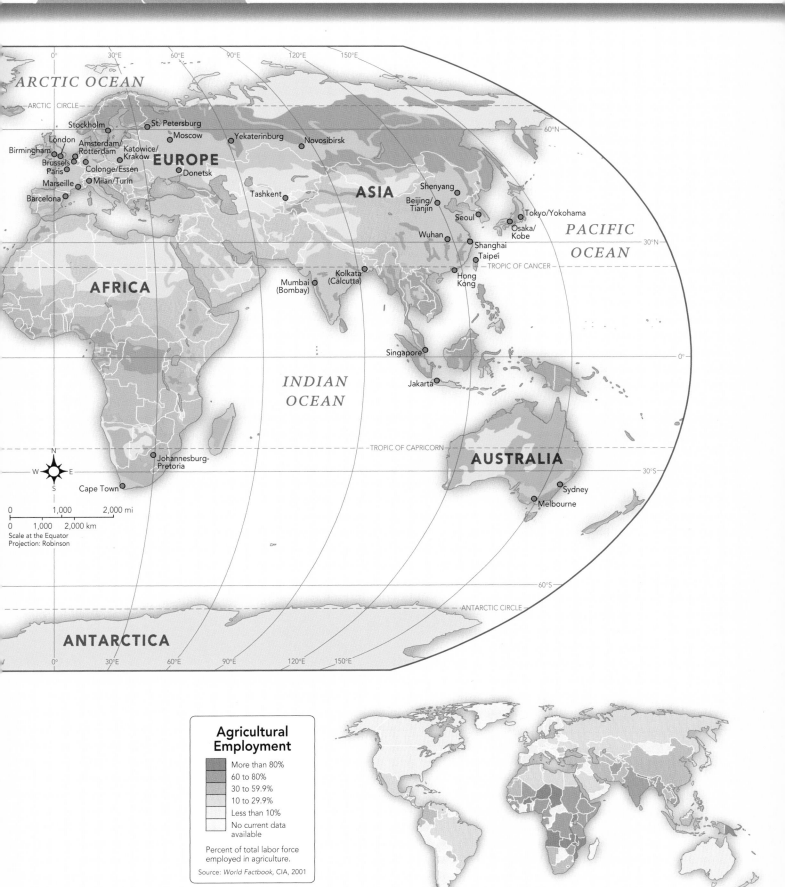

ARCTIC OCEAN

ARCTIC CIRCLE

Stockholm
St. Petersburg
London
Birmingham
Amsterdam/
Rotterdam
Moscow
Yekaterinburg
Novosibirsk
60°N
Brussels
Katowice/
Krakow
EUROPE
Paris
Colonge/Essen
Donetsk
ASIA
Shenyang
Marseille
Milan/Turin
Tashkent
Beijing/
Tianjin
Tokyo/Yokohama
Barcelona
Seoul
Osaka/
Kobe
PACIFIC
OCEAN
Wuhan
Shanghai
30°N
AFRICA
Taipei
TROPIC OF CANCER
Kolkata
(Calcutta)
Mumbai
(Bombay)
Hong
Kong
Singapore
0°
INDIAN
OCEAN
Jakarta
TROPIC OF CAPRICORN
AUSTRALIA
Johannesburg-
Pretoria
30°S
Cape Town
Sydney
Melbourne
0   1,000   2,000 mi
0   1,000   2,000 km
Scale at the Equator
Projection: Robinson
60°S
ANTARCTIC CIRCLE
ANTARCTICA
0°   30°E   60°E   90°E   120°E   150°E

Agricultural Employment

- More than 80%
- 60 to 80%
- 30 to 59.9%
- 10 to 29.9%
- Less than 10%
- No current data available

Percent of total labor force employed in agriculture.

Source: *World Factbook*, CIA, 2001

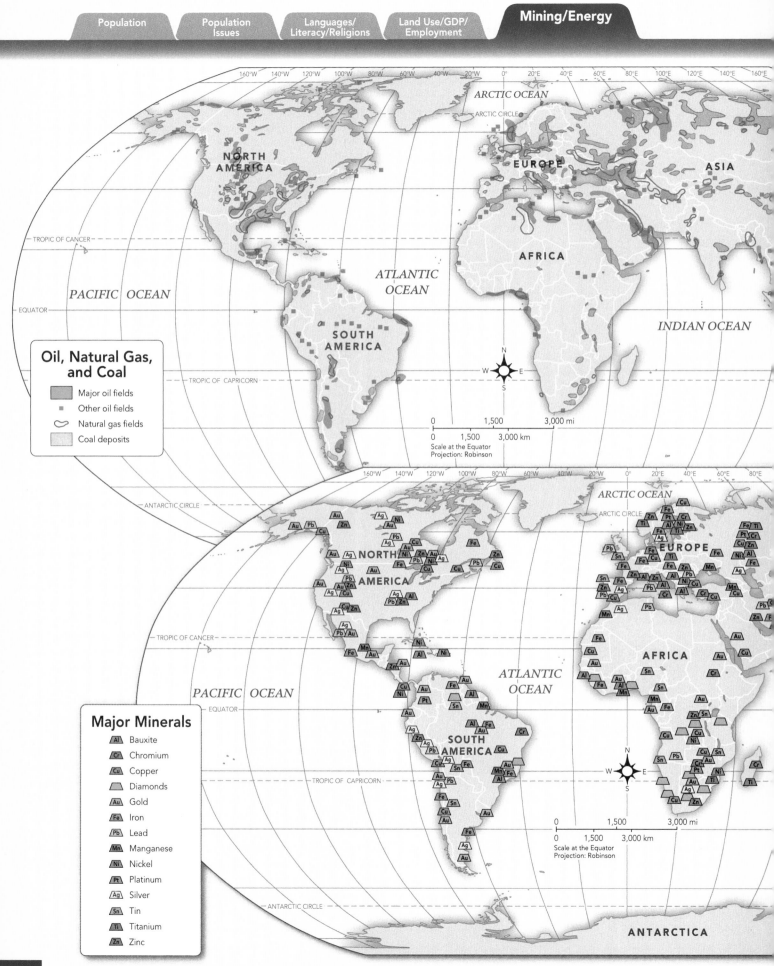

Oil, Natural Gas, and Coal

- Major oil fields
- Other oil fields
- Natural gas fields
- Coal deposits

Major Minerals

- Al Bauxite
- Cr Chromium
- Cu Copper
- Diamonds
- Au Gold
- Fe Iron
- Pb Lead
- Mn Manganese
- Ni Nickel
- Pt Platinum
- Ag Silver
- Sn Tin
- Ti Titanium
- Zn Zinc

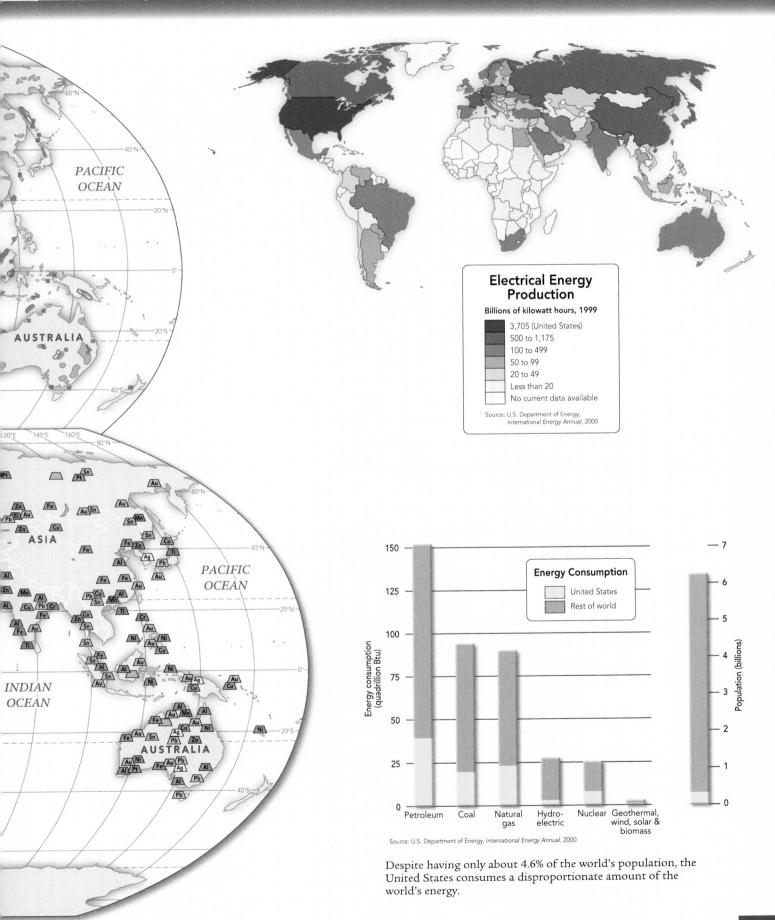

PACIFIC
OCEAN

AUSTRALIA

ASIA

PACIFIC
OCEAN

INDIAN
OCEAN

AUSTRALIA

Electrical Energy Production

Billions of kilowatt hours, 1999

- 3,705 (United States)
- 500 to 1,175
- 100 to 499
- 50 to 99
- 20 to 49
- Less than 20
- No current data available

Source: U.S. Department of Energy,
International Energy Annual, 2000

Energy Consumption

- United States
- Rest of world

Energy consumption (quadrillion Btu)

Population (billions)

Petroleum | Coal | Natural gas | Hydro-electric | Nuclear | Geothermal, wind, solar & biomass

Source: U.S. Department of Energy, *International Energy Annual*, 2000

Despite having only about 4.6% of the world's population, the United States consumes a disproportionate amount of the world's energy.

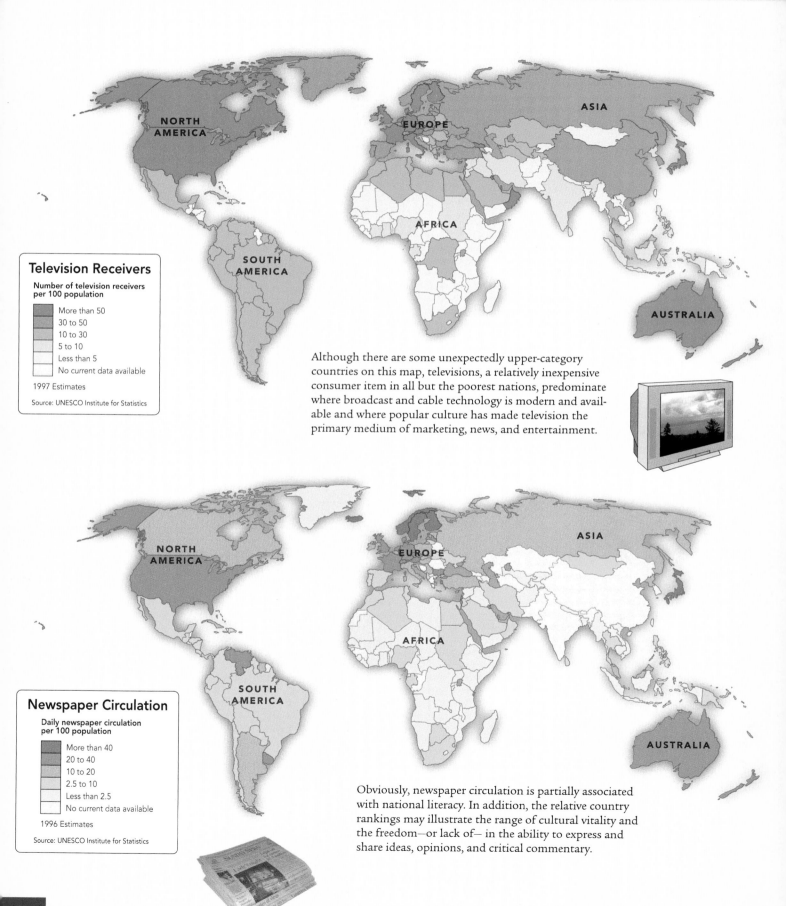

Television Receivers

Number of television receivers per 100 population

- More than 50
- 30 to 50
- 10 to 30
- 5 to 10
- Less than 5
- No current data available

1997 Estimates

Source: UNESCO Institute for Statistics

Although there are some unexpectedly upper-category countries on this map, televisions, a relatively inexpensive consumer item in all but the poorest nations, predominate where broadcast and cable technology is modern and available and where popular culture has made television the primary medium of marketing, news, and entertainment.

Newspaper Circulation

Daily newspaper circulation per 100 population

- More than 40
- 20 to 40
- 10 to 20
- 2.5 to 10
- Less than 2.5
- No current data available

1996 Estimates

Source: UNESCO Institute for Statistics

Obviously, newspaper circulation is partially associated with national literacy. In addition, the relative country rankings may illustrate the range of cultural vitality and the freedom—or lack of— in the ability to express and share ideas, opinions, and critical commentary.

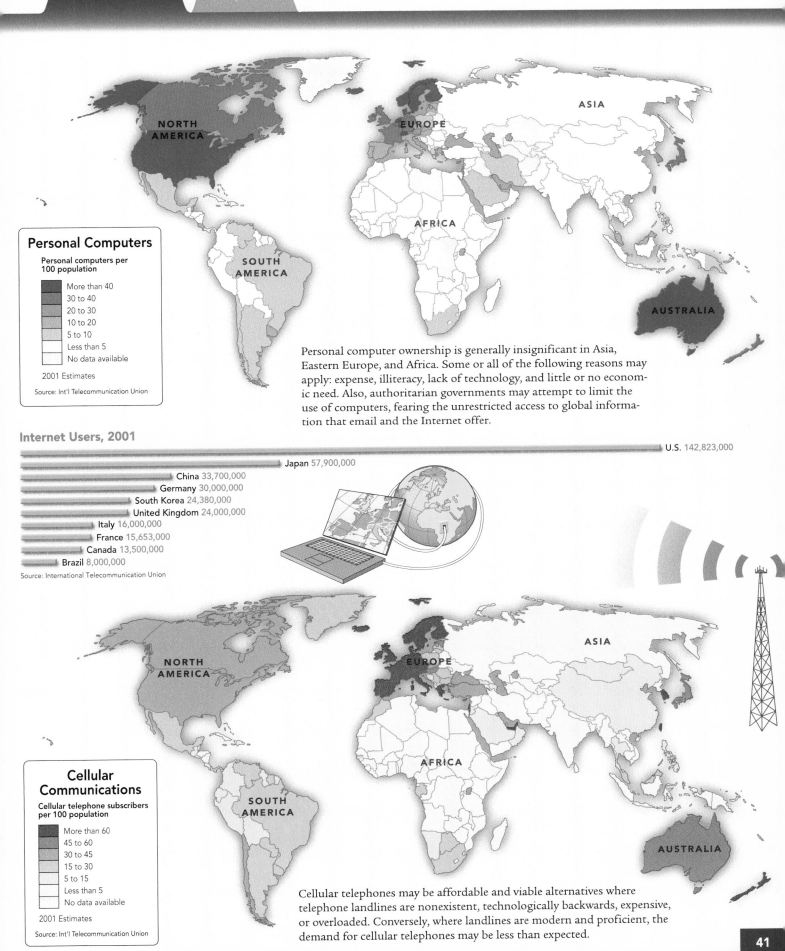

Personal Computers

Personal computers per 100 population

- More than 40
- 30 to 40
- 20 to 30
- 10 to 20
- 5 to 10
- Less than 5
- No data available

2001 Estimates

Source: Int'l Telecommunication Union

Personal computer ownership is generally insignificant in Asia, Eastern Europe, and Africa. Some or all of the following reasons may apply: expense, illiteracy, lack of technology, and little or no economic need. Also, authoritarian governments may attempt to limit the use of computers, fearing the unrestricted access to global information that email and the Internet offer.

Internet Users, 2001

- U.S. 142,823,000
- Japan 57,900,000
- China 33,700,000
- Germany 30,000,000
- South Korea 24,380,000
- United Kingdom 24,000,000
- Italy 16,000,000
- France 15,653,000
- Canada 13,500,000
- Brazil 8,000,000

Source: International Telecommunication Union

Cellular Communications

Cellular telephone subscribers per 100 population

- More than 60
- 45 to 60
- 30 to 45
- 15 to 30
- 5 to 15
- Less than 5
- No data available

2001 Estimates

Source: Int'l Telecommunication Union

Cellular telephones may be affordable and viable alternatives where telephone landlines are nonexistent, technologically backwards, expensive, or overloaded. Conversely, where landlines are modern and proficient, the demand for cellular telephones may be less than expected.

Time Zones

Non-standard tim

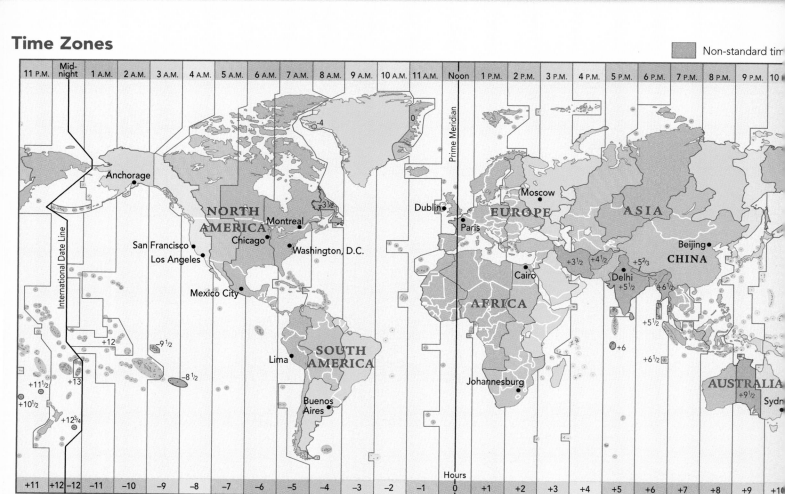

The World is divided into 24 time zones, beginning at the Prime Meridian, which runs through Greenwich, England. The twelve zones east and twelve zones west of the Prime Meridian meet halfway around the globe at the International Date Line.

Traveling in an easterly direction, the time of day moves ahead one hour for each zone crossed. Traveling west, time falls behind one hour per zone. At the International Date Line a traveler gains one day crossing it in an easterly direction, and loses one day traveling west.

Note that the times shown are "standard time." Adjustments are necessary when "daylight saving time" is used.

Average Speeds of
Some Passenger Transportation

Walking 3–4 mph/5-6 kph

Bicycle 10 mph/16 kph

Ocean liner, *Queen Elizabeth II* 33 mph/53 kph

Intercity bus, Greyhound; U.S. 54 mph/87 kph

Air cushion vehicle, United Kingdom 69 mph/111kph

Electric train, Amtrak *Acela Express*; Eastern U.S. 150 mph/241 kph (top speed)

High-speed train, *Shinkansen* (Bullet Train); Japan 164 mph/263 kph (average speed between stations)

Jet airliner, Boeing 737 500 mph/805 kph

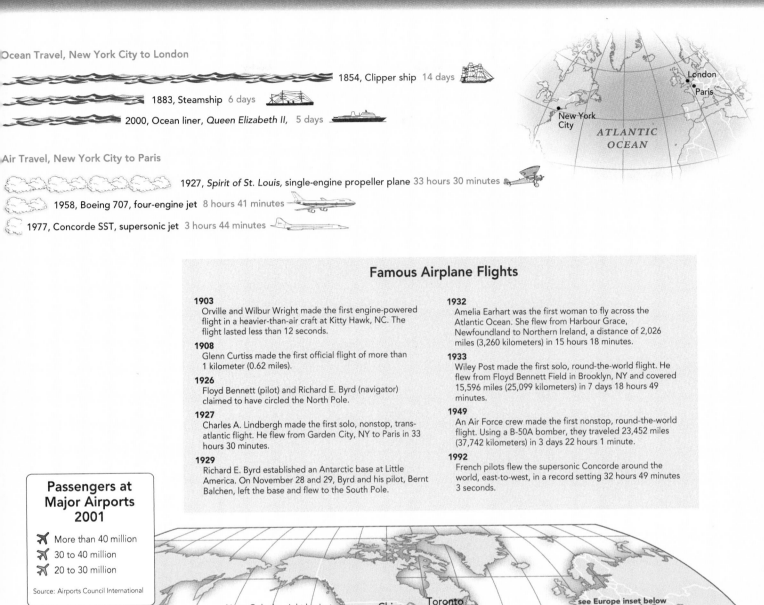

Ocean Travel, New York City to London

1854, Clipper ship 14 days

1883, Steamship 6 days

2000, Ocean liner, *Queen Elizabeth II*, 5 days

ATLANTIC OCEAN

London
Paris
New York City

Air Travel, New York City to Paris

1927, *Spirit of St. Louis,* single-engine propeller plane 33 hours 30 minutes

1958, Boeing 707, four-engine jet 8 hours 41 minutes

1977, Concorde SST, supersonic jet 3 hours 44 minutes

Famous Airplane Flights

1903
Orville and Wilbur Wright made the first engine-powered flight in a heavier-than-air craft at Kitty Hawk, NC. The flight lasted less than 12 seconds.

1908
Glenn Curtiss made the first official flight of more than 1 kilometer (0.62 miles).

1926
Floyd Bennett (pilot) and Richard E. Byrd (navigator) claimed to have circled the North Pole.

1927
Charles A. Lindbergh made the first solo, nonstop, trans-atlantic flight. He flew from Garden City, NY to Paris in 33 hours 30 minutes.

1929
Richard E. Byrd established an Antarctic base at Little America. On November 28 and 29, Byrd and his pilot, Bernt Balchen, left the base and flew to the South Pole.

1932
Amelia Earhart was the first woman to fly across the Atlantic Ocean. She flew from Harbour Grace, Newfoundland to Northern Ireland, a distance of 2,026 miles (3,260 kilometers) in 15 hours 18 minutes.

1933
Wiley Post made the first solo, round-the-world flight. He flew from Floyd Bennett Field in Brooklyn, NY and covered 15,596 miles (25,099 kilometers) in 7 days 18 hours 49 minutes.

1949
An Air Force crew made the first nonstop, round-the-world flight. Using a B-50A bomber, they traveled 23,452 miles (37,742 kilometers) in 3 days 22 hours 1 minute.

1992
French pilots flew the supersonic Concorde around the world, east-to-west, in a record setting 32 hours 49 minutes 3 seconds.

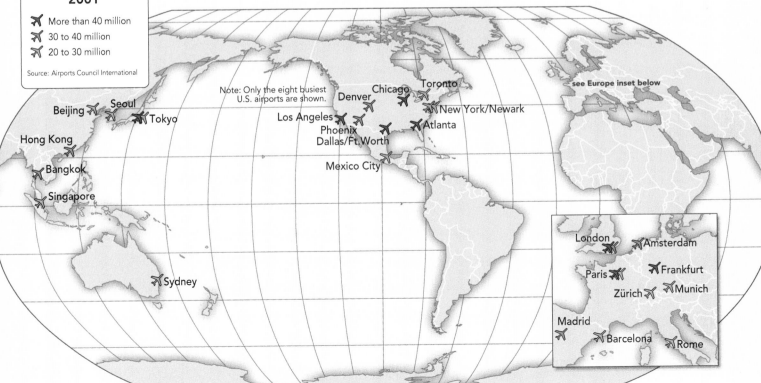

Passengers at Major Airports 2001

✈ More than 40 million

✈ 30 to 40 million

✈ 20 to 30 million

Source: Airports Council International

Note: Only the eight busiest U.S. airports are shown.

Toronto
Chicago
Denver
New York/Newark
Los Angeles
Atlanta
Phoenix
Dallas/Ft.Worth
Mexico City

Beijing
Seoul
Tokyo
Hong Kong
Bangkok
Singapore
Sydney

see Europe inset below

London
Amsterdam
Paris
Frankfurt
Zürich
Munich
Madrid
Barcelona
Rome

North America

Legend

- International boundary
- State or provincial boundary
- ⊛ National capital

Symbol and label sizes indicate relative sizes of cities:
- ● **New York**
- • Baltimore
- · Charlotte

Facts

- Area: 9,361,791 square miles (24,247,038 square kilometers)

- Highest Point: Mt. McKinley, United States, 20,320 ft. (6,194 m)

- Lowest Point: Death Valley, United States, 282 ft. (86 m) below sea level

- Longest River: Mississippi-Missouri-Red Rock, 3,710 mi. (5,971 km)

- Largest Lake: Lake Superior, United States/Canada, 31,700 sq. mi. (82,103 sq. km)

- Largest Country: Canada, 3,851,809 sq. mi. (9,976,140 sq. km)

- Largest City: New York City, United States, 21,200,000 (metropolitan population)

Nations of the Lesser Antilles

Country	Capital	Country	Capital
Antigua and Barbuda	St. John's	St. Vincent and the Grenadines	Kingstown
St. Kitts and Nevis	Basseterre		
Dominica	Roseau	Grenada	St. George's
St. Lucia	Castries	Trinidad and Tobago	Port-of-Spain
Barbados	Bridgetown		

44

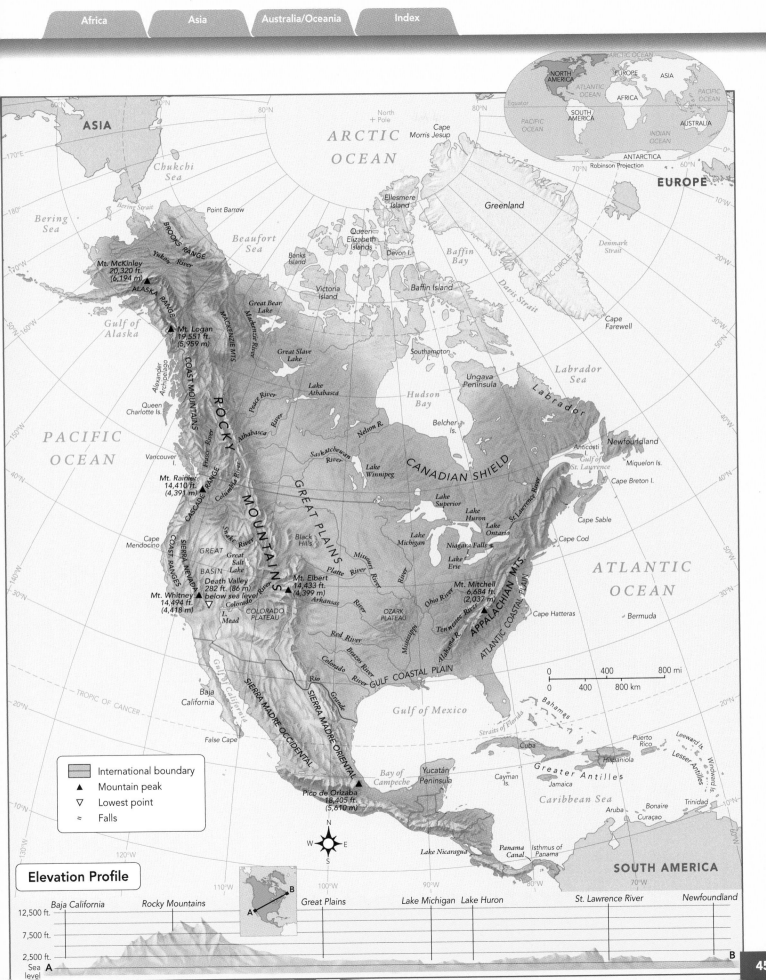

Major Metropolitan Areas

Antigua & Barbuda
St. John's — 22,000

Bahamas
Nassau — 211,000

Barbados
Bridgetown — 6,000

Belize
Belize City — 49,000
Belmopan — 8,000

Canada
Toronto — 5,030,000
Montréal — 3,549,000
Vancouver — 2,123,000
Ottawa — 1,129,000
Calgary — 993,000
Edmonton — 967,000
Québec — 698,000
Hamilton — 687,000
Winnipeg — 686,000

Costa Rica
San José — 1,305,000

Cuba
Havana — 2,192,000

Dominica
Roseau — 16,000

Dominican Republic
Santo Domingo — 2,677,000

El Salvador
San Salvador — 1,909,000

Grenada
St. George's — 5,000

Guatemala
Guatemala City — 1,007,000

Haiti
Port-au-Prince — 991,000

Honduras
Tegucigalpa — 835,000

Jamaica
Kingston — 578,000

Mexico
Mexico City — 16,203,000
Guadalajara — 3,349,000
Monterrey — 3,131,000
Puebla — 1,272,000
Ciudad Juárez — 1,187,000
Tijuana — 1,149,000
León — 1,021,000

Nicaragua
Managua — 1,148,000

Panama
Panama City — 1,002,000

Puerto Rico
San Juan — 2,450,000

St. Kitts & Nevis
Basseterre — 13,000

St. Lucia
Castries — 11,000

St. Vincent & Grenadines
Kingstown — 15,000

Trinidad & Tobago
Port of Spain — 48,000

United States
New York-Newark — 21,200,000
Los Angeles — 16,374,000
Chicago — 9,158,000
Washington-Baltimore — 7,608,000
San Francisco-
 Oakland-San Jose — 7,039,000
Philadelphia — 6,188,000
Boston — 5,819,000
Detroit — 5,456,000
Dallas-Ft. Worth — 5,222,000
Houston — 4,670,000
Atlanta — 4,112,000
Miami — 3,876,000
Seattle-Tacoma — 3,555,000
Phoenix — 3,252,000
Minneapolis-St. Paul — 2,969,000
Cleveland-Akron — 2,946,000
San Diego — 2,814,000
St. Louis — 2,604,000
Denver — 2,582,000
Tampa-St. Petersburg — 2,396,000
Pittsburgh — 2,359,000
Portland — 2,265,000
Cincinnati — 1,979,000
Sacramento — 1,797,000
Kansas City — 1,776,000
Milwaukee — 1,690,000

International comparability of population data is limited by varying census methods. Where metropolitan population is unavailable, core city population is shown.

Population

Persons per sq. mile	Persons per sq. km
Over 520	Over 200
260 to 519	100 to 199
130 to 259	50 to 99
25 to 129	10 to 49
1 to 24	1 to 9
0	0

Major metropolitan areas
● Over 2 million
● 1 million to 2 million
· Under 1 million

Estimated 2002 Population (in millions)
United States 281
Mexico 103
Canada 32
Guatemala 13
Cuba 11
All other countries 51

Source: U.S. Census Bureau

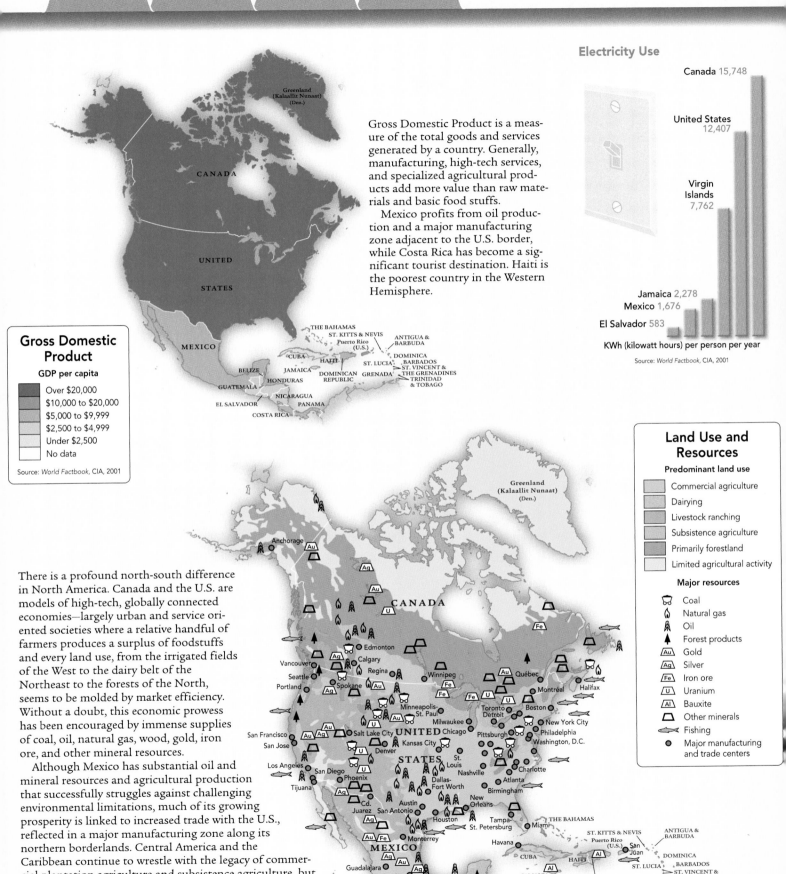

Electricity Use

Canada 15,748
United States 12,407
Virgin Islands 7,762
Jamaica 2,278
Mexico 1,676
El Salvador 583

KWh (kilowatt hours) per person per year

Source: *World Factbook, CIA, 2001*

Gross Domestic Product is a measure of the total goods and services generated by a country. Generally, manufacturing, high-tech services, and specialized agricultural products add more value than raw materials and basic food stuffs.

Mexico profits from oil production and a major manufacturing zone adjacent to the U.S. border, while Costa Rica has become a significant tourist destination. Haiti is the poorest country in the Western Hemisphere.

Gross Domestic Product

GDP per capita

- Over $20,000
- $10,000 to $20,000
- $5,000 to $9,999
- $2,500 to $4,999
- Under $2,500
- No data

Source: *World Factbook, CIA, 2001*

Land Use and Resources

Predominant land use
- Commercial agriculture
- Dairying
- Livestock ranching
- Subsistence agriculture
- Primarily forestland
- Limited agricultural activity

Major resources
- Coal
- Natural gas
- Oil
- Forest products
- Gold (Au)
- Silver (Ag)
- Iron ore (Fe)
- Uranium (U)
- Bauxite (Al)
- Other minerals
- Fishing
- Major manufacturing and trade centers

There is a profound north-south difference in North America. Canada and the U.S. are models of high-tech, globally connected economies—largely urban and service oriented societies where a relative handful of farmers produces a surplus of foodstuffs and every land use, from the irrigated fields of the West to the dairy belt of the Northeast to the forests of the North, seems to be molded by market efficiency. Without a doubt, this economic prowess has been encouraged by immense supplies of coal, oil, natural gas, wood, gold, iron ore, and other mineral resources.

Although Mexico has substantial oil and mineral resources and agricultural production that successfully struggles against challenging environmental limitations, much of its growing prosperity is linked to increased trade with the U.S., reflected in a major manufacturing zone along its northern borderlands. Central America and the Caribbean continue to wrestle with the legacy of commercial plantation agriculture and subsistence agriculture, but tourism, especially in the Caribbean, and small-scale assembly and manufacturing have become economic backbones, as well.

47

Climate

- Tropical wet
- Tropical wet and dry
- Arid
- Semiarid
- Mediterranean
- Humid subtropical
- Marine
- Humid continental
- Subarctic
- Tundra
- Highland
- Ice cap

Surrounded and enveloped by warm water, the countries of southern North America are warm and wet. The Eastern U.S. and most of Canada are striped by climate zones offering adequate precipitation and progressively lower temperatures as one travels north, but the pattern goes topsy-turvy in the West, where swirling arid and semiarid zones abut coastal regions influenced by both rain-bearing winds and cool ocean currents.

See photographs taken in different kinds of climates on pages 24–25.

Snag
Lowest recorded temperature: -81°F (-63°C)

Greenland (Kalaallit Nunaat) (Den.)

Fairbanks

Nuuk

CANADA

St. John's

Vancouver

Minneapolis

New York City

San Francisco

Death Valley
Highest recorded temperature: 134°F (57°C)

UNITED STATES

Phoenix

Atlanta

THE BAHAMAS

ST. KITTS & NEVIS
Puerto Rico (U.S.)

ANTIGUA & BARBUDA

MEXICO

CUBA

HAITI

San Juan

DOMINICA

Mexico City

JAMAICA

DOMINICAN REPUBLIC

ST. LUCIA

BARBADOS

ST. VINCENT & THE GRENADINES

GRENADA

TRINIDAD & TOBAGO

BELIZE

HONDURAS

GUATEMALA

NICARAGUA

EL SALVADOR

San José

COSTA RICA   PANAMA

Fairbanks

Greenland (Kalaallit Nunaat) (Den.)

Nuuk

CANADA

St. John's

Henderson Lake
Highest average annual precipitation: 256" (650 cm)

Vancouver

Minneapolis

New York City

San Francisco

UNITED STATES

Batagues
Lowest average annual precipitation: 1.2" (3.0 cm)

Phoenix

Atlanta

Annual Precipitation

Centimeters	Inches
Over 203	Over 80
152 to 203	60 to 80
102 to 152	40 to 60
51 to 102	20 to 40
25 to 51	10 to 20
Under 25	Under 10

THE BAHAMAS

ST. KITTS & NEVIS
Puerto Rico (U.S.)

ANTIGUA & BARBUDA

MEXICO

CUBA

HAITI

San Juan

DOMINICA

Mexico City

JAMAICA

DOMINICAN REPUBLIC

ST. LUCIA

BARBADOS

ST. VINCENT & THE GRENADINES

GRENADA

TRINIDAD & TOBAGO

BELIZE

HONDURAS

GUATEMALA

NICARAGUA

EL SALVADOR

San José

COSTA RICA   PANAMA

Just as moisture-rich trade winds sweep through the Caribbean to strike and soak Central America, prevailing westerly winds emerge from the North Pacific to collide with the coastal mountains of Canada and the U.S. Leached of rain and snow, the moving air remains dry until it once again approaches warm water—the Gulf of Mexico and the Gulf Stream enriched Atlantic Ocean.

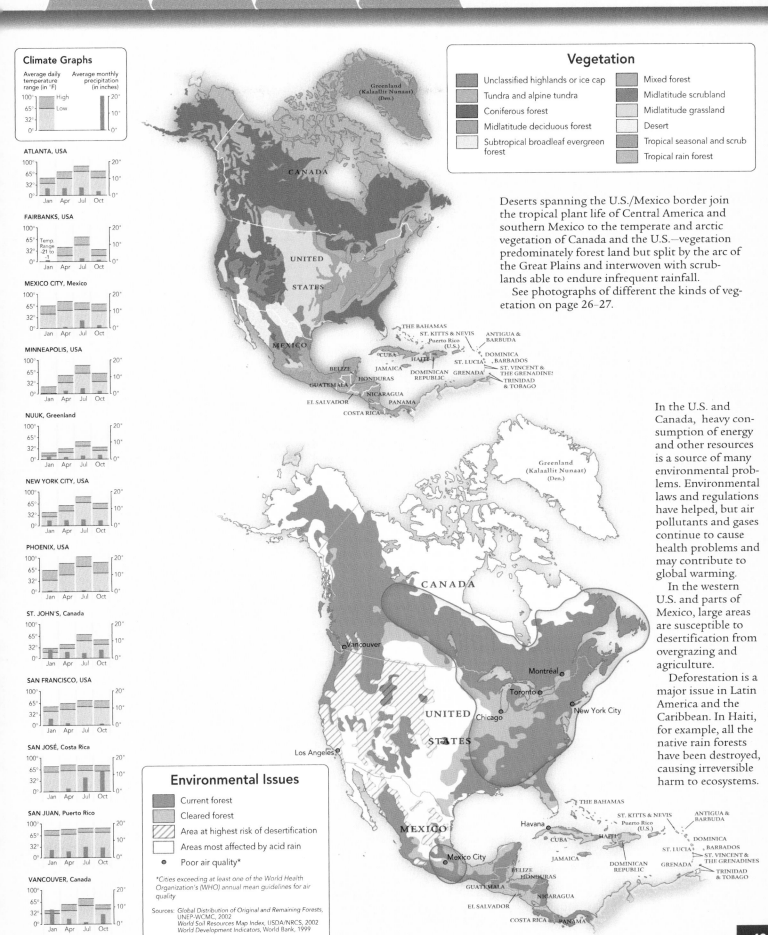

Climate Graphs

Average daily temperature range (in °F) | Average monthly precipitation (in inches)

100° High
65° Low
32°
0°

20"
10"
0"

ATLANTA, USA
FAIRBANKS, USA
MEXICO CITY, Mexico
MINNEAPOLIS, USA
NUUK, Greenland
NEW YORK CITY, USA
PHOENIX, USA
ST. JOHN'S, Canada
SAN FRANCISCO, USA
SAN JOSÉ, Costa Rica
SAN JUAN, Puerto Rico
VANCOUVER, Canada

Vegetation

- Unclassified highlands or ice cap
- Tundra and alpine tundra
- Coniferous forest
- Midlatitude deciduous forest
- Subtropical broadleaf evergreen forest
- Mixed forest
- Midlatitude scrubland
- Midlatitude grassland
- Desert
- Tropical seasonal and scrub
- Tropical rain forest

Deserts spanning the U.S./Mexico border join the tropical plant life of Central America and southern Mexico to the temperate and arctic vegetation of Canada and the U.S.—vegetation predominately forest land but split by the arc of the Great Plains and interwoven with scrublands able to endure infrequent rainfall.

See photographs of different the kinds of vegetation on page 26–27.

In the U.S. and Canada, heavy consumption of energy and other resources is a source of many environmental problems. Environmental laws and regulations have helped, but air pollutants and gases continue to cause health problems and may contribute to global warming.

In the western U.S. and parts of Mexico, large areas are susceptible to desertification from overgrazing and agriculture.

Deforestation is a major issue in Latin America and the Caribbean. In Haiti, for example, all the native rain forests have been destroyed, causing irreversible harm to ecosystems.

Environmental Issues

- Current forest
- Cleared forest
- Area at highest risk of desertification
- Areas most affected by acid rain
- Poor air quality*

*Cities exceeding at least one of the World Health Organization's (WHO) annual mean guidelines for air quality

Sources: Global Distribution of Original and Remaining Forests, UNEP-WCMC, 2002
World Soil Resources Map Index, USDA/NRCS, 2002
World Development Indicators, World Bank, 1999

49

United States

Alabama

Alaska

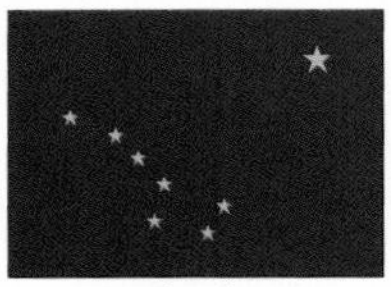

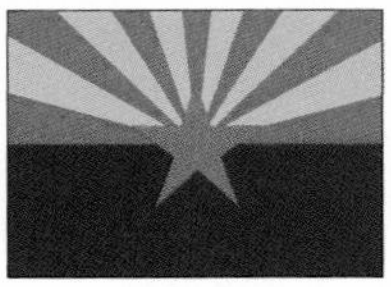

Arizona

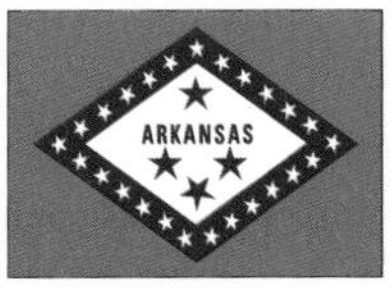

Arkansas

California

Hawaii

Idaho

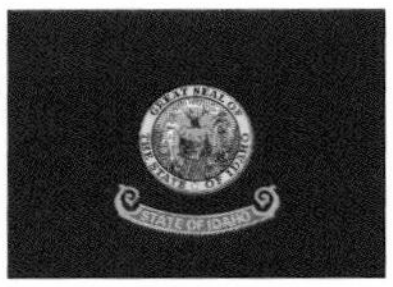

Iowa

Kansas

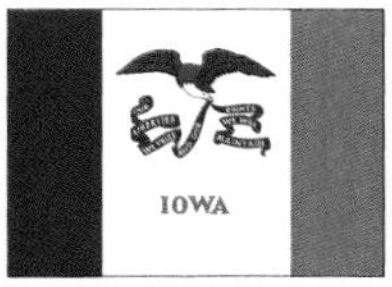

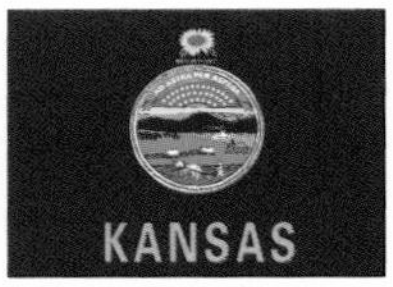

Maine

Maryland

Minnesota

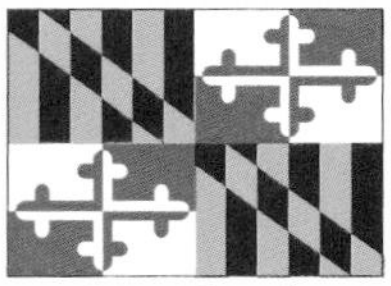

Mississippi

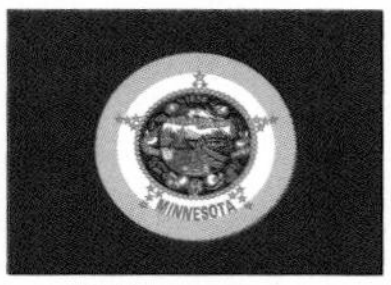

Nebraska

Nevada

New Mexico

New York

Ohio

Oklahoma

Rhode Island

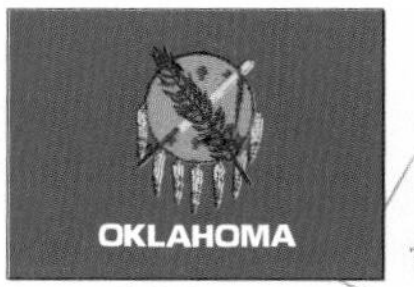

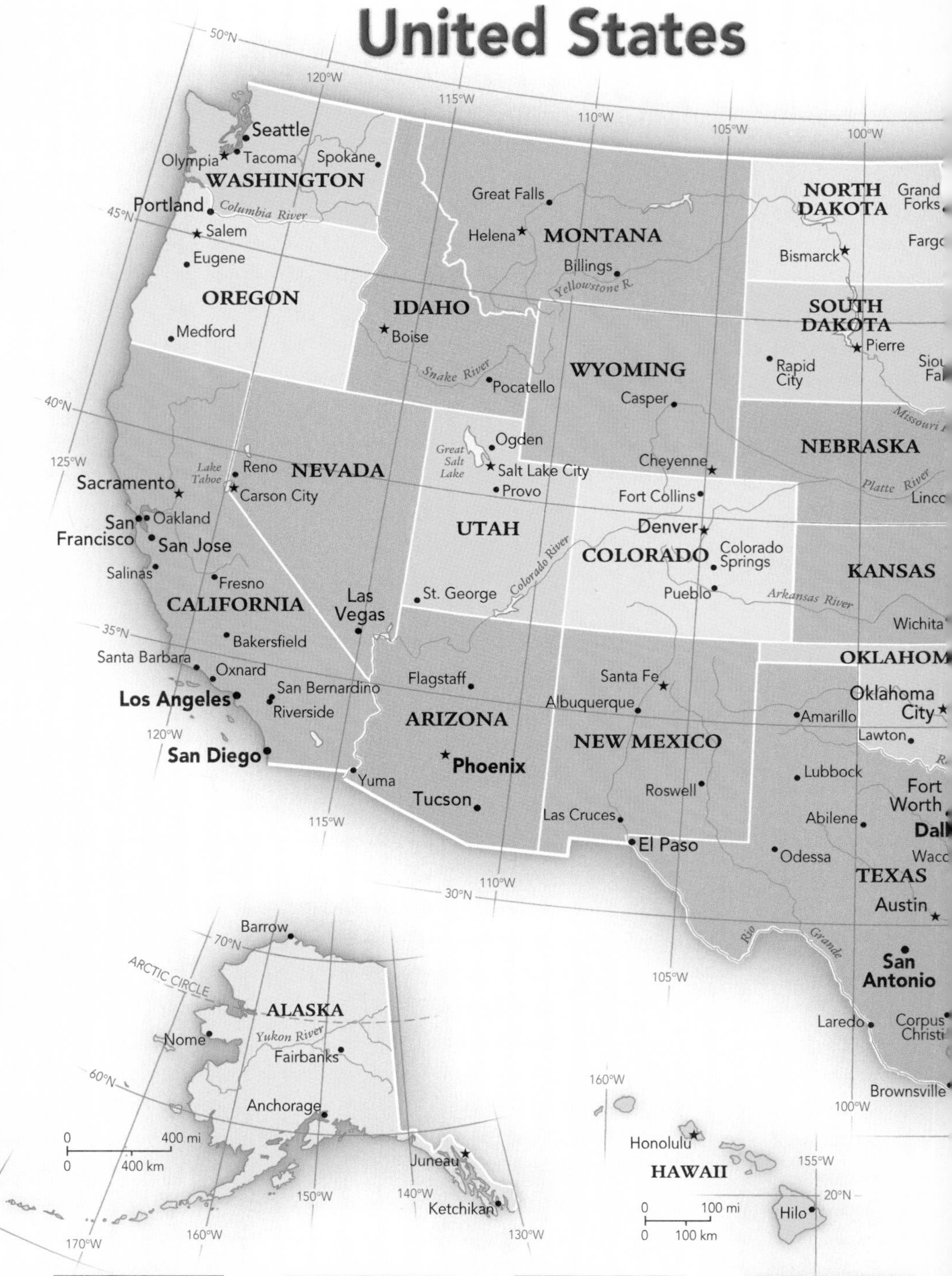

South Carolina

South Dakota

Tennessee

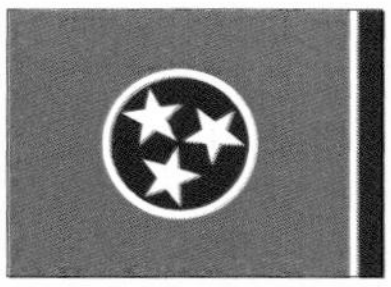

Texas

Utah

United States

50°N
120°W
115°W
110°W
105°W
100°W

Seattle
Olympia ★ Tacoma Spokane
WASHINGTON
Portland Columbia River
45°N Salem
Eugene
OREGON
Medford

Great Falls
Helena ★ MONTANA
Billings
Yellowstone R.
IDAHO
★ Boise
Snake River

NORTH DAKOTA Grand Forks
Bismarck ★ Fargo
SOUTH DAKOTA
★ Pierre Siou
Rapid City Fa
Missouri R.

WYOMING
Pocatello
Casper
Ogden
Great Salt Lake
★ Salt Lake City
Provo
Cheyenne ★
Fort Collins
Denver ★
Colorado Springs
Pueblo
Colorado River
COLORADO
Arkansas River

NEBRASKA
Platte River Linco

40°N
125°W
Lake Tahoe
Reno NEVADA
Carson City
Sacramento ★
San Francisco Oakland
San Jose
Salinas
Fresno
CALIFORNIA
35°N
Bakersfield
Santa Barbara
Oxnard
Los Angeles
San Bernardino
Riverside
120°W
San Diego
115°W

UTAH
St. George

Las Vegas

Flagstaff
Santa Fe ★
Albuquerque
Phoenix ★
ARIZONA
Tucson
Yuma
Roswell
Las Cruces
El Paso
30°N
110°W
105°W

KANSAS
Wichita
OKLAHOM
Oklahoma City
Amarillo
Lawton
Lubbock R
Fort Worth
Abilene Dall
Odessa Wacc
TEXAS
Austin
San Antonio
Laredo Corpus Christi
Brownsville
100°W

NEW MEXICO

Barrow
70°N
ARCTIC CIRCLE
ALASKA
Yukon River
Nome
Fairbanks
60°N
Anchorage
Juneau
Ketchikan
170°W 160°W 150°W 140°W 130°W

0 400 mi
0 400 km

160°W 155°W
Honolulu ★
HAWAII 20°N
Hilo
0 100 mi
0 100 km

Colorado

Connecticut

Delaware

District of Columbia

Florida

Georgia

Illinois

Indiana

Kentucky

Louisiana

Massachusetts

Michigan

Missouri

Montana

New Hampshire

New Jersey

North Carolina

North Dakota

Oregon

Pennsylvania

Map legend:
- State boundary
- ⊛ National capital
- ★ State capital

Symbol and label sizes indicate relative sizes of cities:
- **New York City**
- • St. Louis
- · Carson City

Scale: 0 — 150 — 300 mi / 0 — 150 — 300 km

Facts

- Total Area: 3,717,796 square miles (9,629,091 square kilometers)
- Highest Point: Mt. McKinley, Alaska, 20,320 ft. (6,194 m)
- Lowest Point: Death Valley, California, 282 ft. (86 m) below sea level
- Longest River: Mississippi-Missouri-Red Rock, 3,710 mi. (5,971 km)
- Largest Lake (within U.S.): Lake Michigan, 22,342 sq. mi. (57,866 sq. km)
- Largest State: Alaska, 570,374 sq. mi. (1,477,268 sq. km)
- Largest City: New York City, New York, 8,008,028

Vermont

Virginia

Washington

West Virginia

Wisconsin

Wyoming

State	2000 Population and Rank		Capital	Largest City	Abbreviation		Nickname
					Traditional	Postal Service	
Alabama	4,447,100	23rd	Montgomery	Birmingham	ALA.	AL	Heart of Dixie
Alaska	626,932	48th	Juneau	Anchorage	(none)	AK	The Last Frontier
Arizona	5,130,632	20th	Phoenix	Phoenix	ARIZ.	AZ	Grand Canyon State
Arkansas	2,673,400	33rd	Litttle Rock	Little Rock	ARK.	AR	Land of Opportunity
California	33,871,648	1st	Sacramento	Los Angeles	CALIF.	CA	Golden State
Colorado	4,301,261	24th	Denver	Denver	COLO.	CO	Centennial State
Connecticut	3,405,565	29th	Hartford	Bridgeport	CONN.	CT	Constitution State, Nutmeg State
Delaware	783,600	45th	Dover	Wilmington	DEL.	DE	First State, Diamond State
Florida	15,982,378	4th	Tallahassee	Jacksonville	FLA.	FL	Sunshine State
Georgia	8,186,453	10th	Atlanta	Atlanta	GA.	GA	Empire State of the South, Peach State
Hawaii	1,211,537	42nd	Honolulu	Honolulu	(none)	HI	Aloha State
Idaho	1,293,953	39th	Boise	Boise	IDA.	ID	Gem State
Illinois	12,419,293	5th	Springfield	Chicago	ILL.	IL	Prairie State
Indiana	6,080,485	14th	Indianapolis	Indianapolis	IND.	IN	Hoosier State
Iowa	2,926,324	30th	Des Moines	Des Moines	(none)	IA	Hawkeye State
Kansas	2,688,418	32nd	Topeka	Wichita	KANS.	KS	Sunflower State
Kentucky	4,041,769	25th	Frankfort	Louisville	KY. or KEN.	KY	Bluegrass State
Louisiana	4,468,976	22nd	Baton Rouge	New Orleans	LA.	LA	Pelican State
Maine	1,274,923	40th	Augusta	Portland	(none)	ME	Pine Tree State
Maryland	5,296,486	19th	Annapolis	Baltimore	MD.	MD	Old Line State, Free State
Massachusetts	6,349,097	13th	Boston	Boston	MASS.	MA	Bay State, Old Colony
Michigan	9,938,444	8th	Lansing	Detroit	MICH.	MI	Wolverine State
Minnesota	4,919,479	21st	St. Paul	Minneapolis	MINN.	MN	North Star State, Gopher State
Mississippi	2,844,658	31st	Jackson	Jackson	MISS.	MS	Magnolia State
Missouri	5,595,211	17th	Jefferson City	Kansas City	MO.	MO	Show Me State

State	2000 Population and Rank		Capital	Largest City	Abbreviation		Nickname
					Traditional	Postal Service	
Montana	902,195	44th	Helena	Billings	MONT.	MT	Treasure State
Nebraska	1,711,265	38th	Lincoln	Omaha	NEBR.	NE	Cornhusker State
Nevada	1,998,257	35th	Carson City	Las Vegas	NEV.	NV	Silver State
New Hampshire	1,235,786	41st	Concord	Manchester	N.H.	NH	Granite State
New Jersey	8,414,350	9th	Trenton	Newark	N.J.	NJ	Garden State
New Mexico	1,819,046	36th	Santa Fe	Albuquerque	N. MEX. or N.M.	NM	Land of Enchantment
New York	18,976,457	3rd	Albany	New York	N.Y.	NY	Empire State
North Carolina	8,049,313	11th	Raleigh	Charlotte	N.C.	NC	Tar Heel State
North Dakota	642,200	47th	Bismarck	Fargo	N. DAK. or N.D.	ND	Peace Garden State, Flickertail State
Ohio	11,353,140	7th	Columbus	Columbus	(none)	OH	Buckeye State
Oklahoma	3,450,654	27th	Oklahoma City	Oklahoma City	OKLA.	OK	Sooner State
Oregon	3,421,399	28th	Salem	Portland	ORE.	OR	Beaver State
Pennsylvania	12,281,054	6th	Harrisburg	Philadelphia	PA. or PENN.	PA	Keystone State
Rhode Island	1,048,319	43rd	Providence	Providence	R.I.	RI	Ocean State
South Carolina	4,012,012	26th	Columbia	Columbia	S.C.	SC	Palmetto State
South Dakota	754,844	46th	Pierre	Sioux Falls	S. DAK. or S.D.	SD	Mt. Rushmore State
Tennessee	5,689,283	16th	Nashville	Memphis	TENN.	TN	Volunteer State
Texas	20,851,820	2nd	Austin	Houston	TEX.	TX	Lone Star State
Utah	2,233,169	34th	Salt Lake City	Salt Lake City	(none)	UT	Beehive State
Vermont	608,827	49th	Montpelier	Burlington	VT.	VT	Green Mountain State
Virginia	7,078,515	12th	Richmond	Virginia Beach	VA.	VA	Old Dominion
Washington	5,894,121	15th	Olympia	Seattle	WASH.	WA	Evergreen State
West Virginia	1,808,344	37th	Charleston	Charleston	W. VA.	WV	Mountain State
Wisconsin	5,363,675	18th	Madison	Milwaukee	WIS.	WI	Badger State
Wyoming	493,782	50th	Cheyenne	Cheyenne	WYO.	WY	Equality State

Legend:
- International boundary
- State boundary
- ▲ Mountain peak
- ▽ Lowest point

Strait of Juan de Fuca
Cape Flattery
Puget Sound
Columbia River
Mt. Rainier 14,410 ft. (4,391 m)
Mt. St. Helens 8,366 ft. (2,550 m)
Columbia River
Mt. Hood 11,239 ft. (3,425 m)

COAST RANGES
CASCADE RANGE
COLUMBIA PLATEAU

Snake River
BITTERROOT RANGE
ROCKY

Salmon River
Owyhee River
Snake River
Snake River Plain

Milk River
Missouri River
Fort Peck Lake
Little Missouri River
Lake Sakakawea

Clark Fork
Yellowstone River
Granite Peak 12,799 ft. (3,900 m)
Yellowstone Lake
Bighorn River
Powder River
GREAT

Black Hills
Cheyenne River
White River
Lake Oahe

MOUNTAINS

Cape Mendocino
Mt. Shasta 14,162 ft. (4,316 m)

Sacramento River
Central Valley
Lake Tahoe
San Francisco Bay
San Joaquin River
Monterey Bay

SIERRA NEVADA

GREAT BASIN

Great Salt Lake
Great Salt Lake Desert
WASATCH RANGE
Kings Peak 13,528 ft. (4,123 m)

Green River
Colorado River
N. Platte River
S. Platte River
FRONT RANGE
Mt. Elbert 14,433 ft. (4,398 m)
Pikes Peak 14,110 ft. (4,629 m)
Arkansas River

COAST RANGES

PACIFIC OCEAN

Point Conception

Mt. Whitney 14,494 ft. (4,417 m)

282 ft. (86 m) below sea level
Death Valley

Mojave Desert

Channel Islands

Salton Sea

Sonoran Desert

Lake Tahoe

Lake Powell
Lake Mead
Colorado River
Grand Canyon
COLORADO PLATEAU
Humphreys Peak 12,633 ft. (3,850 m)

Verde River

Gila River
Salt River
Colorado River

San Juan River
SANGRE DE CRISTO
Wheeler Peak 13,161 ft. (4,011 m)
Rio Grande
Pecos River

GREAT PLAINS

LLANO ESTACADO

Guadalupe Peak 8,749 ft. (2,666 m)

EDWARDS PLATEAU

MEXICO

130°W 125°W 120°W 115°W 110°W 105°W
50°N 45°N 40°N 35°N 30°N
100

Alaska inset:
RUSSIA
Pt. Barrow
ARCTIC OCEAN
Bering Strait
Seward Peninsula
St. Lawrence Island
BROOKS RANGE
Yukon River
ALASKA RANGE
Mt. McKinley 20,320 ft. (6,194 m)
Kenai Peninsula
Bering Sea
Gulf of Alaska
Kodiak Island
ALEUTIAN RANGE
Aleutian Is.
ARCTIC CIRCLE
CANADA
70°N 60°N
170°W 160°W 150°W 140°W
N W E S
0 250 500 mi
0 250 500 km

Hawaii inset:
PACIFIC OCEAN
Kauai
Niihau
Oahu
Molokai
Lanai
Maui
Kahoolawe
Hawaiian Islands
Hawaii
Mauna Kea 13,796 ft. (4,205 m)
160°W 155°W
20°N
N W E S
0 100 200 mi
0 100 200 km

Profile (bottom):
Coast Ranges | Sierra Nevada | Great Basin | Wasatch Range | Mount Elbert | Pikes Peak
Lake Tahoe
15,000 ft.
10,000 ft.
5,000 ft.
Sea level
A

CANADA

Lake of
the Woods

Isle
Royale

Lake Superior

MESABI RANGE

Upper Peninsula

Red River of the North

St. Croix River

Minnesota River

James River

Mississippi River

Wisconsin River

Lower
Peninsula

Grand River

Lake Michigan

Lake Huron

Lake
St. Clair

Lake Erie

Lake Ontario

St. Lawrence River

Lake
Champlain

ADIRONDACK
MTS.

GREEN MTS.

WHITE MTS.

Mt. Washington
6,288 ft
(1,917 m)

Merrimack River

Hudson River

Connecticut River

Saint John River

Penobscot River

Quoddy
Head

Gulf
of
Maine

Cape Cod

Long Island
Sound

Long
Island

Delaware Bay

Iowa River

Cedar River

Des Moines River

Rock River

Loup R.

Platte River

Republican River

Missouri

noky Hill R.

Kansas River

FLINT HILLS

Lake of
the Ozarks

Illinois River

CENTRAL   LOWLAND

Kaskaskia River

Wabash

White River

Ohio River

Kentucky R.

Scioto River

River

ALLEGHENY
PLATEAU

Allegheny R.

ALLEGHENY MOUNTAINS

APPALACHIAN   MOUNTAINS

Susquehanna River

Potomac River

James River

Roanoke River

Chesapeake Bay

Cape Hatteras

PIEDMONT

ATLANTIC COASTAL PLAIN

BLUE   RIDGE

CUMBERLAND   PLATEAU

Green River

Cumberland River

Tennessee River

Mt. Mitchell
6,684 ft
(2,037 m)

Pee Dee R.

Savannah River

Oconee River

Ocmulgee River

Cape
Fear

ATLANTIC
OCEAN

OZARK
PLATEAU

BOSTON MTS.

OUACHITA
MOUNTAINS

White River

Arkansas River

Ouachita River

Red

Cimarron River

Canadian River

Brazos River

Trinity River

Colorado River

Sabine River

Mississippi River

Yazoo River

Tombigbee River

Alabama River

Pearl River

Chattahoochee River

Flint River

Apalachicola River

Altamaha River

St. Johns River

GULF   COASTAL   PLAIN

Lake
Pontchartrain

Mobile Bay

Mississippi Delta

Galveston Bay

Tampa Bay

Lake
Okeechobee

Cape Canaveral

Gulf of Mexico

THE
BAHAMAS

Florida Keys

Straits of Florida

Nueces River

Padre
Island

a Grande

N
W   E
S

0   150   300 mi
0   150   300 km

50°N

80°W

75°W

70°W

40°N

70°W

35°N

30°N

25°N

95°W

90°W

85°W

85°W

80°W

75°W

Great Plains

A   B

Mississippi River   Central Lowland   Appalachian Mountains

Chesapeake
Bay   Delaware
Bay

B

State	Land Area and Rank		Highest Point		Temperature °F		Annual Precipitation	
					Highest Recorded	Lowest Recorded	Highest Recorded	Lowest Recorded
Alabama	50,750 sq mi 131,443 sq km	28th	Cheaha Mtn.	2,405 ft 777 m	112°	−27°	106.57"	22.00"
Alaska	570,374 sq mi 1,477,268 sq km	1st	Mt. McKinley	20,320 ft 6,194 m	100°	−80°	332.29"	1.61"
Arizona	113,642 sq mi 294,334 sq km	6th	Humphreys Peak	12,633 ft 3,851 m	128°	−40°	58.92"	0.07"
Arkansas	52,075 sq mi 134,875 sq km	27th	Magazine Mtn.	2,753 ft 839 m	120°	−29°	98.55"	19.11"
California	155,973 sq mi 403,970 sq km	3rd	Mt. Whitney	14,494 ft 4,418 m	134°	−45°	153.54"	0.00"
Colorado	103,730 sq mi 268,660 sq km	8th	Mt. Elbert	14,433 ft 4,399 m	118°	−61°	92.84"	1.69"
Connecticut	4,845 sq mi 12,550 sq km	48th	south slope of Mt. Frissell	2,380 ft 725 m	105°	−32°	78.53"	23.60"
Delaware	1,955 sq mi 5,063 sq km	49th	Ebright Road at DE-PA border	448 ft 137 m	110°	−17°	72.75"	21.38"
Florida	53,997 sq mi 139,852 sq km	26th	Sec. 30, T.6N, R.20W in Walton Co.	345 ft 105 m	109°	−2°	112.43"	21.16"
Georgia	57,919 sq mi 150,010 sq km	21st	Brasstown Bald	4,784 ft 1,458 m	112°	−17°	112.16"	17.14"
Hawaii	6,423 sq mi 16,637 sq km	47th	Pu'u Wekiu, Mauna Kea	13,796 ft 4,205 m	100°	12°	704.83"	0.19"
Idaho	82,751 sq mi 214,325 sq km	11th	Borah Peak	12,662 ft 3,859 m	118°	−60°	81.05"	2.09"
Illinois	55,593 sq mi 143,987 sq km	24th	Charles Mound	1,235 ft 376 m	117°	−35°	74.58"	16.59"
Indiana	35,870 sq mi 92,904 sq km	38th	Franklin Township in Wayne County	1,257 ft 383 m	116°	−35°	97.38"	18.67"
Iowa	55,875 sq mi 144,716 sq km	23rd	Sec. 29, T.100N, R.41W in Osceola Co.	1,670 ft 509 m	118°	−47°	74.50"	12.11"
Kansas	81,823 sq mi 211,922 sq km	13th	Mt. Sunflower	4,039 ft 1,231 m	121°	−40°	67.02"	4.77"
Kentucky	39,732 sq mi 102,907 sq km	36th	Black Mtn.	4,139 ft 1,262 m	114°	−34°	79.68"	14.51"
Louisiana	43,566 sq mi 112,836 sq km	33rd	Driskill Mtn.	535 ft 163 m	114°	−16°	113.74"	26.44"
Maine	30,865 sq mi 79,939 sq km	39th	Mt. Katahdin	5,267 ft 1,605 m	105°	−48°	75.64"	23.06"
Maryland	9,775 sq mi 25,316 sq km	42nd	Backbone Mtn.	3,360 ft 1,024 m	109°	−40°	72.59"	17.76"
Massachusetts	7,838 sq mi 20,300 sq km	45th	Mt. Greylock	3,487 ft 1,063 m	107°	−35°	72.19"	21.76"
Michigan	56,809 sq mi 147,135 sq km	22nd	Mt. Arvon	1,979 ft 603 m	112°	−51°	64.01"	15.64"
Minnesota	79,617 sq mi 206,207 sq km	14th	Eagle Mtn.	2,301 ft 701 m	114°	−59°	51.53"	7.81"
Mississippi	46,914 sq mi 121,506 sq km	31st	Woodall Mtn.	806 ft 246 m	115°	−19°	104.36"	25.97"
Missouri	68,898 sq mi 178,446 sq km	18th	Taum Sauk Mtn.	1,772 ft 540 m	118°	−40°	92.77"	16.14"

State	Land Area and Rank		Highest Point		Temperature °F		Annual Precipitation	
					Highest Recorded	Lowest Recorded	Highest Recorded	Lowest Recorded
Montana	145,556 sq mi 376,991 sq km	4th	Granite Peak	12,799 ft 3,901 m	117°	−70°	55.51"	2.97"
Nebraska	76,878 sq mi 199,113 sq km	15th	Johnson Township in Kimball County	5,424 ft 1,653 m	118°	−47°	64.52"	6.30"
Nevada	109,806 sq mi 284,397 sq km	7th	Boundary Peak	13,140 ft 4,005 m	125°	−50°	59.03"	Trace
New Hampshire	8,969 sq mi 23,231 sq km	44th	Mt. Washington	6,288 ft 1,917 m	106°	−46°	130.14"	22.31"
New Jersey	7,419 sq mi 19,215 sq km	46th	High Point	1,803 ft 550 m	110°	−34°	85.99"	19.85"
New Mexico	121,365 sq mi 314,334 sq km	5th	Wheeler Peak	13,161 ft 4,011 m	122°	−50°	62.45"	1.00"
New York	47,224 sq mi 122,310 sq km	30th	Mt. Marcy	5,344 ft 1,629 m	108°	−52°	82.06"	17.64"
North Carolina	48,718 sq mi 126,180 sq km	29th	Mt. Mitchell	6,684 ft 2,037 m	110°	−34°	129.60"	22.69"
North Dakota	68,994 sq mi 178,695 sq km	17th	White Butte	3,506 ft 1,069 m	121°	−60°	37.98"	4.02"
Ohio	40,953 sq mi 106,067 sq km	35th	Campbell Hill	1,549 ft 472 m	113°	−39°	70.82"	16.96"
Oklahoma	68,679 sq mi 177,878 sq km	19th	Black Mesa	4,973 ft 1,516 m	120°	−27°	84.47"	6.53"
Oregon	96,003 sq mi 248,647 sq km	10th	Mt. Hood	11,239 ft 3,426 m	119°	−54°	168.88"	3.33"
Pennsylvania	44,820 sq mi 116,083 sq km	32nd	Mt. Davis	3,213 ft 979 m	111°	−42°	81.64"	15.71"
Rhode Island	1,045 sq mi 2,707 sq km	50th	Jerimoth Hill	812 ft 247 m	104°	−23°	70.21"	24.08"
South Carolina	30,111 sq mi 77,988 sq km	40th	Sassafras Mtn.	3,560 ft 1,085 m	111°	−19°	101.65"	20.73"
South Dakota	75,891 sq mi 196,575 sq km	16th	Harney Peak	7,242 ft 2,207 m	120°	−58°	48.42"	2.89"
Tennessee	41,220 sq mi 106,759 sq km	34th	Clingmans Dome	6,643 ft 2,025 m	113°	−32°	114.88"	25.23"
Texas	261,914 sq mi 678,358 sq km	2nd	Guadalupe Peak	8,749 ft 2,667 m	120°	−23°	109.38"	1.64"
Utah	82,168 sq mi 212,816 sq km	12th	Kings Peak	13,528 ft 4,123 m	117°	−69°	108.54"	1.34"
Vermont	9,249 sq mi 23,956 sq km	43rd	Mt. Mansfield	4,393 ft 1,339 m	105°	−50°	92.88"	22.98"
Virginia	35,598 sq mi 102,558 sq km	37th	Mt. Rogers	5,729 ft 1,746 m	110°	−30°	81.78"	12.52"
Washington	66,582 sq mi 172,447 sq km	20th	Mt. Rainier	14,410 ft 4,392 m	118°	−48°	184.56"	2.61"
West Virginia	24,087 sq mi 62,384 sq km	41st	Spruce Knob	4,861 ft 1,481 m	112°	−37°	94.01"	9.50"
Wisconsin	54,314 sq mi 104,673 sq km	25th	Timms Hill	1,951 ft 595 m	114°	−54°	62.07"	12.00"
Wyoming	97,105 sq mi 251,501 sq km	9th	Gannett Peak	13,804 ft 4,207 m	114°	−63°	55.46"	1.28"

Divide

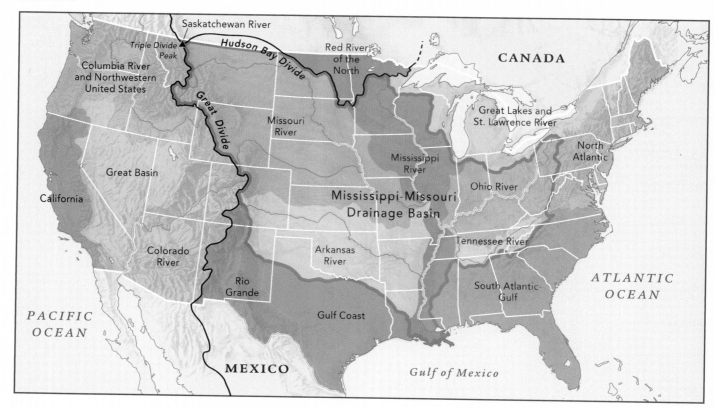

DIVIDE: *The boundary or high ground between river systems.* Streams on one side of the divide flow in a different direction and into a different drainage basin from the streams on the other side. A continental divide is the boundary that separates the rivers flowing toward opposite sides of a continent.

In North America a continental divide called the **Great Divide** runs along the crest of the Rocky Mountains, dividing rivers that flow to the Gulf of Mexico and the Atlantic Ocean from those that flow into the Pacific Ocean. Another much lower divide separates those rivers that flow north through Hudson Bay to the Arctic Ocean. Triple Divide Peak in Montana is located on both these divides. Water from one side of this mountain flows east to the Atlantic; from another side water flows west to the Pacific; and from the north face, water flows to the Arctic Ocean.

Earthquakes

■ Major earthquake

• Other earthquake

The major earthquakes that have occurred in California are distributed along the major fault lines depicted on the California map to the right.

Fall Line

FALL LINE: *A geologic feature where uplands meet lowlands and a series of waterfalls and rapids occur.* Fall lines are formed where a region of hard rock borders softer rock, and the softer rock has eroded away. The erosion creates a ledge that water flows over.

A major fall line exists in the eastern United States. It marks the boundary between the Coastal Plain and the Piedmont and runs between New York and Alabama. Cities have grown into industrial and commercial hubs around each waterfall on the fall line for two reasons. First, the energy of the falling water can be captured and used by industry. Second, the fall line is often the farthest point reachable by ships carrying goods up river, which means that goods are transferred to land-based transport at that point. Some fall line cities on the East Coast include Trenton, Philadelphia, Baltimore, Washington, D.C., Richmond, Petersburg, Columbia, Macon, and Montgomery. If you draw a line on a map connecting these city dots, you will have drawn the Eastern Fall Line.

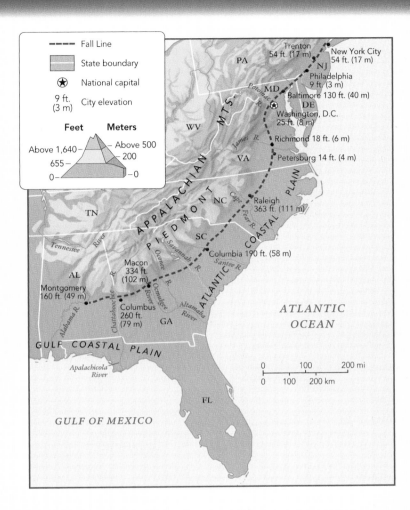

Fault

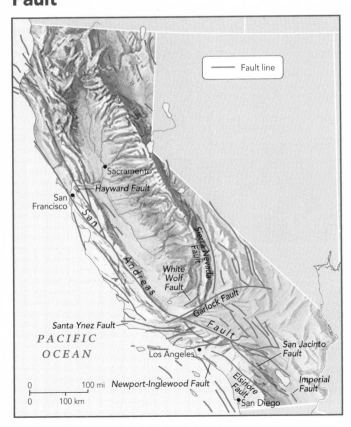

FAULT: *A break in the Earth's crust caused by movement.* Solid rock on one side of the fault no longer matches the solid rock on the other side. The movement may take place in any direction—up, down, or sideways. The movement may be a few inches or thousands of feet.

A fault that moves up or down is called a **dip-slip fault**. Niagara Falls cascades over an escarpment caused by this kind of movement.

A fault that moves sideways is called a **strike-slip fault**. The San Andreas fault is an example of this kind. Horizontal movement along this fault caused the devastating San Francisco earthquake in 1906 and will cause more earthquakes in the future. This happens because this fault marks the boundary between the Pacific Plate and the North American Plate (see page 20).

Where two parallel faults pull away from each other, they create a long, sunken valley between them called a **rift**. The Great Rift Valley in Africa is the world's most visible example (see page 91). Underwater, the huge Mid-Ocean Ridge is the longest rift on Earth (see pages 18–19).

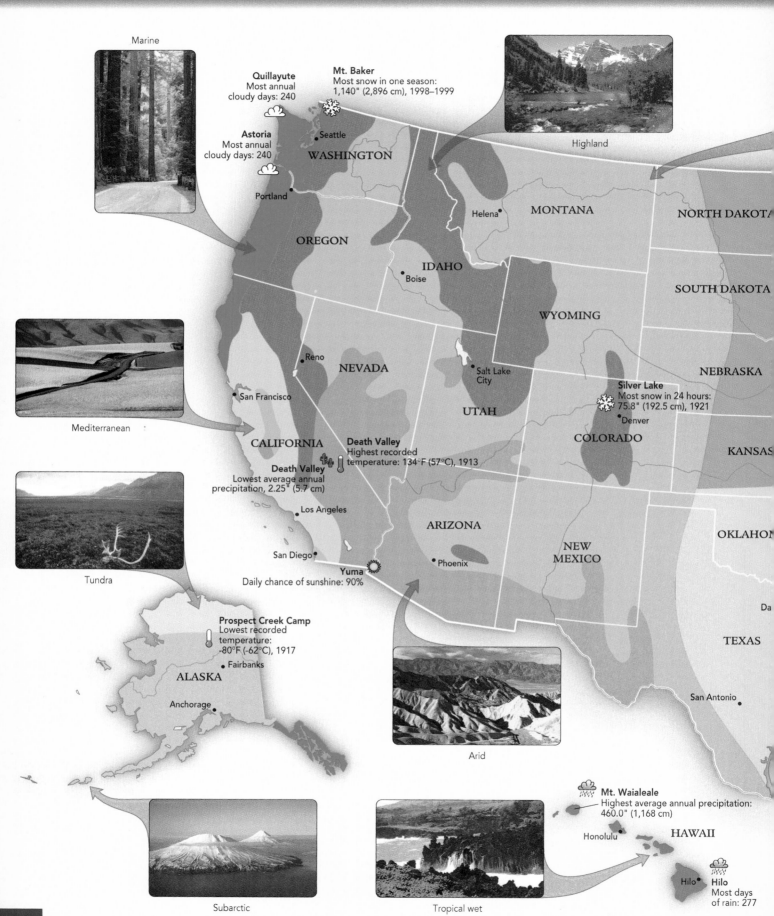

Marine

Quillayute
Most annual cloudy days: 240

Astoria
Most annual cloudy days: 240

Mt. Baker
Most snow in one season: 1,140" (2,896 cm), 1998–1999

Highland

WASHINGTON
Seattle

Portland

OREGON

MONTANA
Helena

NORTH DAKOTA

IDAHO
Boise

SOUTH DAKOTA

WYOMING

Mediterranean

Reno

NEVADA

Salt Lake City

NEBRASKA

Silver Lake
Most snow in 24 hours: 75.8" (192.5 cm), 1921
Denver

San Francisco

UTAH

COLORADO

KANSAS

CALIFORNIA

Death Valley
Highest recorded temperature: 134°F (57°C), 1913

Death Valley
Lowest average annual precipitation, 2.25" (5.7 cm)

Los Angeles

Tundra

San Diego

ARIZONA

OKLAHOM

Phoenix

NEW MEXICO

Yuma
Daily chance of sunshine: 90%

Prospect Creek Camp
Lowest recorded temperature: -80°F (-62°C), 1917

Fairbanks

ALASKA

Anchorage

TEXAS

San Antonio

Da

Arid

Subarctic

Tropical wet

Mt. Waialeale
Highest average annual precipitation: 460.0" (1,168 cm)

Honolulu

HAWAII

Hilo

Hilo
Most days of rain: 277

Semiarid

Humid continental

MAINE

Mt. Washington
Highest wind gust:
231 mph (372 kph), 1934

Lake Superior

MINNESOTA

MICHIGAN

Lake Huron

Portland

VT

NH

NEW YORK

Lake Ontario

Blue Hill
Highest average annual wind speed:
15.4 mph (24.8 kph)

Boston

MA

WISCONSIN

Lake Michigan

Minneapolis

Buffalo

RI

CT

Detroit

Lake Erie

IOWA

Chicago

PENNSYLVANIA
Johnstown
Deadliest flood: over 2,200 dead, 1889

New York City

Philadelphia

Great Midwest Flood
Costliest flood damage: $18 billion, 1993

OHIO

INDIANA

Baltimore

NEW JERSEY

DELAWARE

ILLINOIS

Indianapolis

WEST
VIRGINIA

Washington, D.C.

MARYLAND

MISSOURI

St. Louis

Lexington

VIRGINIA

Tri-State Tornado
Deadliest tornado: 689 dead, 1925

KENTUCKY

Raleigh

Nashville

NORTH CAROLINA

ARKANSAS

TENNESSEE

SOUTH
CAROLINA

Atlanta

MISSISSIPPI

ALABAMA

GEORGIA

LOUISIANA

Alvin
Most rain in 24 hours:
43.0" (109.2 cm), 1979

FLORIDA

Houston

New Orleans

Galveston
Deadliest hurricane: over 8,000 dead, 1900

Miami

Hurricane Andrew
Costliest hurricane
damage: $26.5 billion,
1992

Climate

- Tropical wet
- Tropical wet and dry
- Arid
- Semiarid
- Mediterranean
- Humid subtropical
- Marine
- Humid continental
- Subarctic
- Tundra
- Highland

Humid subtropical

Tropical wet and dry

61

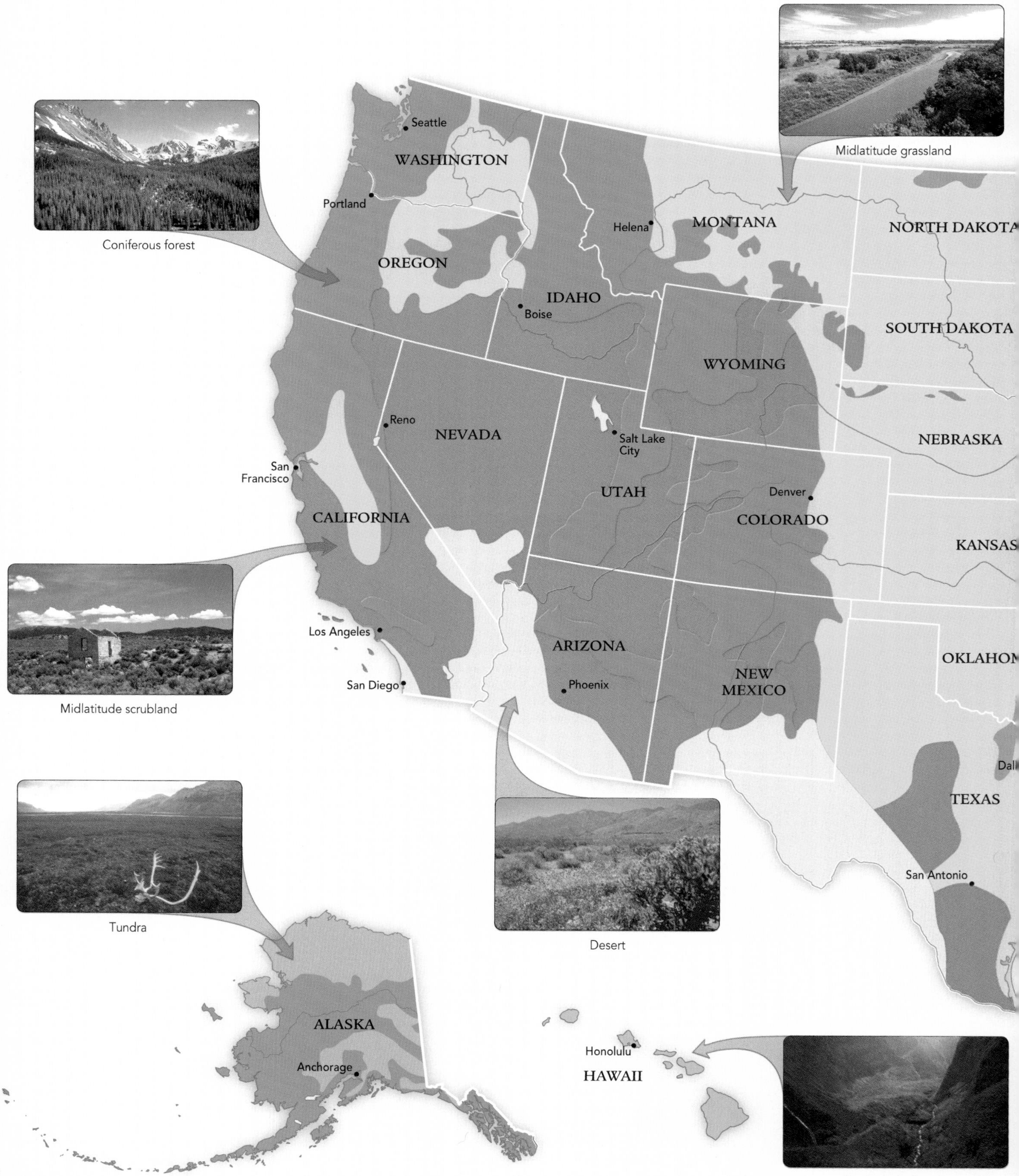

Midlatitude grassland

Coniferous forest

Midlatitude scrubland

Tundra

Desert

Tropical rain forest

WASHINGTON

Seattle

Portland

OREGON

IDAHO

Boise

MONTANA

Helena

NORTH DAKOTA

SOUTH DAKOTA

WYOMING

NEBRASKA

NEVADA

Reno

Salt Lake City

San Francisco

UTAH

Denver

COLORADO

KANSAS

CALIFORNIA

Los Angeles

San Diego

ARIZONA

Phoenix

NEW MEXICO

OKLAHOMA

Dall

TEXAS

San Antonio

ALASKA

Anchorage

Honolulu

HAWAII

MINNESOTA

Lake Superior

MICHIGAN

Lake Huron

WISCONSIN

Lake Michigan

Minneapolis

Lake Ontario

Detroit

Lake Erie

NEW YORK

Buffalo

VERMONT

MAINE

Portland

NEW HAMPSHIRE

MASSACHUSETTS

Boston

RHODE ISLAND

CONNECTICUT

IOWA

Chicago

PENNSYLVANIA

New York City

NEW JERSEY

Philadelphia

ILLINOIS   INDIANA   OHIO

Indianapolis

Baltimore

Washington, D.C.

DELAWARE

MARYLAND

WEST VIRGINIA

VIRGINIA

St. Louis

Lexington

MISSOURI

KENTUCKY

Raleigh

NORTH CAROLINA

Nashville

TENNESSEE

ARKANSAS

SOUTH CAROLINA

Atlanta

MISSISSIPPI

ALABAMA

GEORGIA

LOUISIANA

Houston   New Orleans

FLORIDA

Miami

Deciduous forest

Vegetation

- Tundra and alpine tundra
- Coniferous forest
- Midlatitude deciduous forest
- Subtropical broadleaf evergreen forest
- Mixed forest
- Midlatitude scrubland
- Midlatitude grassland
- Desert
- Tropical rain forest

Mixed forest

Subtropical broadleaf evergreen forest

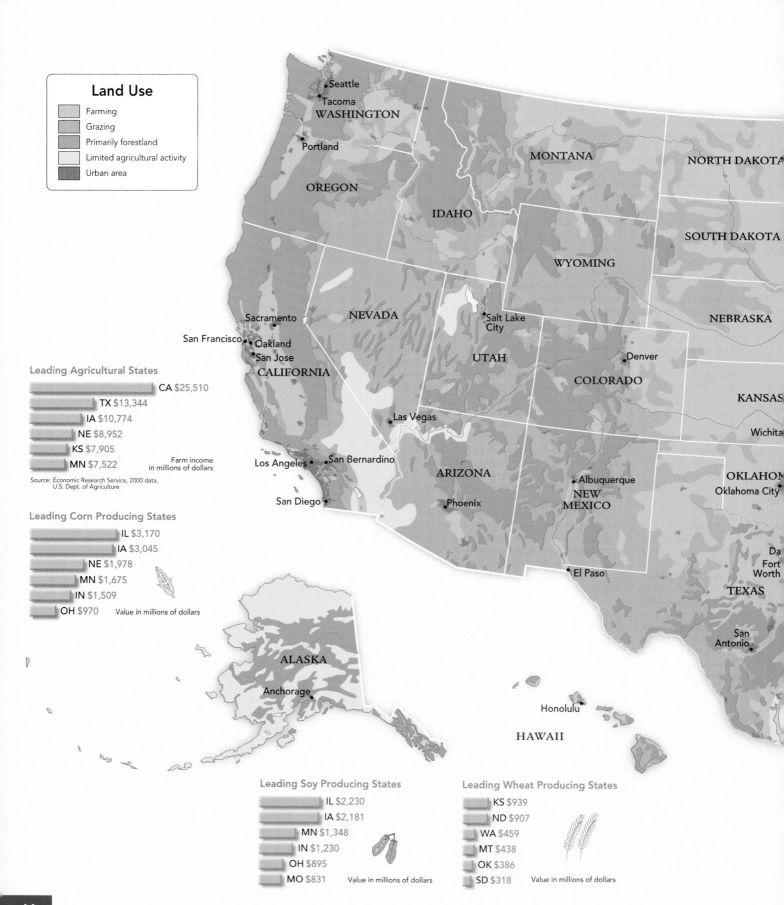

Land Use

- Farming
- Grazing
- Primarily forestland
- Limited agricultural activity
- Urban area

Leading Agricultural States

- CA $25,510
- TX $13,344
- IA $10,774
- NE $8,952
- KS $7,905
- MN $7,522

Farm income in millions of dollars

Source: Economic Research Service, 2000 data, U.S. Dept. of Agriculture

Leading Corn Producing States

- IL $3,170
- IA $3,045
- NE $1,978
- MN $1,675
- IN $1,509
- OH $970

Value in millions of dollars

Leading Soy Producing States

- IL $2,230
- IA $2,181
- MN $1,348
- IN $1,230
- OH $895
- MO $831

Value in millions of dollars

Leading Wheat Producing States

- KS $939
- ND $907
- WA $459
- MT $438
- OK $386
- SD $318

Value in millions of dollars

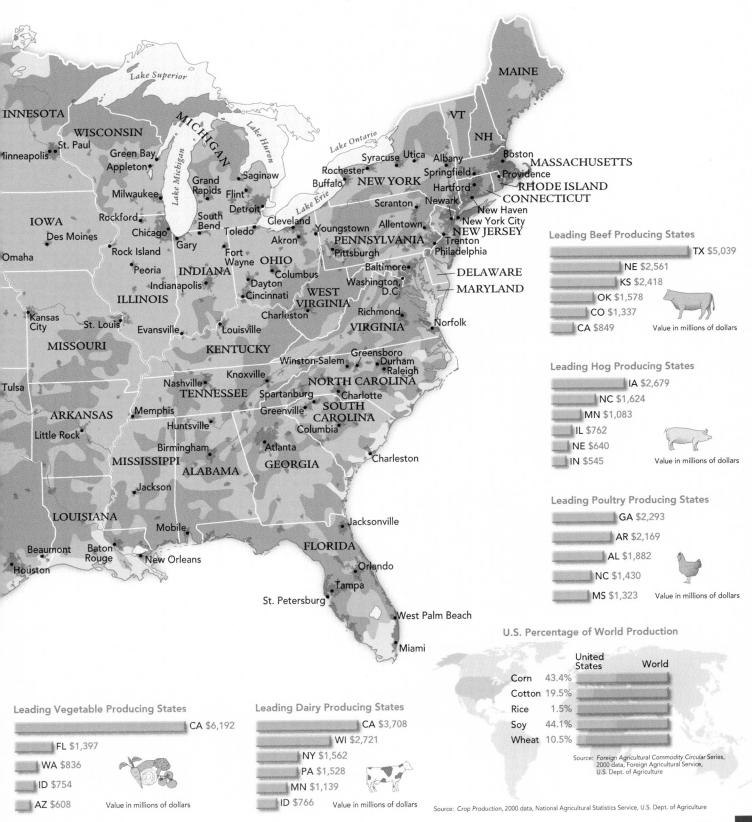

MAINE

MINNESOTA
WISCONSIN
MICHIGAN
VT
NH
MASSACHUSETTS
RHODE ISLAND
CONNECTICUT

St. Paul
Minneapolis
Green Bay
Appleton
Milwaukee
Lake Superior
Lake Michigan
Lake Huron
Lake Ontario
Lake Erie

Grand Rapids
Saginaw
Flint
Detroit
Cleveland

Syracuse Utica
Rochester
Buffalo
NEW YORK
Albany Boston
Springfield Providence
Hartford
Scranton Newark
New Haven
New York City

IOWA
Rockford
Des Moines
Chicago
Gary
Rock Island
Omaha
Peoria
South Bend
Toledo
Fort Wayne
OHIO
Columbus
Dayton
Cincinnati

Youngstown
Akron
PENNSYLVANIA
Pittsburgh
Allentown
Trenton
Philadelphia
Baltimore
Washington, D.C.
NEW JERSEY
DELAWARE
MARYLAND

Kansas City
St. Louis
INDIANA
Indianapolis
ILLINOIS
Evansville
Louisville
WEST VIRGINIA
Charleston
Richmond
Norfolk

MISSOURI
KENTUCKY
VIRGINIA
Tulsa

Nashville
Knoxville
TENNESSEE
Winston-Salem Greensboro
Durham Raleigh
NORTH CAROLINA
Spartanburg Charlotte
Greenville
SOUTH CAROLINA
Columbia

ARKANSAS
Little Rock
Memphis
Huntsville
Birmingham
MISSISSIPPI
ALABAMA
Atlanta
GEORGIA
Charleston

LOUISIANA
Jackson
Mobile
Beaumont Baton Rouge
Houston New Orleans
FLORIDA
Jacksonville
Orlando
Tampa
St. Petersburg
West Palm Beach
Miami

Leading Beef Producing States

TX $5,039
NE $2,561
KS $2,418
OK $1,578
CO $1,337
CA $849

Value in millions of dollars

Leading Hog Producing States

IA $2,679
NC $1,624
MN $1,083
IL $762
NE $640
IN $545

Value in millions of dollars

Leading Poultry Producing States

GA $2,293
AR $2,169
AL $1,882
NC $1,430
MS $1,323

Value in millions of dollars

U.S. Percentage of World Production

		United States	World
Corn	43.4%		
Cotton	19.5%		
Rice	1.5%		
Soy	44.1%		
Wheat	10.5%		

Source: *Foreign Agricultural Commodity Circular* Series, 2000 data, Foreign Agricultural Service, U.S. Dept. of Agriculture

Leading Vegetable Producing States

CA $6,192
FL $1,397
WA $836
ID $754
AZ $608

Value in millions of dollars

Leading Dairy Producing States

CA $3,708
WI $2,721
NY $1,562
PA $1,528
MN $1,139
ID $766

Value in millions of dollars

Source: *Crop Production*, 2000 data, National Agricultural Statistics Service, U.S. Dept. of Agriculture

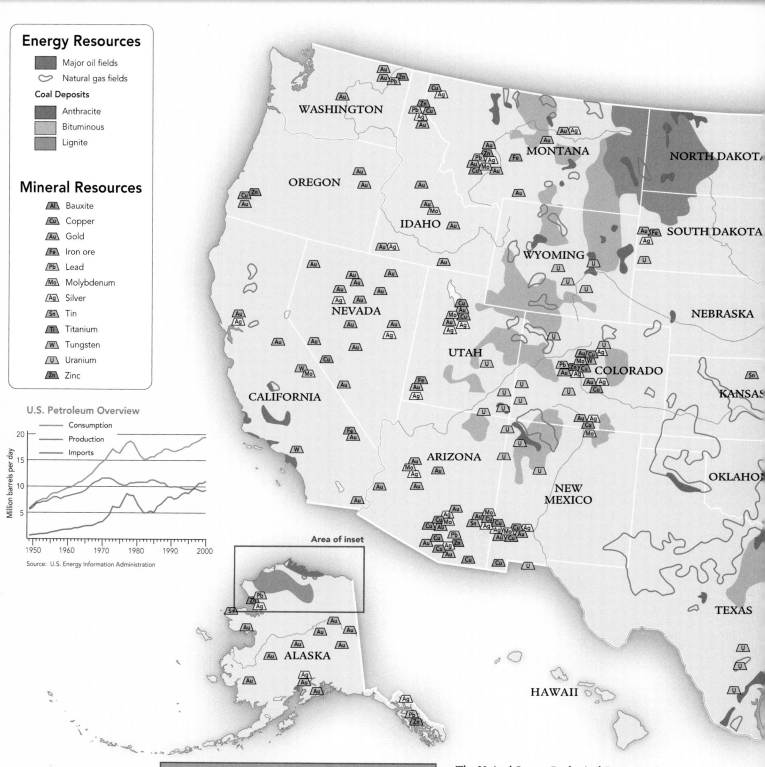

Energy Resources

- Major oil fields
- Natural gas fields

Coal Deposits
- Anthracite
- Bituminous
- Lignite

Mineral Resources

Al	Bauxite
Cu	Copper
Au	Gold
Fe	Iron ore
Pb	Lead
Mo	Molybdenum
Ag	Silver
Sn	Tin
Ti	Titanium
W	Tungsten
U	Uranium
Zn	Zinc

U.S. Petroleum Overview

- Consumption
- Production
- Imports

Million barrels per day — 1950 1960 1970 1980 1990 2000

Source: U.S. Energy Information Administration

WASHINGTON, OREGON, IDAHO, NEVADA, CALIFORNIA, MONTANA, WYOMING, UTAH, ARIZONA, NEW MEXICO, NORTH DAKOTA, SOUTH DAKOTA, NEBRASKA, COLORADO, KANSAS, OKLAHOMA, TEXAS, HAWAII, ALASKA

Area of inset

The United States Geological Survey estimates that there is a 50% chance of extracting 5 billion barrels of oil from the coastal plain within the Arctic National Wildlife Refuge. Debate surrounds the issue of drilling and production and its impact on the environment.

ARCTIC OCEAN — Barrow — Prudhoe Bay — Beaufort Sea — TRANS-ALASKA PIPELINE — NOATAK NATL. PRES. — KOBUK VALLEY N.P. — GATES OF THE ARCTIC N.P. AND PRES. — ARCTIC NATIONAL WILDLIFE REFUGE — CANADA — U.S. — 100 mi — 100 km

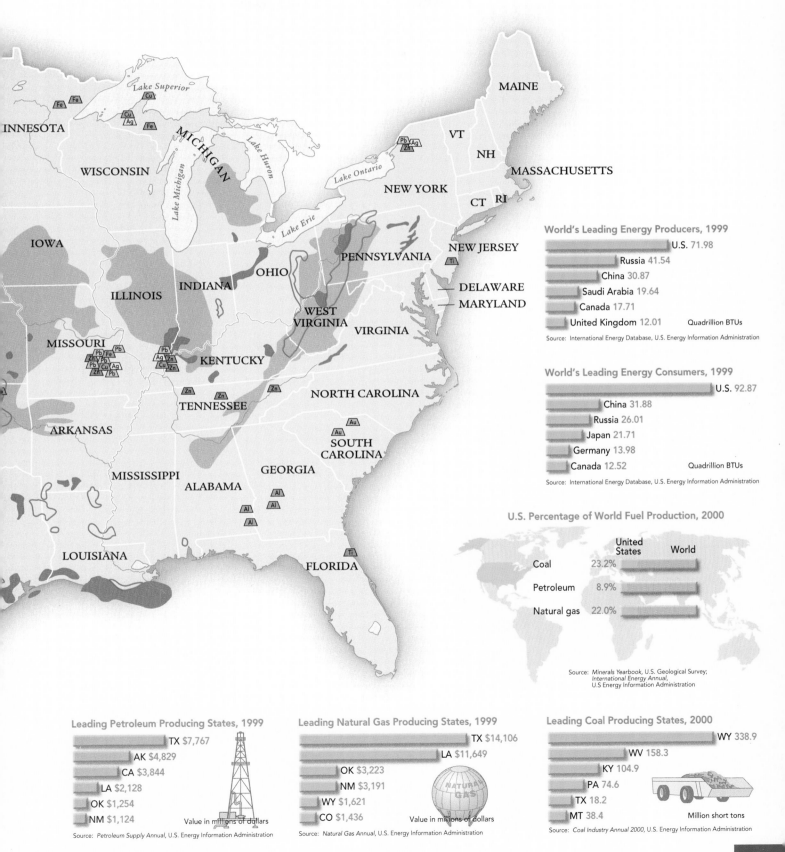

MAINE

MICHIGAN

INNESOTA

WISCONSIN

IOWA

ILLINOIS

INDIANA

OHIO

MISSOURI

KENTUCKY

TENNESSEE

ARKANSAS

MISSISSIPPI

ALABAMA

GEORGIA

LOUISIANA

FLORIDA

VT

NH

MASSACHUSETTS

NEW YORK

CT   RI

PENNSYLVANIA

NEW JERSEY

DELAWARE

MARYLAND

WEST VIRGINIA

VIRGINIA

NORTH CAROLINA

SOUTH CAROLINA

Lake Superior
Lake Huron
Lake Michigan
Lake Ontario
Lake Erie

World's Leading Energy Producers, 1999

- U.S. 71.98
- Russia 41.54
- China 30.87
- Saudi Arabia 19.64
- Canada 17.71
- United Kingdom 12.01   Quadrillion BTUs

Source: International Energy Database, U.S. Energy Information Administration

World's Leading Energy Consumers, 1999

- U.S. 92.87
- China 31.88
- Russia 26.01
- Japan 21.71
- Germany 13.98
- Canada 12.52   Quadrillion BTUs

Source: International Energy Database, U.S. Energy Information Administration

U.S. Percentage of World Fuel Production, 2000

	United States	World
Coal	23.2%	
Petroleum	8.9%	
Natural gas	22.0%	

Source: Minerals Yearbook, U.S. Geological Survey;
International Energy Annual,
U.S Energy Information Administration

Leading Petroleum Producing States, 1999

- TX $7,767
- AK $4,829
- CA $3,844
- LA $2,128
- OK $1,254
- NM $1,124

Value in millions of dollars

Source: Petroleum Supply Annual, U.S. Energy Information Administration

Leading Natural Gas Producing States, 1999

- TX $14,106
- LA $11,649
- OK $3,223
- NM $3,191
- WY $1,621
- CO $1,436

Value in millions of dollars

Source: Natural Gas Annual, U.S. Energy Information Administration

Leading Coal Producing States, 2000

- WY 338.9
- WV 158.3
- KY 104.9
- PA 74.6
- TX 18.2
- MT 38.4

Million short tons

Source: Coal Industry Annual 2000, U.S. Energy Information Administration

WA
Seattle
Olympia
Tacoma
Spokane

OR
Portland
Salem
Eugene

MT
Helena

ND
Bismarck

SD
Pierre

ID
Boise

WY
Cheyenne

NE

NV
Reno
Carson City
Sacramento
Oakland
Stockton
San Francisco
San Jose
Salinas
Fresno

CA

UT
Salt Lake City

CO
Denver
Colorado Springs

KS
Wichita

Las Vegas
Bakersfield
Los Angeles
San Bernardino
Long Beach
Riverside
San Diego

AZ
Phoenix
Tucson

NM
Santa Fe
Albuquerque

OK
Amarillo
Oklahoma City
Lubbock

TX
Dallas
Ft. Worth
Abilene
Waco
Austin
San Antonio
Laredo
Brownsville
Corpus Christi

El Paso

PACIFIC TIME ZONE
MOUNTAIN TIME ZONE
MOUNTAIN T.Z.
CENTRAL T.Z.

ALASKA TIME ZONE
Barrow
Nome
Circle
Fairbanks
ALASKA
Bethel
Anchorage
Valdez
Homer
Seward
Haines
Skagway
Juneau
Kodiak
Ketchikan

0   200   400 mi
0   200   400 km

Niihau
Kauai
Lihue
Oahu
Kaneohe
Honolulu
Molokai
Lanai
Lahaina
Kahului
Maui
Kahoolawe
HAWAII
HAWAII-ALEUTIAN TIME ZONE
Kailua-Kona
Hilo
Hawaii

0   100 mi
0   100 km

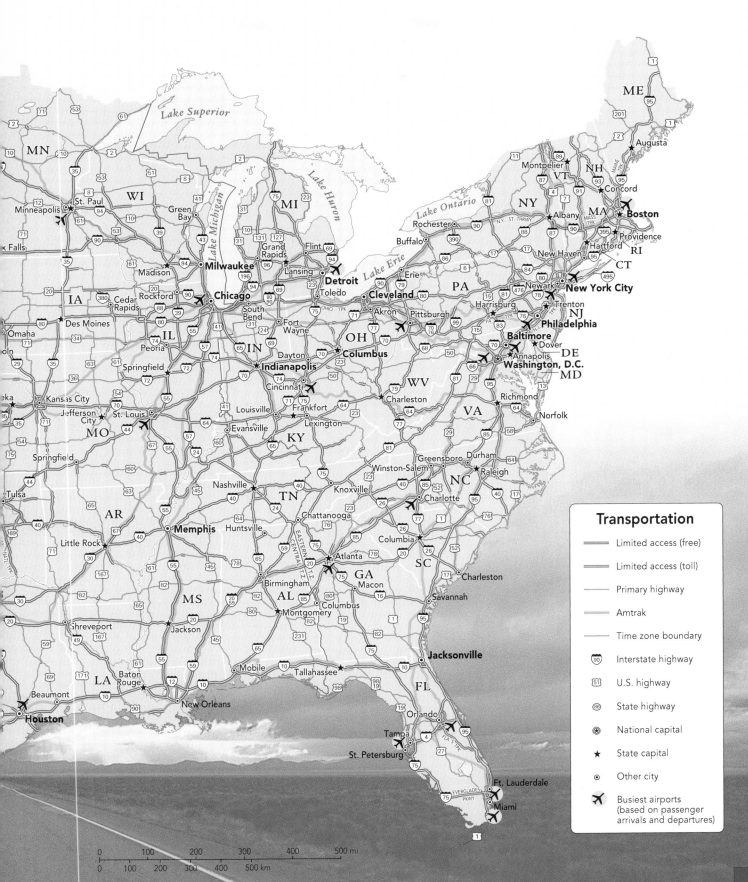

Transportation

- Limited access (free)
- Limited access (toll)
- Primary highway
- Amtrak
- Time zone boundary
- 🛡 Interstate highway
- 🛡 U.S. highway
- ◉ State highway
- ◎ National capital
- ★ State capital
- ◉ Other city
- ✈ Busiest airports (based on passenger arrivals and departures)

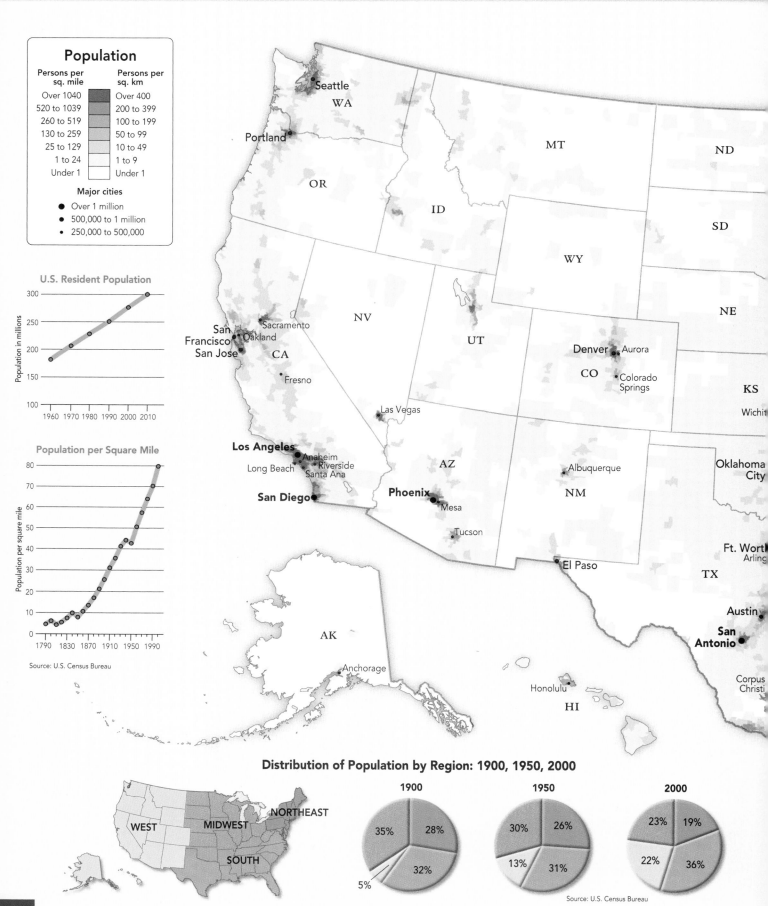

Population

Persons per sq. mile	Persons per sq. km
Over 1040	Over 400
520 to 1039	200 to 399
260 to 519	100 to 199
130 to 259	50 to 99
25 to 129	10 to 49
1 to 24	1 to 9
Under 1	Under 1

Major cities

● Over 1 million
• 500,000 to 1 million
· 250,000 to 500,000

U.S. Resident Population

Population in millions

1960 1970 1980 1990 2000 2010

Population per Square Mile

Population per square mile

1790 1830 1870 1910 1950 1990

Source: U.S. Census Bureau

Distribution of Population by Region: 1900, 1950, 2000

WEST | MIDWEST | NORTHEAST | SOUTH

1900
35% | 28% | 32% | 5%

1950
30% | 26% | 13% | 31%

2000
23% | 19% | 22% | 36%

Source: U.S. Census Bureau

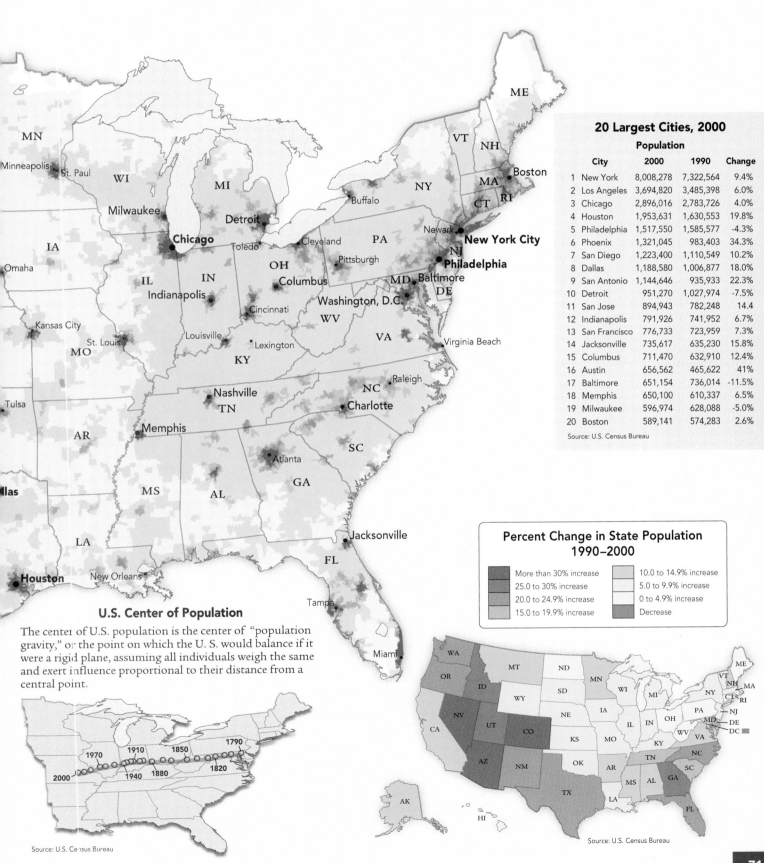

20 Largest Cities, 2000

	City	Population 2000	Population 1990	Change
1	New York	8,008,278	7,322,564	9.4%
2	Los Angeles	3,694,820	3,485,398	6.0%
3	Chicago	2,896,016	2,783,726	4.0%
4	Houston	1,953,631	1,630,553	19.8%
5	Philadelphia	1,517,550	1,585,577	-4.3%
6	Phoenix	1,321,045	983,403	34.3%
7	San Diego	1,223,400	1,110,549	10.2%
8	Dallas	1,188,580	1,006,877	18.0%
9	San Antonio	1,144,646	935,933	22.3%
10	Detroit	951,270	1,027,974	-7.5%
11	San Jose	894,943	782,248	14.4
12	Indianapolis	791,926	741,952	6.7%
13	San Francisco	776,733	723,959	7.3%
14	Jacksonville	735,617	635,230	15.8%
15	Columbus	711,470	632,910	12.4%
16	Austin	656,562	465,622	41%
17	Baltimore	651,154	736,014	-11.5%
18	Memphis	650,100	610,337	6.5%
19	Milwaukee	596,974	628,088	-5.0%
20	Boston	589,141	574,283	2.6%

Source: U.S. Census Bureau

Percent Change in State Population 1990–2000

- More than 30% increase
- 25.0 to 30% increase
- 20.0 to 24.9% increase
- 15.0 to 19.9% increase
- 10.0 to 14.9% increase
- 5.0 to 9.9% increase
- 0 to 4.9% increase
- Decrease

U.S. Center of Population

The center of U.S. population is the center of "population gravity," or the point on which the U. S. would balance if it were a rigid plane, assuming all individuals weigh the same and exert influence proportional to their distance from a central point.

Source: U.S. Census Bureau

Source: U.S. Census Bureau

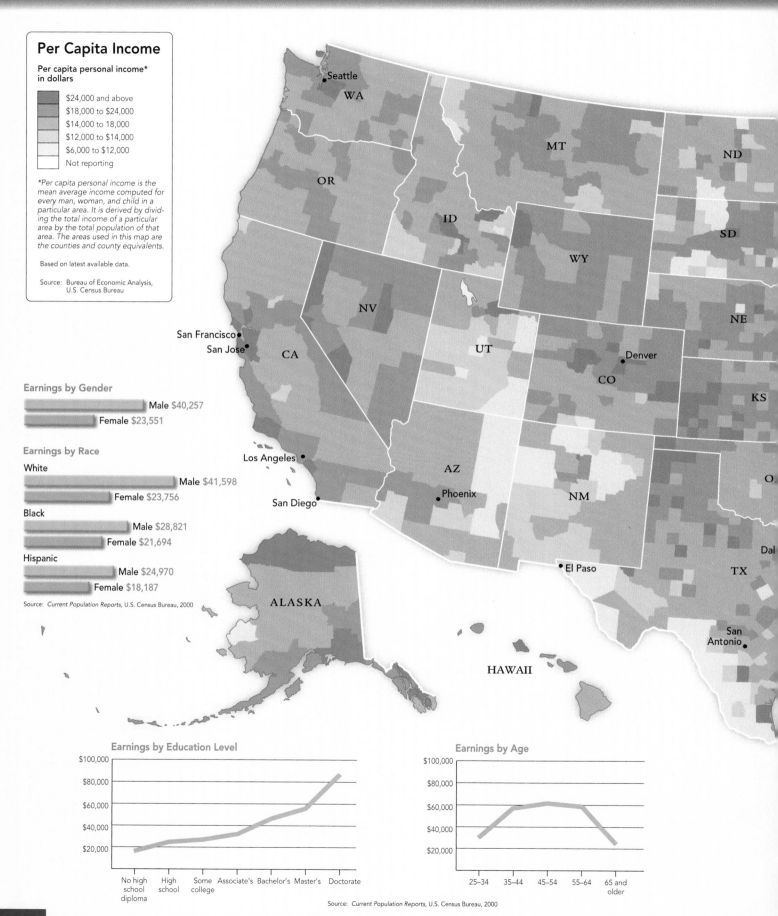

Per Capita Income

Per capita personal income* in dollars

- $24,000 and above
- $18,000 to $24,000
- $14,000 to 18,000
- $12,000 to $14,000
- $6,000 to $12,000
- Not reporting

*Per capita personal income is the mean average income computed for every man, woman, and child in a particular area. It is derived by dividing the total income of a particular area by the total population of that area. The areas used in this map are the counties and county equivalents.

Based on latest available data.

Source: Bureau of Economic Analysis, U.S. Census Bureau

Earnings by Gender
Male $40,257
Female $23,551

Earnings by Race
White
Male $41,598
Female $23,756
Black
Male $28,821
Female $21,694
Hispanic
Male $24,970
Female $18,187

Source: *Current Population Reports, U.S. Census Bureau, 2000*

Earnings by Education Level

$100,000 / $80,000 / $60,000 / $40,000 / $20,000

No high school diploma — High school — Some college — Associate's — Bachelor's — Master's — Doctorate

Earnings by Age

$100,000 / $80,000 / $60,000 / $40,000 / $20,000

25–34 — 35–44 — 45–54 — 55–64 — 65 and older

Source: *Current Population Reports, U.S. Census Bureau, 2000*

MN

WI

MI

IA

IL   IN

Milwaukee

Detroit

Chicago

Cleveland

OH   PA

Columbus

Indianapolis

MO

KY

WV

VA

AR   TN

Memphis

NC

MS   AL   GA   SC

LA

Houston

FL

Jacksonville

ME

VT   NH

NY   MA   Boston

CT   RI

New York City

NJ

Philadelphia

MD   Baltimore

DE

Washington, D.C.

Highest Per Capita Income*

Luxembourg	$36,400
United States	$36,200
Bermuda	$33,000
San Marino	$32,000
Switzerland	$28,600
Aruba	$28,000
Norway	$27,700
Monaco	$27,000
Singapore	$26,500
Denmark	$25,500
Belgium	$25,300
Austria	$25,000
Japan	$24,900
Canada	$24,800
Iceland	$24,800
France	$24,400
Netherlands	$24,400
Germany	$23,400
Australia	$23,200

*estimated, 2000

Source: *The World Factbook 2000*, CIA

Persons Below the Poverty Level

30% and above
25% to 30%
20% to 25%
15% to 20%
10% to 15%
Less than 10%

Poverty level is based on the income a household needs so that no more than a third of income must be used for adequate food. Households with incomes below this level are considered to be poor. The U.S. government adjusts the poverty level according to household size, and revises it each year for changes in the cost of living.

Source: Census 2000, U.S. Census Bureau

73

Canada

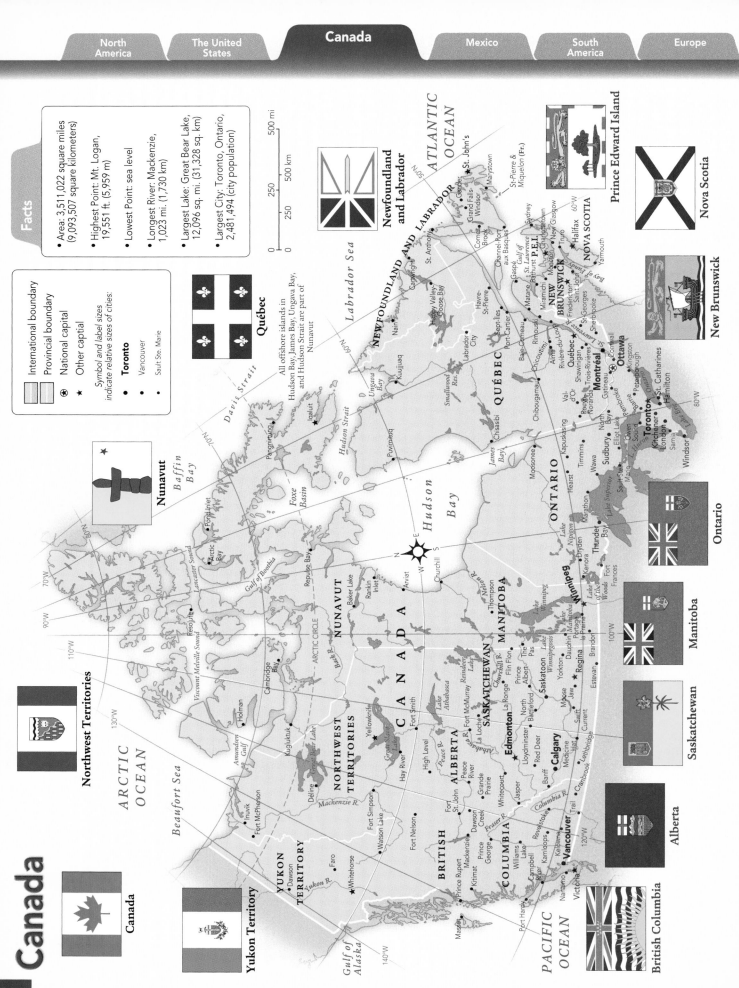

Facts

- Area: 3,511,022 square miles (9,093,507 square kilometers)
- Highest Point: Mt. Logan, 19,551 ft. (5,959 m)
- Lowest Point: sea level
- Longest River: Mackenzie, 1,023 mi. (1,730 km)
- Largest Lake: Great Bear Lake, 12,096 sq. mi. (31,328 sq. km)
- Largest City: Toronto, Ontario, 2,481,494 (city population)

500 mi
500 km
250
250
0

International boundary
Provincial boundary
⊛ National capital
★ Other captial

Symbol and label sizes indicate relative sizes of cities:

Toronto
Vancouver
Sault Ste. Marie

All offshore islands in Hudson Bay, James Bay, Ungava Bay, and Hudson Strait are part of Nunavut

Newfoundland and Labrador

Québec

Prince Edward Island

Nova Scotia

New Brunswick

Nunavut

Ontario

Manitoba

Saskatchewan

Alberta

Northwest Territories

British Columbia

Yukon Territory

Canada

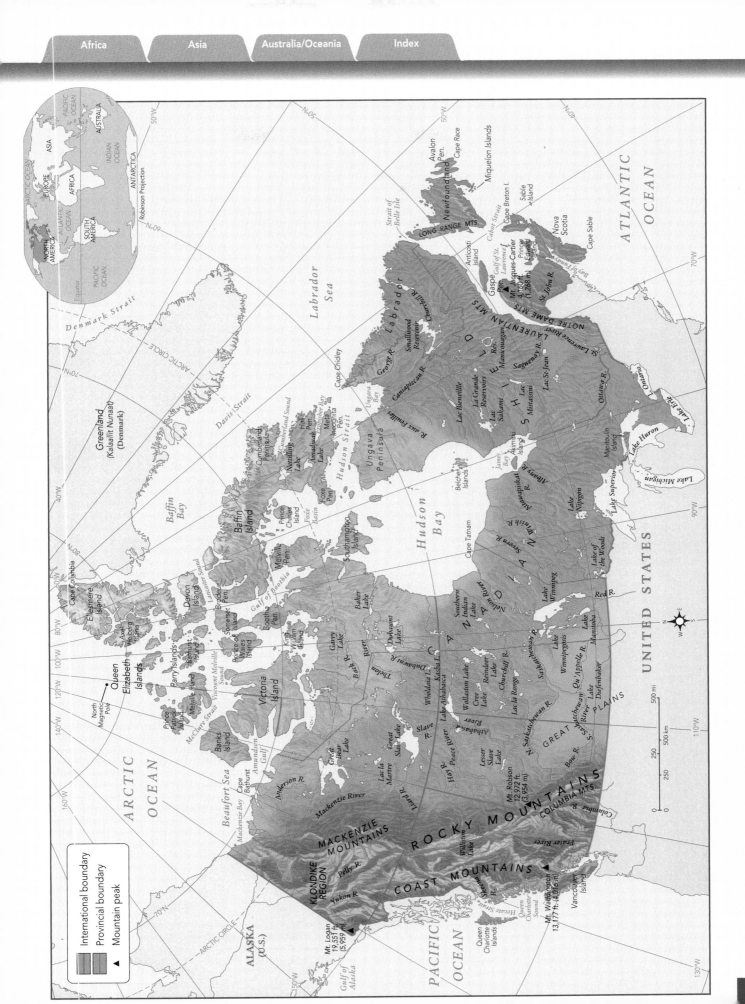

Mexico

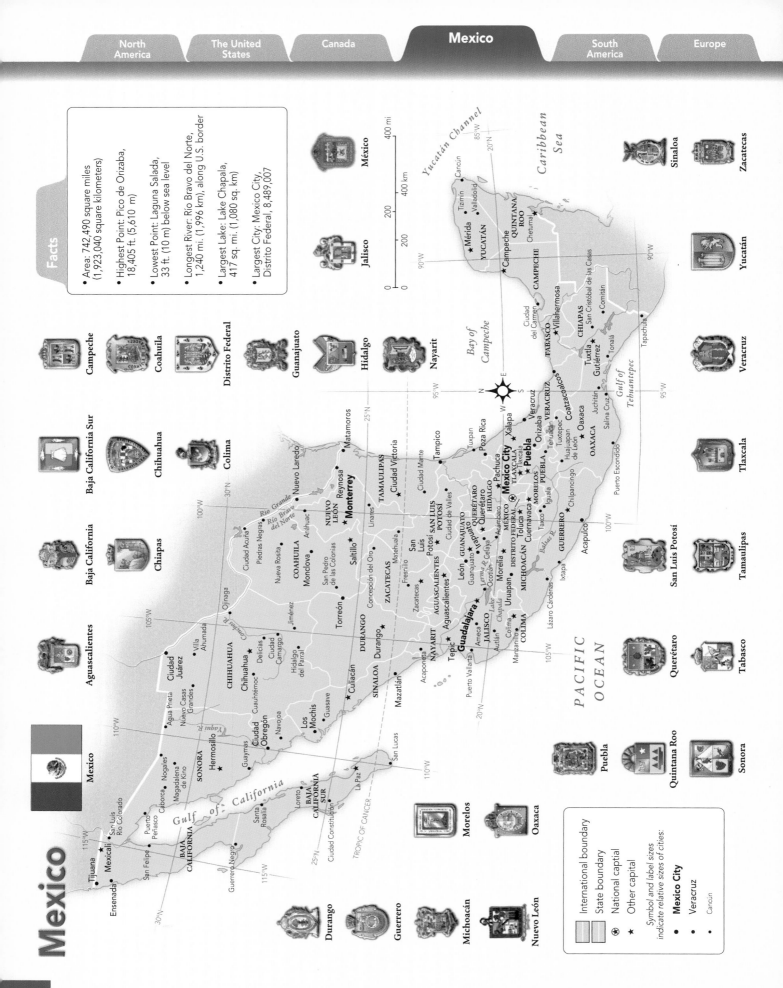

Facts

- Area: 742,490 square miles (1,923,040 square kilometers)
- Highest Point: Pico de Orizaba, 18,405 ft. (5,610 m)
- Lowest Point: Laguna Salada, 33 ft. (10 m) below sea level
- Longest River: Rio Bravo del Norte, 1,240 mi. (1,996 km), along U.S. border
- Largest Lake: Lake Chapala, 417 sq. mi. (1,080 sq. km)
- Largest City: Mexico City, Distrito Federal, 8,489,007

México

Jalisco

Campeche

Coahuila

Distrito Federal

Guanajuato

Hidalgo

Nayarit

Baja California Sur

Chihuahua

Colima

Baja California

Chiapas

Aguascalientes

Mexico

Morelos

Oaxaca

Durango

Guerrero

Michoacán

Nuevo León

Sinaloa

Zacatecas

Yucatán

Veracruz

Tlaxcala

San Luis Potosí

Tamaulipas

Querétaro

Tabasco

Puebla

Quintana Roo

Sonora

Legend:
- International boundary
- State boundary
- ⊛ National capital
- ★ Other capital
- Symbol and label sizes indicate relative sizes of cities:
  - **Mexico City**
  - Veracruz
  - Cancún

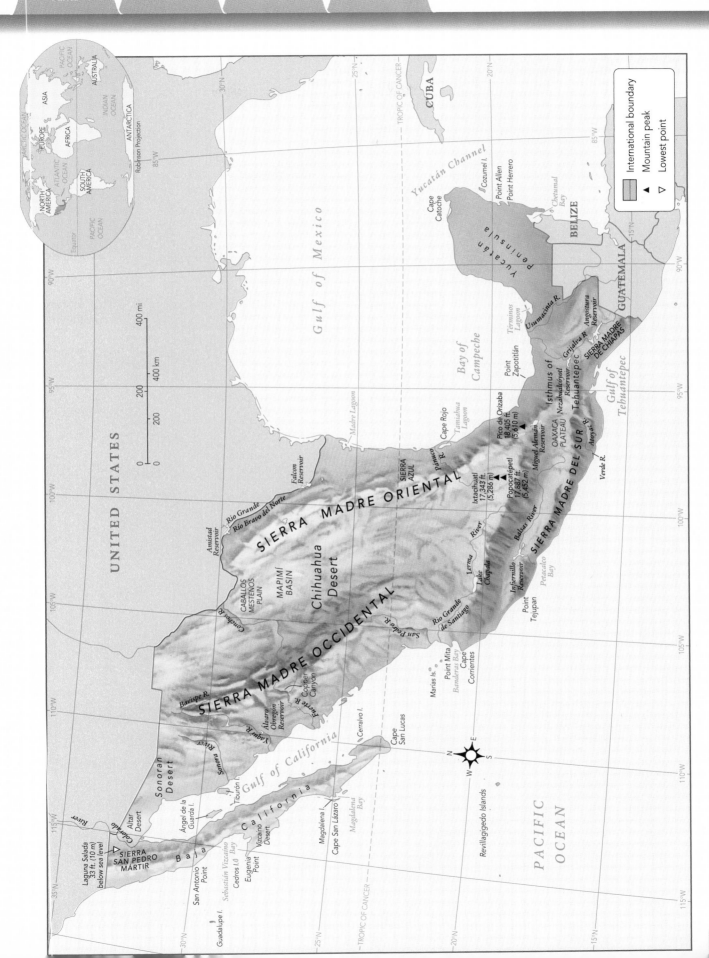

PACIFIC OCEAN
PACIFIC OCEAN
ASIA
AUSTRALIA
INDIAN OCEAN
ANTARCTICA
EUROPE
AFRICA
ATLANTIC OCEAN
NORTH AMERICA
SOUTH AMERICA
Equator
PACIFIC OCEAN
Robinson Projection

Legend:
International boundary
▲ Mountain peak
▽ Lowest point

UNITED STATES

Gulf of Mexico

CUBA

TROPIC OF CANCER

Yucatán Channel

Cape Catoche

Cozumel I.
Point Allen
Point Herrero

Chetumal Bay

BELIZE

Yucatán Peninsula

Bay of Campeche

Términos Lagoon

Usumacinta R.

GUATEMALA

Angostura Reservoir

Grijalva R.

SIERRA MADRE DE CHIAPAS

Gulf of Tehuantepec

Point Zapotlán

Isthmus of Tehuantepec

Nezahualcóyotl Reservoir

Madre Lagoon

Tamiahua Lagoon

Cape Rojo

Pánuco R.

SIERRA AZUL

Pico de Orizaba 18,405 ft. (5,610 m) ▲

Miguel Alemán Reservoir

OAXACA PLATEAU

Arroyo R.

Verde R.

SIERRA MADRE DEL SUR

Ixtlahuatl 17,343 ft. (5,286 m) ▲
Popocatépetl 17,887 ft. (5,452 m) ▲

Balsas River

Lerma River

Lake Chapala

Infiernillo Reservoir

Petacalco Bay

Point Tejupan

Río Grande de Santiago

San Pedro R.

400 mi
400 km
200
200
0
0

SIERRA MADRE ORIENTAL

Falcon Reservoir

Rio Grande
Rio Bravo del Norte

Amistad Reservoir

Chihuahua Desert

CABALLOS MESTEÑOS PLAIN

MAPIMÍ BASIN

Conchos R.

SIERRA MADRE OCCIDENTAL

Bavispe R.

Fuerte R.

Copper Canyon

Álvaro Obregón Reservoir

Yaqui R.

Sonora River

Sonoran Desert

Colorado River

Altar Desert

Laguna Salada 33 ft. (10 m) below sea level

SIERRA SAN PEDRO MÁRTIR

▽

Baja California

Ángel de la Guarda I.

Tiburón I.

Gulf of California

Cerralvo I.

Cape San Lucas

Marías Is.

Point Mita

Banderas Bay

Cape Corrientes

Revillagigedo Islands

PACIFIC OCEAN

N E S W

TROPIC OF CANCER

Magdalena I.

Cape San Lázaro

Magdalena Bay

Vizcaíno Desert

Sebastián Vizcaíno Bay

Eugenia Point

Cedros I.

San Antonio Point

Guadalupe I.

35°N
30°N
25°N
20°N
15°N

115°W
110°W
105°W
100°W
95°W
90°W
85°W

77

South America

Caribbean Sea

Legend:
- International boundary
- National capital
- Other capital

Symbol and label sizes indicate relative sizes of cities:
- **Rio de Janeiro**
- Santos
- Jatai

VENEZUELA
Barranquilla, Maracaibo, Valencia, **Caracas**, Cumaná
Cartagena, Barquisimeto, Maracay, El Tigre, Ciudad Guayana
Sincelejo, Valera
Montería, Mérida
Cúcuta, San Cristóbal, Ciudad Bolívar
Medellín, Bucaramanga, Barrancabermeja
Manizales, Puerto Ayacucho
Pereira, **Bogotá**, Boa Vista
Armenia, Ibagué
Buenaventura, Cali, **COLOMBIA**
Neiva
Pasto, Florencia
Esmeraldas, Macapá

Georgetown, Paramaribo
GUYANA, **SURINAME**, **FRENCH GUIANA (Fr.)**, Cayenne

ECUADOR
Guayaquil, Cuenca
Machala, Iquitos
Tumbes
Piura
PERU
Chiclayo, Cajamarca
Trujillo, Pucallpa
Chimbote, Huánuco
Callao, Huancayo, Puerto Maldonado
Lima, Ayacucho, Cuzco
Ica, Juliaca
Arequipa
Tacna, **Lake Titicaca**
Arica
Iquique

EQUATOR

Quito

Benjamin Constant
Cruzeiro do Sul
Rio Branco, Pôrto Velho
Riberalta, Guajará-Mirim
BOLIVIA
Trinidad
La Paz, Cochabamba, Santa Cruz
Oruro, **Sucre**
Potosí
Tarija

Manaus, Santarém, Belém, São Luís, Parnaíba
BRAZIL
Imperatriz, Fortaleza, Teresina, Floriano, Juàzeiro do Norte, Natal, Campina Grande, João Pessoa, Petrolina, **Recife**, Maceió
Cuiabá, Gurupi, Feira de Santana, Aracaju, Vitória da Conquista, **Salvador**, Ilhéus
Goiânia, **Brasília**, Montes Claros
Jataí, Uberlândia
Corumbá, **Belo Horizonte**, Governador Valadares
Campo Grande, São José do Rio Prêto, Vitória
Dourados, Grande, Bauru, Ribeirão Prêto, Campinas, Volta Redonda
Concepción, Londrina, **São Paulo**, Niterói, Santos, **Rio de Janeiro**
Curitiba

PARAGUAY
Asunción
Encarnación, Florianópolis
Resistencia, Corrientes, Reconquista, Passo Fundo
Salta, San Salvador de Jujuy
San Miguel de Tucumán
Catamarca, Santiago del Estero, Santa Maria, Rivera
Copiapó, La Rioja, Salto, Melo
CHILE
La Serena, Córdoba, Santa Fe, Paraná, Rivera, Pelotas
Calama, Antofagasta
Pôrto Alegre
URUGUAY
Valparaíso, Mendoza, Rosario, **Montevideo**
Rancagua, Río Cuarto, **Buenos Aires**, La Plata
Santiago
Talca
Chillán, Santa Rosa
Concepción, **ARGENTINA**, Mar del Plata
Temuco, Neuquén, Bahía Blanca, Necochea
Valdivia
Puerto Montt, San Carlos de Bariloche, Viedma
Esquel, Rawson

PACIFIC OCEAN

San Ambrosio Island (Chile)
San Félix Island (Chile)
Galápagos Islands (Ecuador)
Juan Fernández Islands (Chile)

ATLANTIC OCEAN

Comodoro Rivadavia

Río Gallegos, Stanley, *Falkland Islands (U.K.) (Islas Malvinas)*
Punta Arenas
Ushuaia

N W E S

0   300   600 mi
0   300   600 km

Facts

- Area: 6,900,000 square miles (17,800,000 square kilometers)
- Highest Point: Mt. Aconcagua, Argentina, 22,834 ft (6,960 m)
- Lowest Point: Valdés Peninsula, Argentina, 131 ft (40 m) below sea level
- Longest River: Amazon, 4,000 mi (6,400 km)
- Largest Lake: Lake Titicaca, Peru/Bolivia, 3,200 sq. mi (8,300 sq. km)
- Largest Country: Brazil, 6,880,000 sq. mi (17,819,000 sq. km) (slightly smaller than the United States)
- Largest City: São Paulo, Brazil, 17,834,000

78

NORTH AMERICA

Caribbean Sea

ATLANTIC OCEAN

ARCTIC OCEAN
NORTH AMERICA
EUROPE
ASIA
ATLANTIC OCEAN
AFRICA
PACIFIC OCEAN
Equator
PACIFIC OCEAN
SOUTH AMERICA
INDIAN OCEAN
AUSTRALIA
ANTARCTICA
Robinson Projection

Lake Maracaibo

LLANOS
Orinoco River
Angel Falls ≈
GUIANA
HIGHLANDS

Cauca River
Magdalena River

Orinoco River

Rio Negro

AMAZON BASIN

Amazon

River

Galápagos Islands

EQUATOR

Gulf of Guayaquil

Putumayo River

Marañón River

Ucayali River

Amazon (Solimões) River
Jurua River
Purus River
Madeira River

Topajós River
Teles Pires
River
Xingu
River
Tocantins River
Parnaíba
River

Cape São Roque

Pariñas Pt.

Mt. Huascarán
22,133 ft.
(6,746 m)

Paracas Peninsula

ANDES

Beni River

Guaporé River

MATO GROSSO PLATEAU

Araguaia River
São Francisco River

BRAZILIAN

HIGHLANDS

PACIFIC OCEAN

Volcán Misti
19,098 ft.
(5,821 m)

Lake Titicaca
Mt. Illimani
20,741 ft.
(6,322 m)
Lake Poopó

ALTIPLANO

Mamore River

Paraguay River

San Félix I.   San Ambrosio I.

Atacama Desert

GRAN CHACO
Pilcomayo River
Salado River

Paraná River

Grande River

SERRA DO MAR

Paraná

Iguazú Falls

Uruguay River

TROPIC OF CAPRICORN

ANDES

Juan Fernández Is.

Mt. Aconcagua
22,834 ft.
(6,960 m)

Río de la Plata

ATLANTIC OCEAN

Colorado River

PAMPAS

Negro River

Gulf of San Matías
▽ Valdés Peninsula
131 ft (40 m) below sea level

Chiloé I.

Los Chonos Archipelago

Patagonia

Gulf of San Jorge

	International boundary
▲	Mountain peak
▽	Lowest point
≈	Falls

0   300   600 mi
0   300   600 km

N
W E
S

Santa Cruz River

Strait of Magellan

Falkland Islands
(Islas Malvinas)

South Georgia

Tierra del Fuego

Cape Horn

A   B

Elevation Profile

Paracas Peninsula   Lake Titicaca   Andes Mountains

Mato Grosso Plateau

Brazilian Highlands

20,000 ft.
10,000 ft.
5,000 ft.
Sea level
A

B

Major Metropolitan Areas

Argentina
Buenos Aires	11,298,000
Córdoba	1,209,000
Rosario	1,119,000

Bolivia
La Paz	1,484,000
Santa Cruz	1,136,000
Cochabamba	517,000

Brazil
São Paulo	17,834,000
Rio de Janeiro	10,612,000
Belo Horizonte	4,800,000
Pôrto Alegre	3,655,000
Recife	3,332,000
Salvador	3,018,000
Fortaleza	2,975,000
Brasília	2,942,000
Curitiba	2,726,000
Belém	1,816,000
Manaus	1,011,000

Chile
Santiago	4,647,000
Viña del Mar	299,000

Colombia
Bogotá	6,422,000
Cali	2,129,000
Medellín	1,885,000
Barranquilla	1,549,000

Ecuador
Guayaquil	2,118,000
Quito	1,616,000

French Guiana
Cayenne	50,000

Guyana
Georgetown	187,000

Paraguay
Asunción	513,000

Peru
Lima	6,988,000
Arequipa	830,000
Chiclayo	766,000

Suriname
Paramaribo	291,000

Uruguay
Montevideo	1,303,000

Venezuela
Caracas	3,061,000
Maracaibo	1,220,000
Barquisimeto	896,000
Valencia	742,000

International comparability of population data is limited by varying census methods. Where metropolitan population is unavailable, core city population is shown.

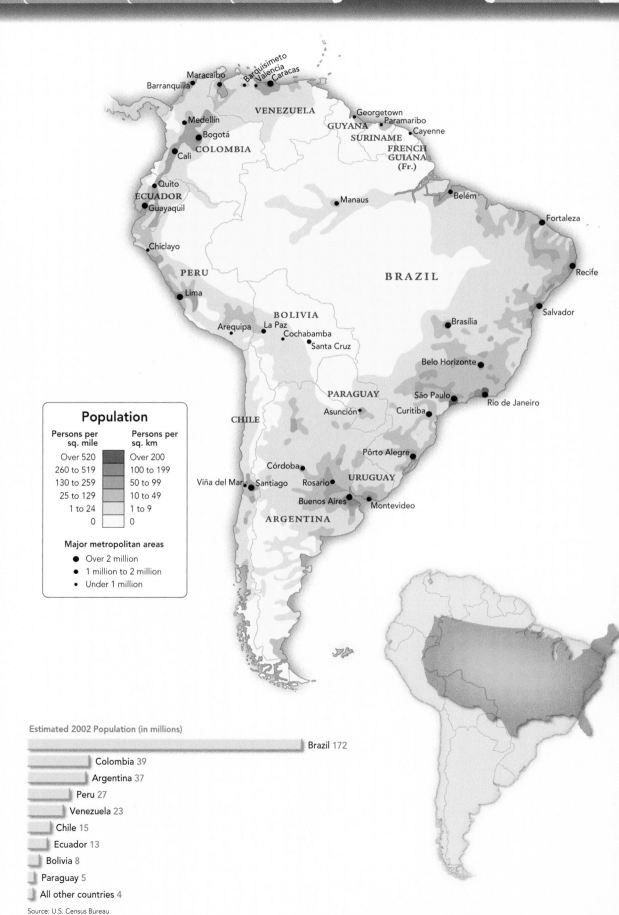

Population

Persons per sq. mile	Persons per sq. km
Over 520	Over 200
260 to 519	100 to 199
130 to 259	50 to 99
25 to 129	10 to 49
1 to 24	1 to 9
0	0

Major metropolitan areas
- ● Over 2 million
- ● 1 million to 2 million
- • Under 1 million

Estimated 2002 Population (in millions)

- Brazil 172
- Colombia 39
- Argentina 37
- Peru 27
- Venezuela 23
- Chile 15
- Ecuador 13
- Bolivia 8
- Paraguay 5
- All other countries 4

Source: U.S. Census Bureau

Gross Domestic Product

GDP per capita

- Over $20,000
- $10,000 to $20,000
- $5,000 to $9,999
- $2,500 to $4,999
- Less than $2,500
- No data

Source: *World Factbook*, CIA, 2001

Gross Domestic Product is a measure of the total goods and services generated by a country. Generally, manufacturing, high-tech services, and specialized agricultural products add more value than raw materials and basic food stuffs.

Electricity Use

United States 12,407
Suriname 4,150
Chile 2,311
Columbia 1,005
Paraguay 334

KWh (kilowatt hours) per person per year

Source: *World Factbook*, CIA, 2001

Non-manufacturing economic activity is generated primarily by commercial plantation agriculture, livestock raising, and the harvest of forest products, plus the extraction of oil and minerals. Manufacturing, like population, is concentrated in the continent's coastal areas.

Land Use and Resources

Predominant land use
- Commercial agriculture
- Livestock ranching
- Subsistence agriculture
- Primarily forestland
- Limited agricultural activity

Major resources
- Coal
- Natural gas
- Oil
- Forest products
- Gold (Au)
- Silver (Ag)
- Iron ore (Fe)
- Uranium (U)
- Bauxite (Al)
- Diamonds
- Other minerals
- Fishing
- Major manufacturing and trade centers

81

Most of the continent is under the influence of wet and tropical air. Warm currents in the Atlantic Ocean as well as wet lowland elevations lying within the confines of the tropical latitudes directly affect the climate of the majority of the land area. The Andes Mountains and cold currents that hug the Pacific coast keep the Western and Southern regions of the continent temperate but dry.

See photographs taken in different kinds of climates on pages 24–25.

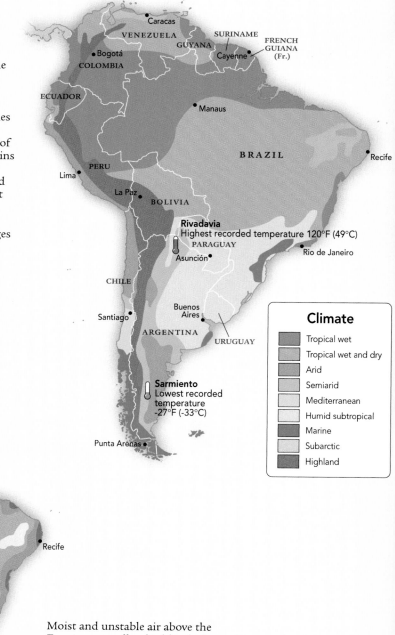

Rivadavia
Highest recorded temperature 120°F (49°C)

Sarmiento
Lowest recorded temperature -27°F (-33°C)

Climate

- Tropical wet
- Tropical wet and dry
- Arid
- Semiarid
- Mediterranean
- Humid subtropical
- Marine
- Subarctic
- Highland

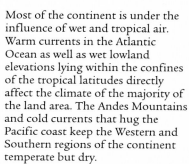

Quibdo
Highest average annual precipitation: 354" (899 cm)

Arica
Lowest average annual precipitation: 0.03" (0.08 cm)

Moist and unstable air above the Equator—as well as highlands that wring out waterlogged clouds—produce heavy rainfall, but along the coast of Chile and elsewhere, cold ocean water and mountainous barriers keep rainfall at a minimum.

Annual Precipitation

Centimeters		Inches
Over 200		Over 80
150 to 200		60 to 80
100 to 150		40 to 60
50 to 100		20 to 40
25 to 50		10 to 20
Under 25		Under 10

Climate Graphs

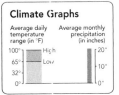

Average daily temperature range (in °F)
100°
65° High
32° Low
0°

Average monthly precipitation (in inches)
20"
10"
0"

ASUNCIÓN, Paraguay
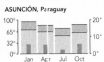

BOGOTÁ, Colombia
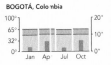

BUENOS AIRES, Argentina
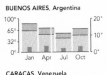

CARACAS, Venezuela
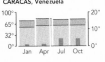

CAYENNE, French Guiana
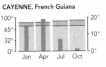

LA PAZ, Bolivia

LIMA, Peru
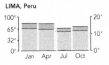

MANAUS, Brazil

PUNTA ARENAS, Chile

RECIFE, Brazil
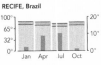

RIO DE JANEIRO, Brazil
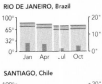

SANTIAGO, Chile
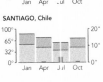

South America is dominated by tropical vegetation, including Earth's most extensive rain forest. Farther south, a vast grassland, the Pampa, fades gradually into the dry and meager vegetation of Patagonia.

See photographs of the different kinds of vegetation on pages 26–27.

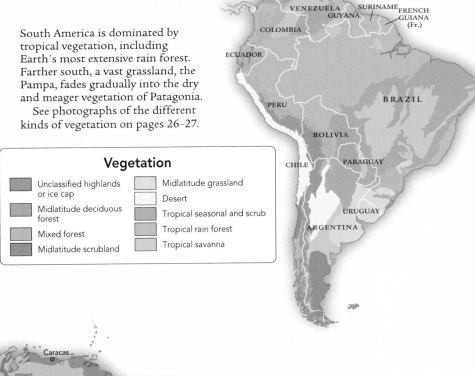

Vegetation

- Unclassified highlands or ice cap
- Midlatitude deciduous forest
- Mixed forest
- Midlatitude scrubland
- Midlatitude grassland
- Desert
- Tropical seasonal and scrub
- Tropical rain forest
- Tropical savanna

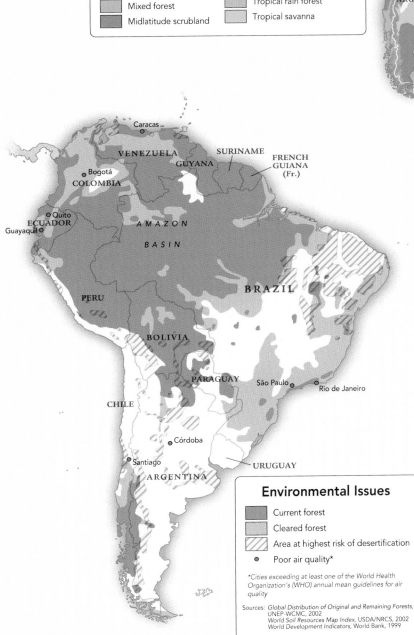

The destruction of forest areas—especially in the Amazon Basin—is one of the leading environmental issues in South America. In Brazil, it is estimated that an average of 15,000 acres of forest are lost each day as people clear land for timber and to grow crops. Human activities have impacted other types of vegetation, as well. For example, over-grazing has caused damage to grasslands in many areas, putting them at risk of becoming infertile deserts. Poor urban air quality is another serious concern in the region, with nearly 80 percent of the population living in cities.

Environmental Issues

- Current forest
- Cleared forest
- Area at highest risk of desertification
- Poor air quality*

*Cities exceeding at least one of the World Health Organization's (WHO) annual mean guidelines for air quality

Sources: Global Distribution of Original and Remaining Forests, UNEP-WCMC, 2002
World Soil Resources Map Index, USDA/NRCS, 2002
World Development Indicators, World Bank, 1999

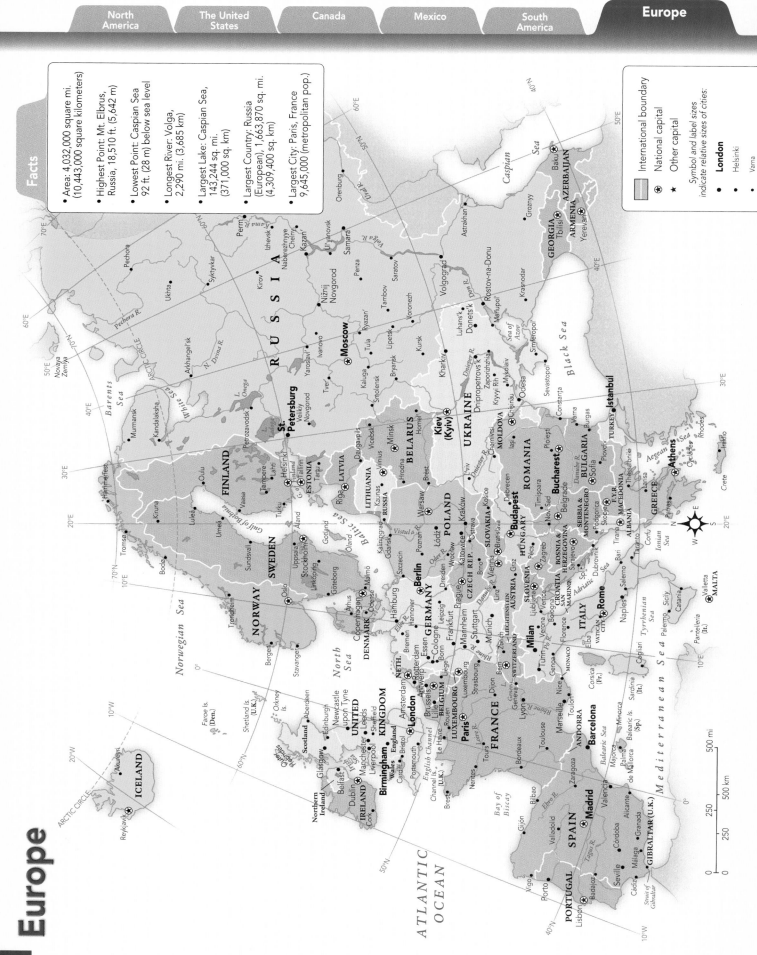

Europe

Facts

- Area: 4,032,000 square mi. (10,443,000 square kilometers)
- Highest Point: Mt. Elbrus, Russia, 18,510 ft. (5,642 m)
- Lowest Point: Caspian Sea 92 ft. (28 m) below sea level
- Longest River: Volga, 2,290 mi. (3,685 km)
- Largest Lake: Caspian Sea, 143,244 sq. mi. (371,000 sq. km)
- Largest Country: Russia (European), 1,663,870 sq. mi. (4,309,400 sq. km)
- Largest City: Paris, France 9,645,000 (metropolitan pop.)

International boundary
National capital
Other capital
Symbol and label sizes indicate relative sizes of cities:
London
Helsinki
Varna

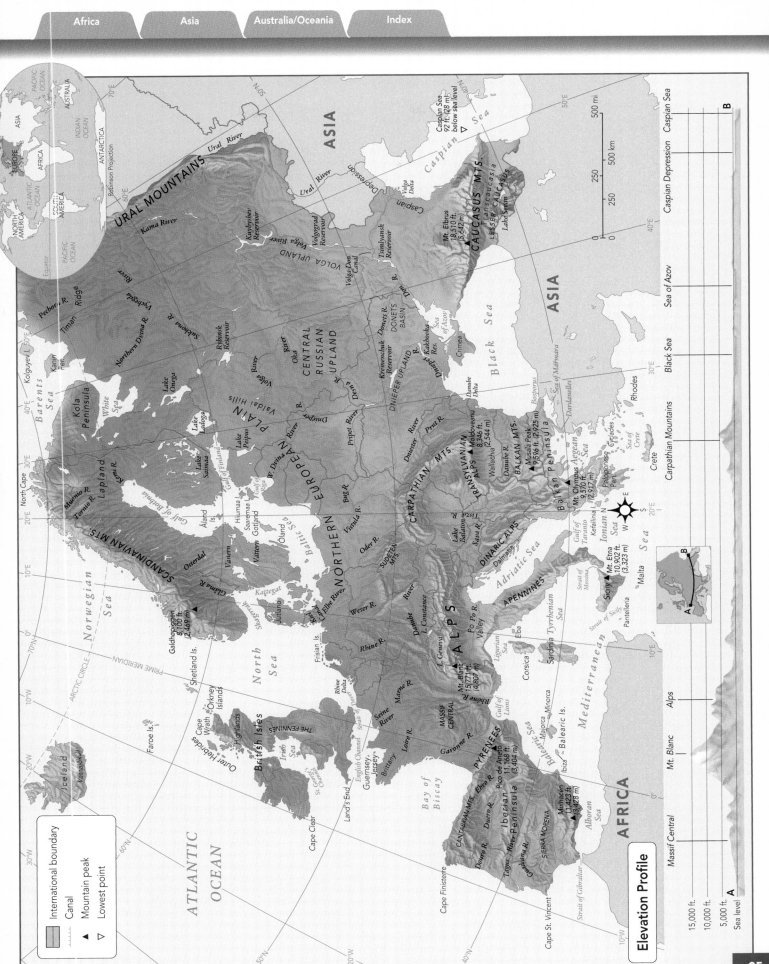

ASIA

URAL MOUNTAINS

Ural River

Caspian Depression

Caspian Sea
92 ft. (28 m)
below sea level

Caspian Sea

Ural River

Volga River
Kama River

Kaybyshev
Reservoir

Volga Delta

VOLGA UPLAND

Volgograd Reservoir

Volga-Don
Canal

Tsimlyansk
Reservoir

Don R.

Mt. Elbrus
18,510 ft.
(5,642 m) ▲

CAUCASUS MTS.

Transcaucasia

LESSER CAUCASUS

Lake Sevan

ASIA

Pechora R.

Timan Ridge

Vychegda River

Rybinsk
Reservoir

Northern Dvina R.

Sukhona R.

Oka River

Volga R.

CENTRAL
RUSSIAN
UPLAND

Kremenchuk Reservoir

Donets R.

DONETS
BASIN

Desna R.

Kakhovka
Res.

Sea
of
Azov

Sea
of Azov

Crimea

Black Sea

Kolguyev I.

Kanin
Pen.

*White
Sea*

Kola
Peninsula

*Barents
Sea*

Lake
Onega

NORTHERN

Valdai Hills

EUROPEAN

Pripet River

Dnieper River

Dniester River

Prut R.

Danube R.

Danube
Delta

Black Sea

Lake
Ladoga

Lake
Peipus

Lake
Saimaa

Gulf of Finland

PLAIN

W. Dvina R.

Dnieper River

Bug R.

CARPATHIAN
MTS.

TRANSYLVANIAN
ALPS

Moldoveanu
8,346 ft.
(2,544 m) ▲

Tisza R.

Wallachia

BALKAN MTS.

Musala Peak
9,596 ft. (2,925 m) ▲

Danube R.

Bosporus

Sea of Marmara

Dardanelles

Balkan Peninsula

Mt. Olympus
9,570 ft.
(2,917 m) ▲

Aegean
Sea

Sea of
Crete

Peloponnese
Pen.

Cyclades

Rhodes

Crete

Carpathian Mountains

Lapland

North Cape

Scandinavian Mts.

Muonio R.

Tornio R.

Kemi R.

Torne R.

Gulf of
Bothnia

Aland
Is.

Hiiumaa

Saaremaa

Öland

Gotland

Baltic Sea

SUDETEN
MTS.

Oder R.

Vistula R.

Lake
Balaton

Sava R.

DINARIC ALPS

Dalmatia

Gulf of
Taranto

Ionian
Sea

Kefallinia

Ionian
Sea

Malta

Galdhøpiggen
8,100 ft.
(2,469 m) ▲

Vänern

Klara R.

Österdal

Glåma R.

Kattegat

Vättern

Jutland

Skagerrak

Frisian
Is.

Weser R.

Elbe River

Rhine R.

Danube

L. Constance

L. Geneva

A L P S

Po R.
Valley

Po R.

APENNINES

Adriatic Sea

Tyrrhenian
Sea

Sardinia

Elba

Liguridan
Sea

Corsica

Strait of
Messina

Sicily

Mt. Etna
10,902 ft.
(3,323 m) ▲

Pantelleria

Strait of Sicily

Shetland Is.

North
Sea

*Rhine
Delta*

Faroe Is.

Orkney
Islands

Cape
Wrath

Highlands

THE PENNINES

Outer Hebrides

British Isles

Irish
Sea

Rhine R.

Marne R.

Seine River

Loire R.

MASSIF
CENTRAL

Garonne R.

Gulf of
Lions

Balearic
Sea

Minorca

Majorca

Ibiza

Balearic Is.

Mediterranean

Sea

Iceland

Vatnajökull

ATLANTIC
OCEAN

Cape Clear

Cape Finisterre

Cape St. Vincent

Cape
Wrath

St. George's Channel

English Channel

Land's End

Guernsey,
Jersey

Brittany

Strait of Dover

Bay of
Biscay

PYRENEES

Pico de Aneto
11,168 ft.
(3,404 m) ▲

Ebro R.

CANTABRIAN MTS.

Duero R.

Iberian
Peninsula

Douro R.

Tagus River

SIERRA MORENA

Guadiana R.

Mulhacén
11,423 ft.
(3,428 m) ▲

Alboran
Sea

Strait of Gibraltar

AFRICA

Norwegian
Sea

Elevation Profile

Massif Central   Mt. Blanc   Alps   Carpathian Mountains   Black Sea   Sea of Azov   Caspian Depression   Caspian Sea

15,000 ft.
10,000 ft.
5,000 ft.
Sea level

A   B

International boundary
Canal
▲ Mountain peak
▽ Lowest point

0   250   500 mi
0   250   500 km

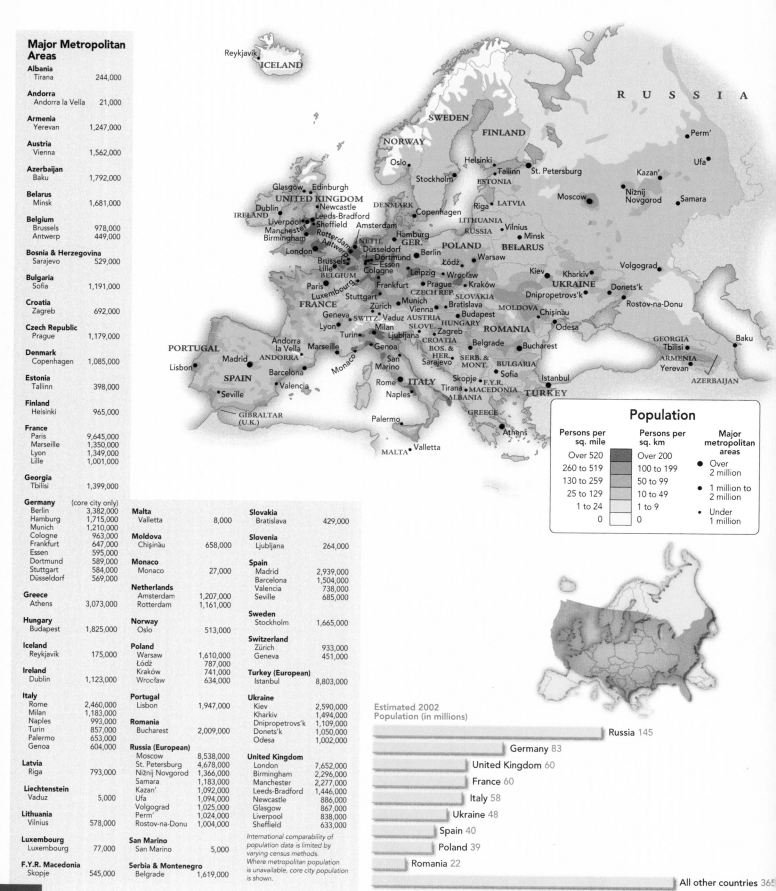

Major Metropolitan Areas

Albania
Tirana — 244,000

Andorra
Andorra la Vella — 21,000

Armenia
Yerevan — 1,247,000

Austria
Vienna — 1,562,000

Azerbaijan
Baku — 1,792,000

Belarus
Minsk — 1,681,000

Belgium
Brussels — 978,000
Antwerp — 449,000

Bosnia & Herzegovina
Sarajevo — 529,000

Bulgaria
Sofia — 1,191,000

Croatia
Zagreb — 692,000

Czech Republic
Prague — 1,179,000

Denmark
Copenhagen — 1,085,000

Estonia
Tallinn — 398,000

Finland
Helsinki — 965,000

France
Paris — 9,645,000
Marseille — 1,350,000
Lyon — 1,349,000
Lille — 1,001,000

Georgia
Tbilisi — 1,399,000

Germany (core city only)
Berlin — 3,382,000
Hamburg — 1,715,000
Munich — 1,210,000
Cologne — 963,000
Frankfurt — 647,000
Essen — 595,000
Dortmund — 589,000
Stuttgart — 584,000
Düsseldorf — 569,000

Greece
Athens — 3,073,000

Hungary
Budapest — 1,825,000

Iceland
Reykjavik — 175,000

Ireland
Dublin — 1,123,000

Italy
Rome — 2,460,000
Milan — 1,183,000
Naples — 993,000
Turin — 857,000
Palermo — 653,000
Genoa — 604,000

Latvia
Riga — 793,000

Liechtenstein
Vaduz — 5,000

Lithuania
Vilnius — 578,000

Luxembourg
Luxembourg — 77,000

F.Y.R. Macedonia
Skopje — 545,000

Malta
Valletta — 8,000

Moldova
Chişinău — 658,000

Monaco
Monaco — 27,000

Netherlands
Amsterdam — 1,207,000
Rotterdam — 1,161,000

Norway
Oslo — 513,000

Poland
Warsaw — 1,610,000
Łódź — 787,000
Kraków — 741,000
Wrocław — 634,000

Portugal
Lisbon — 1,947,000

Romania
Bucharest — 2,009,000

Russia (European)
Moscow — 8,538,000
St. Petersburg — 4,678,000
Nižnij Novgorod — 1,366,000
Samara — 1,183,000
Kazan' — 1,092,000
Ufa — 1,094,000
Volgograd — 1,025,000
Perm' — 1,024,000
Rostov-na-Donu — 1,004,000

San Marino
San Marino — 5,000

Serbia & Montenegro
Belgrade — 1,619,000

Slovakia
Bratislava — 429,000

Slovenia
Ljubljana — 264,000

Spain
Madrid — 2,939,000
Barcelona — 1,504,000
Valencia — 738,000
Seville — 685,000

Sweden
Stockholm — 1,665,000

Switzerland
Zürich — 933,000
Geneva — 451,000

Turkey (European)
Istanbul — 8,803,000

Ukraine
Kiev — 2,590,000
Kharkiv — 1,494,000
Dnipropetrovs'k — 1,109,000
Donets'k — 1,050,000
Odesa — 1,002,000

United Kingdom
London — 7,652,000
Birmingham — 2,296,000
Manchester — 2,277,000
Leeds-Bradford — 1,446,000
Newcastle — 886,000
Glasgow — 867,000
Liverpool — 838,000
Sheffield — 633,000

International comparability of population data is limited by varying census methods. Where metropolitan population is unavailable, core city population is shown.

Population

Persons per sq. mile	Persons per sq. km	Major metropolitan areas
Over 520	Over 200	● Over 2 million
260 to 519	100 to 199	
130 to 259	50 to 99	● 1 million to 2 million
25 to 129	10 to 49	
1 to 24	1 to 9	· Under 1 million
0	0	

Estimated 2002 Population (in millions)

Russia 145
Germany 83
United Kingdom 60
France 60
Italy 58
Ukraine 48
Spain 40
Poland 39
Romania 22
All other countries 365

Source: U.S. Census Bureau

Gross Domestic Product

GDP per capita

- Over $20,000
- $10,000 to $20,000
- $5,000 to $9,999
- $2,500 to $4,999
- Under $2,500
- No data

Source: *World Factbook*, CIA, 2001

Gross Domestic Product is a measure of the total goods and services generated by a country. Generally, manufacturing, high-tech services, and specialized agricultural products add more value than raw materials and basic food stuffs.

Electricity Use

- Iceland 23,655
- Finland 15,768
- United States 12,407
- France 6,696
- Germany 5,964
- United Kingdom 5,583
- Moldova 1,304

KWh (kilowatt hours) per person per year

Source: *World Factbook*, CIA, 2001

Land Use and Resources

Predominant land use

- Commercial agriculture
- Dairying
- Livestock ranching
- Nomadic herding
- Subsistence agriculture
- Primarily forestland
- Limited agricultural activity

Major resources

- Coal
- Natural gas
- Oil
- Au Gold
- Fe Iron ore
- Ag Silver
- U Uranium
- Al Bauxite
- Other minerals
- Fishing
- Major manufacturing and trade centers

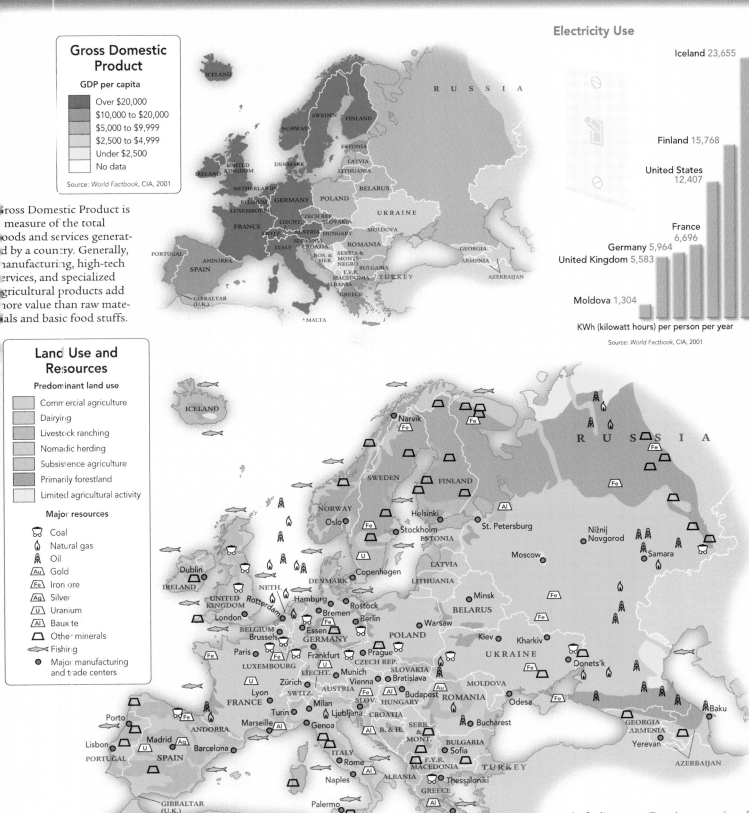

Europe, particularly Western Europe, is a consolidation of high-tech, market-driven, globally connected economies, where manufacturing and commercial agriculture predominate. Crucial to continental economic integration is the European Union, a partnership of 15 member nations whose combined economic clout rivals the U.S. Russia and former Soviet-satellite nations are, in large part, reaching harmony with the rest of Europe after an initial and unsettling period of adjustment. Despite centuries of exploration and exploitation, commercially-valuable mineral resources continue to be mined, notably in Russia, the Ukraine, and Scandinavia. The bountiful oil and gas fields of the North Sea are one of the most important and most recent discoveries.

Climate

- Semiarid
- Mediterranean
- Humid subtropical
- Marine
- Humid continental
- Subarctic
- Tundra
- Ice cap
- Highland

The far-reaching influence and effects of warm ocean currents cannot be overstated. The ceaseless torrent distributed by the Gulf Stream along the coasts of Western Europe, even to the shores of Iceland and Norway, produces much milder weather than would be expected at its latitudes and provides a ready source of moisture. Along the Mediterranean margin of Europe the typical weather—mild, wet winters and hot, dry summers—has been defined as a climate category that is now used worldwide.

See photographs taken in different kinds of climates on pages 24–25.

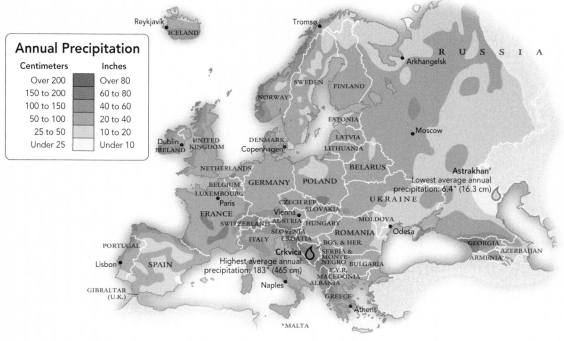

Annual Precipitation

Centimeters	Inches
Over 200	Over 80
150 to 200	60 to 80
100 to 150	40 to 60
50 to 100	20 to 40
25 to 50	10 to 20
Under 25	Under 10

Though regionally formidable mountains rise to extract snow and rain, no continental-scale alpine barrier exists—thereby permitting moisture-laden, westerly winds springing from warm oceanic waters to distribute precipitation uniformly across Europe. However, by the time these currents of air reach the landlocked heart of Eastern Europe, northeast of the Black Sea, much of the moisture has already been spent.

Climate Graphs

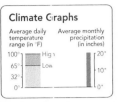

Average daily temperature range (in °F)
High
Low

Average monthly precipitation (in inches)

ARKHANGELSK, Russia

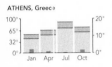
ATHENS, Greece

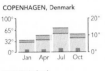
COPENHAGEN, Denmark

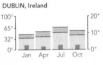
DUBLIN, Ireland

LISBON, Portugal

MOSCOW, Russia

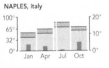
NAPLES, Italy

ODESA, Ukraine

PARIS, France

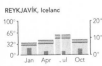
REYKJAVÍK, Iceland

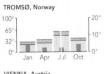
TROMSØ, Norway

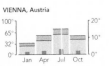
VIENNA, Austria

Vegetation

- Unclassified highlands or ice cap
- Tundra and alpine tundra
- Coniferous forest
- Midlatitude deciduous forest
- Mixed forest
- Midlatitude scrubland
- Midlatitude grassland

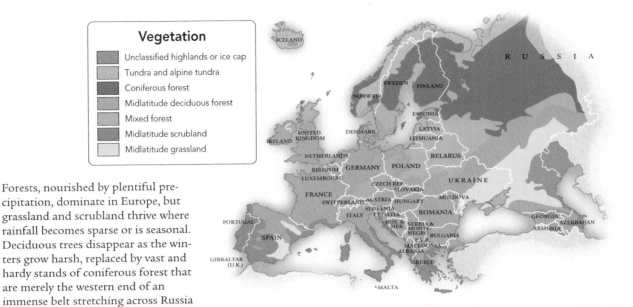

Forests, nourished by plentiful precipitation, dominate in Europe, but grassland and scrubland thrive where rainfall becomes sparse or is seasonal. Deciduous trees disappear as the winters grow harsh, replaced by vast and hardy stands of coniferous forest that are merely the western end of an immense belt stretching across Russia to the Pacific Ocean.

See photographs of the different kinds of vegetation on pages 26–27.

Environmental Issues

- Current forest
- Cleared forest
- Area at highest risk of desertification
- Areas most affected by acid rain
- Poor air quality*

*Cities exceeding at least one of the World Health Organization's (WHO) annual mean guidelines for air quality

Sources: *Global Distribution of Original and Remaining Forests*, UNEP-WCMC, 2002
World Soil Resources Map Index, USDA/NRCS, 2002
World Development Indicators, World Bank, 1999

Emissions from the many cars, trucks, and factories in Europe have led to problems with air pollution and acid rain over a large part of the continent. Land and water pollution (from fertilizers, pesticides, and industrial waste) is also widespread. Since the 1960's, the amount of forest area in Western and Central Europe has actually increased, but many forests (nearly 60%) are damaged due to acidification, pollution, drought, or fires. Overfishing—especially in the North Sea—is a serious problem for marine ecosystems.

Africa

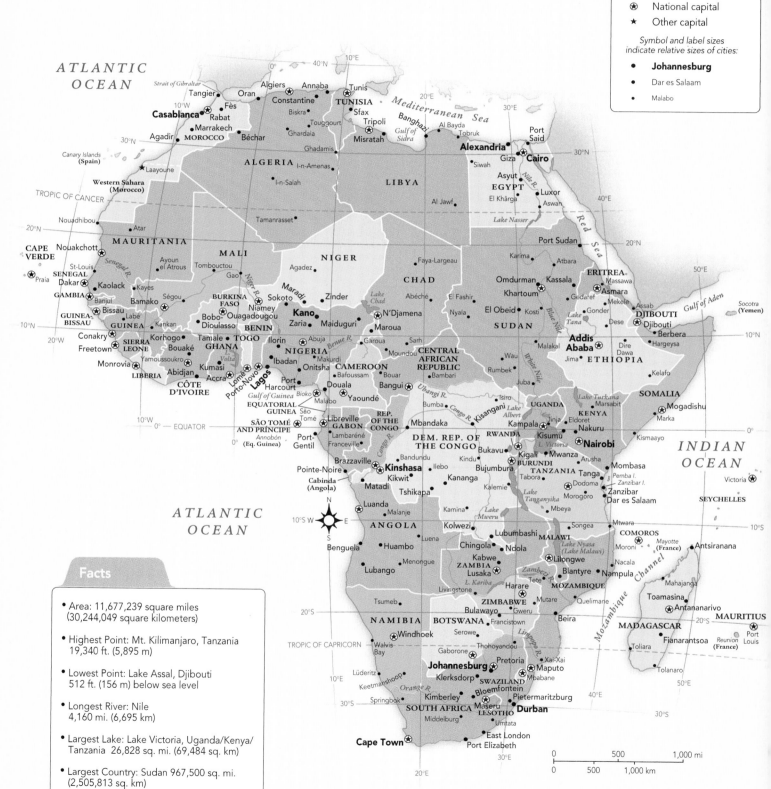

Legend:
- International boundary
- ⊛ National capital
- ★ Other capital

Symbol and label sizes indicate relative sizes of cities:
- ● **Johannesburg**
- ● Dar es Salaam
- ● Malabo

Facts

- Area: 11,677,239 square miles (30,244,049 square kilometers)
- Highest Point: Mt. Kilimanjaro, Tanzania 19,340 ft. (5,895 m)
- Lowest Point: Lake Assal, Djibouti 512 ft. (156 m) below sea level
- Longest River: Nile 4,160 mi. (6,695 km)
- Largest Lake: Lake Victoria, Uganda/Kenya/Tanzania 26,828 sq. mi. (69,484 sq. km)
- Largest Country: Sudan 967,500 sq. mi. (2,505,813 sq. km)
- Largest City: Cairo, Egypt 6,801,000

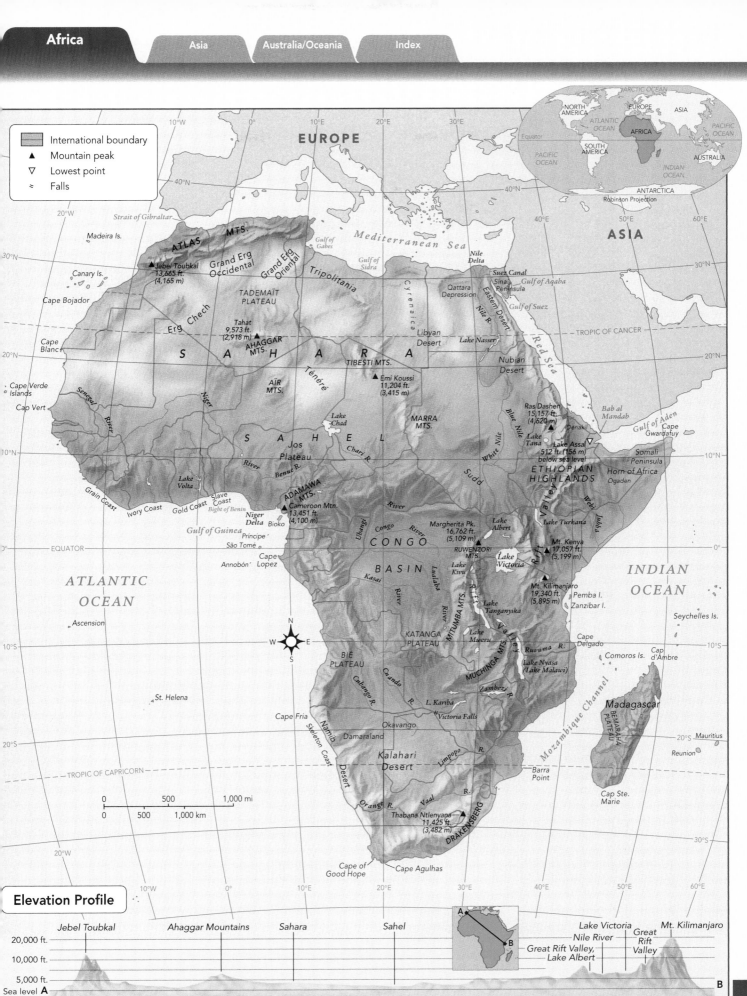

Legend

- International boundary
- ▲ Mountain peak
- ▽ Lowest point
- ≈ Falls

Elevation Profile

Jebel Toubkal	Ahaggar Mountains	Sahara	Sahel		Lake Victoria		Mt. Kilimanjaro

Nile River
Great Rift Valley
Great Rift Valley, Lake Albert

20,000 ft.
10,000 ft.
5,000 ft.
Sea level A   B

Major Metropolitan Areas

Algeria
Algiers 1,904,000 (metro)
Oran 745,000
Constantine 564,000

Angola
Luanda 1,822,000

Benin
Cotonou 537,000
Porto-Novo 179,000

Botswana
Gaborone 186,000

Burkina Faso
Ouagadougou 634,000

Burundi
Bujumbura 234,000

Cameroon
Douala 810,000
Yaoundé 649,000

Cape Verde
Praia 103,000

Central African Republic
Bangui 452,000

Chad
N'Djamena 547,000

Comoros
Moroni 30,000

Congo, Democratic Republic of the
Kinshasa 4,657,000
Lubumbashi 565,000

Congo, Republic of the
Brazzaville 596,000

Côte d'Ivoire
Abidjan 1,929,000
Yamoussoukro 107,000

Djibouti
Djibouti 62,000

Egypt
Cairo 6,801,000
Alexandria 3,339,000
Giza 2,222,000

Equatorial Guinea
Malabo 30,000

Eritrea
Asmara 358,000

Ethiopia
Addis Ababa 2,424,000

Gabon
Libreville 420,000

The Gambia
Banjul 271,000

Ghana
Accra 1,155,000

Guinea
Conakry 705,000

Guinea-Bissau
Bissau 109,000

Kenya
Nairobi 2,143,000
Mombasa 465,000

Lesotho
Maseru 138,000

Liberia
Monrovia 421,000

Libya
Tripoli 1,500,000

Madagascar
Antananarivo 1,103,000

Malawi
Blantyre 502,000
Lilongwe 440,000

Mali
Bamako 1,179,000

Mauritania
Nouakchott 612,000

Mauritius
Port Louis 128,000

Morocco
Casablanca 2,943,000
Rabat 1,220,000
Marrakesh 602,000

Mozambique
Maputo 989,000

Namibia
Windhoek 147,000

Niger
Niamey 397,000

Nigeria
Lagos 5,195,000
Kano 2,167,000
Ibadan 1,835,000

Rwanda
Kigali 234,000

São Tomé & Príncipe
São Tomé 6,000

Senegal
Dakar 1,977,000

Seychelles
Victoria 25,000

Sierra Leone
Freetown 470,000

Somalia
Mogadishu 230,000

South Africa
Durban 2,992,000
Cape Town 2,898,000
Johannesburg 2,885,000
Pretoria 2,086,000
Port Elizabeth 1,312,000

Sudan
Omdurman 1,271,000
Khartoum 947,000

Swaziland
Mbabane 38,000

Tanzania
Dar es Salaam 1,361,000

Togo
Lomé 450,000

Tunisia
Tunis 674,000

Uganda
Kampala 1,209,000

Western Sahara
el-Aaiún 90,000

Zambia
Lusaka 1,270,000

Zimbabwe
Harare 1,189,000

International comparability of population data is limited by varying census methods. Where metropolitan population is unavailable, core city population is shown.

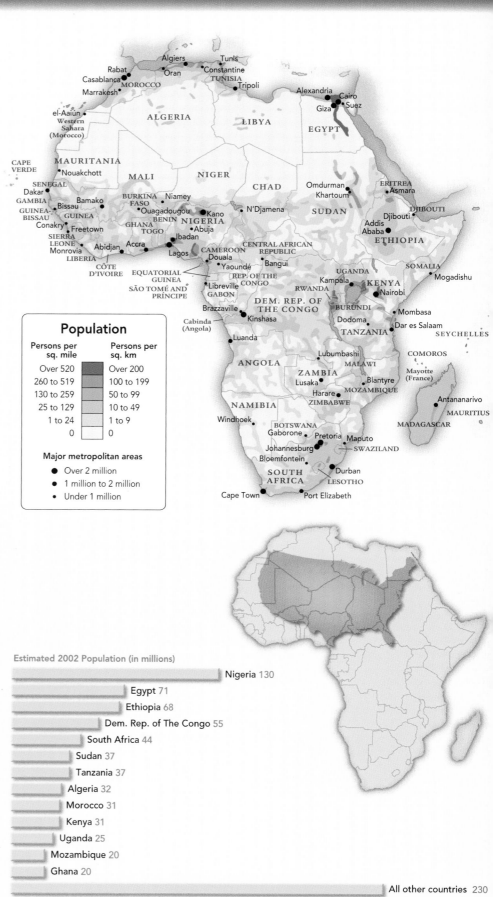

Population

Persons per sq. mile / **Persons per sq. km**

Persons per sq. mile	Persons per sq. km
Over 520	Over 200
260 to 519	100 to 199
130 to 259	50 to 99
25 to 129	10 to 49
1 to 24	1 to 9
0	0

Major metropolitan areas
● Over 2 million
• 1 million to 2 million
· Under 1 million

Estimated 2002 Population (in millions)

Nigeria 130
Egypt 71
Ethiopia 68
Dem. Rep. of The Congo 55
South Africa 44
Sudan 37
Tanzania 37
Algeria 32
Morocco 31
Kenya 31
Uganda 25
Mozambique 20
Ghana 20
All other countries 230

Source: U.S. Census Bureau

Gross Domestic Product is a measure of the total goods and services generated by a country. Generally, manufacturing, high-tech services, and specialized agricultural products add more value than raw materials and basic food stuffs.

South Africa is the only African nation considered to have a developed economy, even though their GDP is less then half that of the United States.

Gross Domestic Product

GDP per capita

- Over $20,000
- $10,000 to $20,000
- $5,000 to $9,999
- $2,500 to $4,999
- Under $2,500
- No data

Source: *World Factbook*, CIA, 2001

Electricity Use

United States 12,407

South Africa 3,955

Seychelles 1,867

Namibia 1,084
Zimbabwe 611
Cameroon 204

KWh (kilowatt hours) per person per year

Source: *World Factbook*, CIA, 2001

Agriculture supplies the livelihood for the vast majority of Africans. Agricultural exports include coffee, cocoa beans, peanuts, palm oil, and spices. These important export crops are mainly cultivated on plantations and large farms. Areas of subsistence farming supply the needs of local communities.

Unfortunately, poor soils and unfavorable climate conditions, as well as political unrest and unstable economies, all have an adverse impact on agricultural activity and therefore the standard of living.

Minerals account for more then one half of Africa's exports. Oil, diamonds, gold, cobalt, and several other minerals are leading exports. However, important mineral deposits are limited to a handful of countries.

Manufacturing has been slow to develop on the continent. Lack of money and skilled labor are the main deterrents.

Land Use and Resources

Predominant land use

- Commercial agriculture
- Livestock ranching
- Subsistence agriculture
- Nomadic herding
- Primarily forestland
- Limited agricultural activity

Major resources

- Coal
- Natural gas
- Oil
- Au Gold
- Fe Iron ore
- Pt Platinum
- U Uranium
- Al Bauxite
- Diamonds
- Other minerals
- Fishing
- Major manufacturing and trade centers

The climate of Africa is clearly a study in geographic contrasts. Perpetually wet and tropical areas surrounding the Equator quickly acquire seasonal variety as you move north and south. Roaming even farther leads to the vast, hot and arid zones of northern and southern Africa. The influence of neighboring water bodies is limited to small regions of northern Africa, namely Morocco, Algeria, and Libya, where the mild currents of the Mediterranean Sea temper the climate, and eastern South Africa, where the mixture of warm currents flowing close to shore and the seasonal onshore winds striking the Drakensberg uplands provide for a moist and temperate marine coast climate.

See photographs taken in different kinds of climates on pages 24–25.

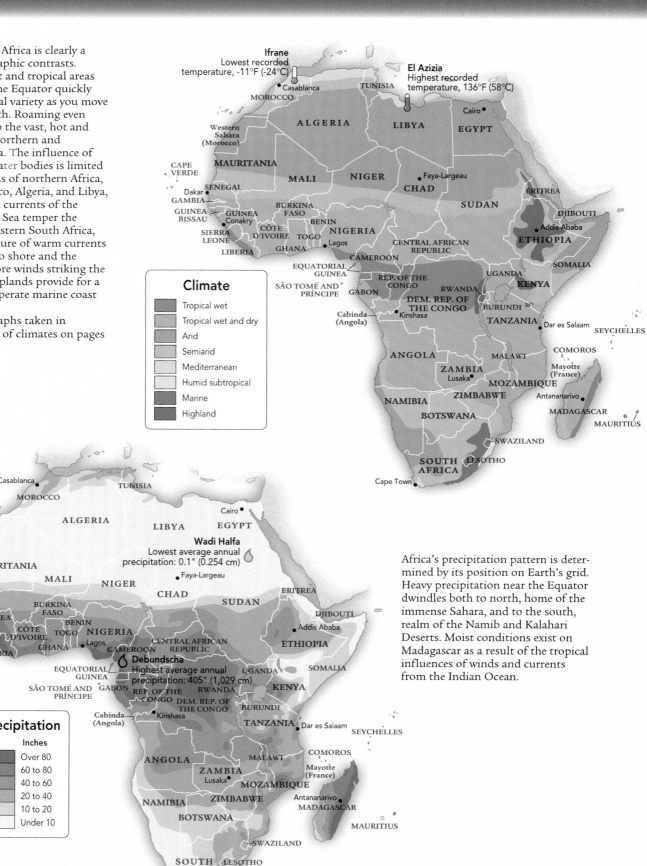

Climate

- Tropical wet
- Tropical wet and dry
- Arid
- Semiarid
- Mediterranean
- Humid subtropical
- Marine
- Highland

Ifrane
Lowest recorded temperature, -11°F (-24°C)

El Azizia
Highest recorded temperature, 136°F (58°C)

Wadi Halfa
Lowest average annual precipitation: 0.1" (0.254 cm)

Debundscha
Highest average annual precipitation: 405" (1,029 cm)

Annual Precipitation

Centimeters	Inches
Over 203	Over 80
152 to 203	60 to 80
102 to 152	40 to 60
51 to 102	20 to 40
25 to 51	10 to 20
Under 25	Under 10

Africa's precipitation pattern is determined by its position on Earth's grid. Heavy precipitation near the Equator dwindles both to north, home of the immense Sahara, and to the south, realm of the Namib and Kalahari Deserts. Moist conditions exist on Madagascar as a result of the tropical influences of winds and currents from the Indian Ocean.

Climate Graphs

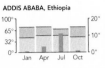

Average daily temperature range (in °F) | Average monthly precipitation (in inches)

High
Low

ADDIS ABABA, Ethiopia

ANTANANARIVO, Madagascar

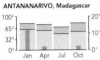

CAIRO, Egypt

CAPE TOWN, South Africa

CASABLANCA, Morocco

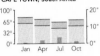

CONAKRY, Guinea
51.1

DAKAR, Senegal

DAR ES SALAAM, Tanzania

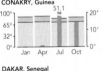

FAYA-LARGEAU, Chad

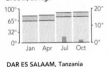

KINSHASA, Dem. Rep. of the Congo

LAGOS, Nigeria

LUSAKA, Zambia

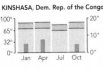

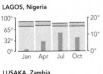

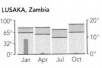

The dense, tropical rain forest surrounding the Equator is offset by the contrastingly sparse vegetation on the rest of the continent. Vast areas consist of grassland and scrub vegetation with trees only occasionally dotting the landscape. Evergreen and mixed forests of more temperate climates are limited to the Mediterranean areas of Morocco and Algeria, the Ethiopian Highlands, and Kenya.

See photographs of the different kinds of vegetation on pages 26–27.

Vegetation

- Coniferous forest
- Mixed forest
- Midlatitude scrubland
- Midlatitude grassland
- Desert
- Tropical seasonal and scrub
- Tropical rain forest
- Tropical savanna

Environmental Issues

- Current forest
- Cleared forest
- Area at highest risk of desertification
- Poor air quality*

*Cities exceeding at least one of the World Health Organization's (WHO) annual mean guidelines for air quality

Sources: *Global Distribution of Original and Remaining Forests*, UNEP-WCMC, 2002
World Soil Resources Map Index, USDA/NRCS, 2002
World Development Indicators, World Bank, 1999

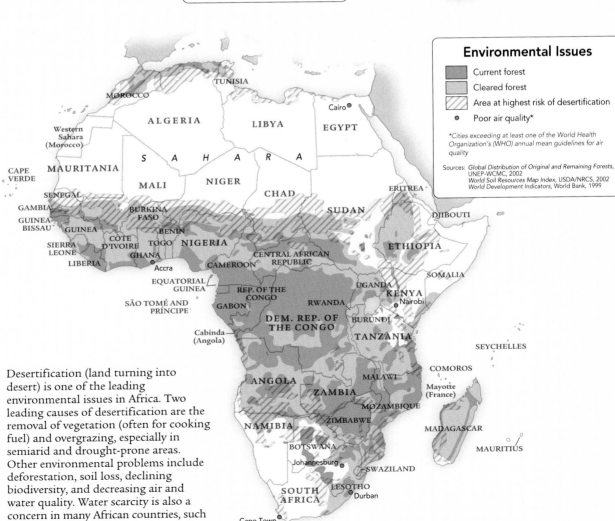

Desertification (land turning into desert) is one of the leading environmental issues in Africa. Two leading causes of desertification are the removal of vegetation (often for cooking fuel) and overgrazing, especially in semiarid and drought-prone areas. Other environmental problems include deforestation, soil loss, declining biodiversity, and decreasing air and water quality. Water scarcity is also a concern in many African countries, such as Egypt, Libya, Algeria, Tunisia, and Morocco.

Asia

Facts

- Area: 17,139,000 square miles (44,390,000 square kilometers)
- Highest Point: Mt. Everest, China/Nepal 29,035 ft. (8,850 m)
- Lowest Point: Dead Sea, Israel/Jordan 1,310 ft. (399 m) below sea level
- Longest River: Chang (Yangtze), China 3,964 mi. (6,379 km)
- Largest Lake: Caspian Sea 143,244 sq. mi. (371,000 sq. km)
- Largest Country: Russia (Asian) 4,928,980 sq. mi. (12,766,000 sq. km)
- Largest City: Mumbai, India 16,368,000

Legend

- International boundary
- ⊛ National capital
- ★ Other capital

Symbol and label sizes indicate relative sizes of cities:

- **Bangalore**
- Chengdu
- Magadan

Oceans and Seas

ARCTIC OCEAN
PACIFIC OCEAN
INDIAN OCEAN

Chukchi Sea
East Siberian Sea
Laptev Sea
Kara Sea
Barents Sea
Bering Sea
Sea of Okhotsk
Sea of Japan
Yellow Sea
East China Sea
South China Sea
Philippine Sea
Celebes Sea
Java Sea
Arafura Sea
Andaman Sea
Bay of Bengal
Arabian Sea
Laccadive
Gulf of Thailand
Luzon Strait
Black Sea
Caspian Sea
Mediterranean Sea
Red Sea
Persian Gulf
Gulf of Aden
Gulf of Oman
Aral Sea

Countries and Places

RUSSIA
CHINA
MONGOLIA
KAZAKHSTAN
INDIA
IRAN
SAUDI ARABIA
TURKEY
SYRIA
IRAQ
JORDAN
LEBANON
ISRAEL
CYPRUS
KUWAIT
QATAR
BAHRAIN
UNITED ARAB EMIRATES
OMAN
YEMEN
AFGHANISTAN
PAKISTAN
UZBEKISTAN
TURKMENISTAN
TAJIKISTAN
KYRGYZSTAN
NEPAL
BHUTAN
BANGLADESH
MYANMAR (BURMA)
THAILAND
LAOS
VIETNAM
CAMBODIA
MALAYSIA
INDONESIA
SINGAPORE
BRUNEI
PHILIPPINES
SRI LANKA
MALDIVES
TAIWAN
N. KOREA
S. KOREA
JAPAN
EAST TIMOR
IRIAN JAYA (WEST PAPUA)

Cities

Anadyr'
Petropavlovsk-Kamchatskiy
Magadan
Komsomol'sk-na-Amure
Khabarovsk
Vladivostok
Yakutsk
Sapporo
Sendai
Tokyo
Yokohama
Kyoto
Osaka
Kitakyushu
Busan
Seoul
Pyongyang
N. KOREA
Shenyang
Changchun
Harbin
Chita
Ulan-Ude
Irkutsk
Bratsk
Krasnoyarsk
Kemerovo
Novokuznetsk
Tomsk
Novosibirsk
Omsk
Surgut
Yekaterinburg
Chelyabinsk
Noril'sk
Ulaanbaatar
Baotou
Beijing
Tianjin
Taiyuan
Jinan
Qingdao
Zhengzhou
Nanjing
Shanghai
Wuhan
Nanchang
Changsha
Fuzhou
Taipei
Hong Kong
Guangzhou
Macao
Hainan
Nanning
Kunming
Chongqing
Chengdu
Lanzhou
Xi'an
Yumen
Urumqi
Hotan
Kashi
Lhasa
Thimphu
Kathmandu
Dhaka
Kolkata (Calcutta)
Lucknow
Kanpur
Jaipur
New Delhi
Delhi
Faisalabad
Lahore
Islamabad
Srinagar
Almaty
Bishkek
Tashkent
Samarqand
Dushanbe
Kabul
Karachi
Ahmadabad
Mumbai (Bombay)
Nagpur
Hyderabad
Bangalore
Chennai (Madras)
Madurai
Colombo
Male
Astana
Qaraghandy
Qostanay
Pavlodar
Semey
Mangghystau
Ashgabat
Mashhad
Tehran
Esfahan
Shiraz
Tabriz
Baghdad
Basra
Kuwait
Riyadh
Manamah
Doha
Abu Dhabi
Muscat
Jeddah
Mecca
Sanaa
Aden
Ankara
Bursa
Izmir
Nicosia
Beirut
Damascus
Amman
Jerusalem
Da Nang
Hanoi
Vientiane
Mandalay
Yangon (Rangoon)
Bangkok
Phnom Penh
Ho Chi Minh City
Kuala Lumpur
Medan
Padang
Palembang
Jakarta
Bandung
Surabaya
Banjarmasin
Makassar
Manado
Pontianak
Bandar Seri Begawan
Kuching
Kota Kinabalu
Singapore
Manila
Quezon City
Cebu
Davao
Dili
Jayapura

Physical Features

North Pole
ARCTIC CIRCLE
TROPIC OF CANCER
EQUATOR
Lena River
Ob' R.
Irtysh River
Yenisey River
Angara River
Lake Baikal
Amur River
Huang (Yellow) R.
Chang (Yangtze) R.
Mekong River
Ganges R.
Brahmaputra R.
Indus R.
Tigris R.
Euphrates R.
Ural River
Lake Balkhash
Socotra (Yemen)
Aleutian Islands (U.S.)
Kuril Islands (Russia)
Sakhalin
Hainan
Andaman Islands (India)
Nicobar Islands (India)
Lakshadweep (India)

Scale

1,000 mi
1,000 km
500
0

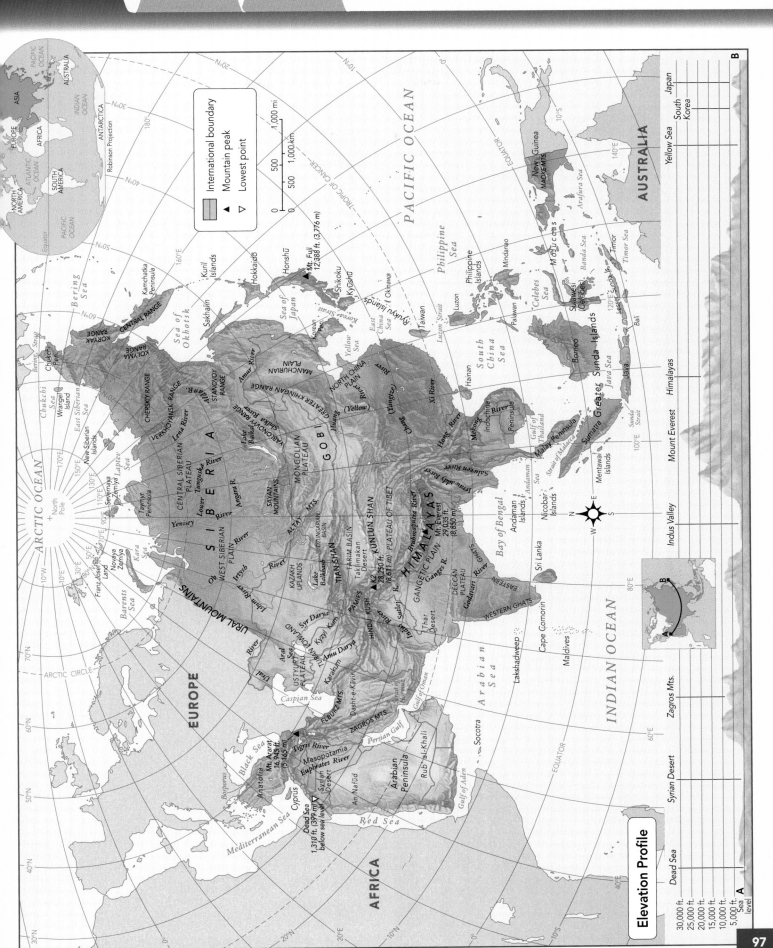

ARCTIC OCEAN

North Pole

PACIFIC OCEAN

INDIAN OCEAN

EUROPE

AFRICA

AUSTRALIA

S I B E R I A

URAL MOUNTAINS

CENTRAL RANGE
KORYAK RANGE
KOLYMA RANGE
CHERSKIY RANGE
VERKHOYANSK RANGE
STANOVOY RANGE
YABLONOVYY RANGE
SAYAN MOUNTAINS
MONGOLIAN PLATEAU
GOBI
ALTAI MTS.
TIAN SHAN
KUNLUN SHAN
PLATEAU OF TIBET
HINDU KUSH
PAMIRS
H I M A L A Y A S
ZAGROS MTS.
ELBURZ MTS.

CENTRAL SIBERIAN PLATEAU
WEST SIBERIAN PLAIN
KAZAKH UPLANDS
TURAN LOWLAND
DZUNGARIAN BASIN
TARIM BASIN
Taklimakan Desert
GANGETIC PLAIN
DECCAN PLATEAU
EASTERN GHATS
WESTERN GHATS
NORTH CHINA PLAIN
MANCHURIAN PLAIN
Thar Desert
USTYURT PLATEAU
Dasht-e-Kavir
Syrian Desert
An Nafud
Rub' al-Khali
Arabian Peninsula
Anatolia
Mesopotamia

Bering Strait
Chukchi Sea
Chukchi Pen.
Wrangel Island
East Siberian Sea
New Siberian Islands
Laptev Sea
Severnaya Zemlya
Taymyr Peninsula
Kara Sea
Novaya Zemlya
Franz Josef Land
Barents Sea
Yenisey
Ob River
Irtysh River
Ishim River
Tobol River
Lower Tunguska River
Angara R.
Lena River
Lake Baikal
Vilyuy
Aldan
Amur River
Shilka River
Argun River
Sakhalin
Kamchatka Peninsula
Sea of Okhotsk
Kuril Islands
Hokkaidō
Honshū
Mt. Fuji 12,388 ft. (3,776 m)
Sea of Japan
Korean Pen.
Korea Strait
Shikoku
Kyūshū
Ryukyu Islands
Okinawa
East China Sea
Yellow Sea
Huang (Yellow)
Chang (Yangtze)
Xi River
Hainan
South China Sea
Taiwan
Luzon Strait
Philippine Islands
Luzon
Mindanao
Palawan
Philippine Sea
Celebes Sea
Sulawesi (Celebes)
Borneo
Moluccas
New Guinea
MACKE MTS.
Arafura Sea
Timor Sea
Banda Sea
Timor
Bali
Java
Java Sea
Sumatra
Greater Sunda Islands
Lesser Sunda Is.
Sunda Strait
Mentawai Islands
Malay Peninsula
Strait of Malacca
Gulf of Thailand
Indochina Peninsula
Mekong River
Hong River
Salween River
Irrawaddy River
Brahmaputra River
Ganges R.
Sutlej R.
Indus River
Godavari River
Bay of Bengal
Andaman Islands
Andaman Sea
Nicobar Islands
Sri Lanka
Cape Comorin
Lakshadweep
Maldives
Socotra
Gulf of Aden
Red Sea
Gulf of Oman
Strait of Hormuz
Persian Gulf
Tigris River
Euphrates River
Mt. Ararat 16,945 ft. (5,165 m)
Black Sea
Bosporus
Cyprus
Dead Sea 1,310 ft. (399 m) below sea level
Mediterranean Sea
Caspian Sea
Aral Sea
Ural River
Amu Darya
Syr Darya
Kyzyl Kum
Karakum
K2
28,250 ft. (8,611 m)
Mt. Everest 29,035 ft. (8,850 m)
TROPIC OF CANCER
EQUATOR
ARCTIC CIRCLE
Arabian Sea

Legend

- International boundary
- ▲ Mountain peak
- ▽ Lowest point

0   500   1,000 km
0   500   1,000 mi

Robinson Projection

Elevation Profile

30,000 ft.	
25,000 ft.	
20,000 ft.	
15,000 ft.	
10,000 ft.	
5,000 ft.	
Sea level	

A — Syrian Desert — Dead Sea — Zagros Mts. — Indus Valley — Mount Everest — Himalayas — South Korea — Japan — B

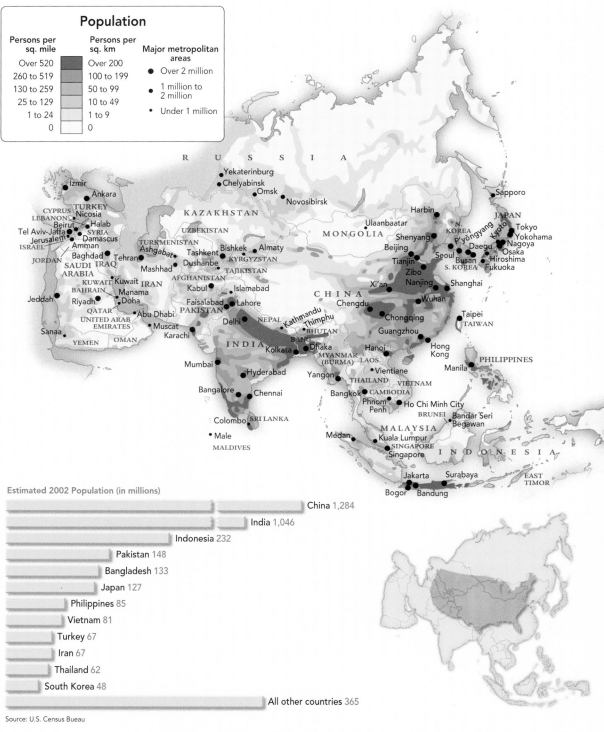

Population

Persons per sq. mile	Persons per sq. km
Over 520	Over 200
260 to 519	100 to 199
130 to 259	50 to 99
25 to 129	10 to 49
1 to 24	1 to 9
0	0

Major metropolitan areas
● Over 2 million
● 1 million to 2 million
• Under 1 million

Estimated 2002 Population (in millions)

China 1,284
India 1,046
Indonesia 232
Pakistan 148
Bangladesh 133
Japan 127
Philippines 85
Vietnam 81
Turkey 67
Iran 67
Thailand 62
South Korea 48
All other countries 365

Source: U.S. Census Bueau

Major Metropolitan Areas

Afghanistan
Kabul 2,029,000

Bahrain
Manama 151,000

Bangladesh
Dhaka 6,487,000

Bhutan
Thimphu 8,900

Brunei
Bandar Seri Begawan 50,000

Cambodia
Phnom Penh 1,000,000

China
Shanghai 12,910,000
Beijing 10,820,000
Tianjin 8,970,000
Hong Kong 6,708,000
Shenyang 4,740,000
Wuhan 4,450,000
Chongqing 4,070,000
Guangzhou 3,910,000
Chengdu 3,120,000
Xi'an 2,990,000
Harbin 2,960,000
Nanjing 2,670,000

Cyprus
Nicosia 273,000

East Timor
Dili 140,000

India
Mumbai (Bombay) 16,368,000
Kolkata (Calcutta) 13,217,000
Delhi 12,791,000
Chennai (Madras) 6,425,000
Bangalore 5,687,000
Hyderabad 5,534,000

Indonesia
Jakarta 9,374,000
Bandung 5,919,000
Bogor 5,000,000
Malang 3,174,000

Iran
Tehran 6,759,000
Mashhad 1,887,000

Iraq
Baghdad 4,336,000

Israel
Tel Aviv-Jaffa 2,595,000
Jerusalem 628,000

Japan
Tokyo 12,059,000
Yokohama 3,427,000
Osaka 2,599,000
Nagoya 2,171,000
Sapporo 1,822,000
Kobe 1,494,000
Kyoto 1,468,000
Fukuoka 1,341,000
Kawasaki 1,250,000
Hiroshima 1,126,000

Jordan
Amman 1,147,000

Kazakhstan
Almaty 1,129,000

North Korea
P'yŏngyang 2,741,000

South Korea (core city only)
Seoul 9,854,000
Busan 3,655,000
Daegu 2,474,000

Kuwait
Kuwait 193,000

Kyrgyzstan
Bishkek 753,000

Laos
Vientiane 331,000

Lebanon
Beirut 1,500,000

Malaysia
Kuala Lumpur 1,379,000

Maldives
Male 74,000

Mongolia
Ulaanbaatar 760,000

Myanmar (Burma)
Yangon (Rangoon) 4,101,000

Nepal
Kathmandu 421,000

Oman
Muscat 477,000

Pakistan
Karachi 9,339,000
Lahore 5,143,000
Faisalabad 2,009,000
Islamabad 529,000

Philippines
Manila 9,933,000

Qatar
Doha 264,000

Russia (Asian)
Novosibirsk 1,400,000
Yekaterinburg 1,314,000
Omsk 1,177,000
Chelyabinsk 1,111,000

Saudi Arabia
Riyadh 2,776,000
Jeddah 2,046,000

Singapore
Singapore 4,131,000

Sri Lanka
Colombo 642,000

Syria
Halab (Aleppo) 1,813,000
Damascus 1,394,000

Taiwan
Taipei 2,720,000

Tajikistan
Dushanbe 529,000

Thailand
Bangkok 6,320,000

Turkey (Asian)
Ankara 3,203,000
Izmir 2,232,000

Turkmenistan
Ashgabat 407,000

United Arab Emirates
Abu Dhabi 904,000

Uzbekistan
Tashkent 2,142,000

Vietnam
Ho Chi Minh City 4,990,000
Hanoi 2,464,000

Yemen
Sanaa 927,000

International comparability of population data is limited by varying census methods. Where metropolitan population is unavailable, core city population is shown.

ross Domestic Product is a measure of the total goods
d services generated by a country. Generally, manu-
cturing, high-tech services, and specialized agricul-
ral products add more value than raw materi-
s and basic food stuffs. The high-tech and
producing countries on the fringes of
ia are the exceptions in this gener-
y poor continent.

Gross Domestic Product

GDP per capita

Over $20,000
$10,000 to $20,000
$5,000 to $9,999
$2,500 to $4,999
Less than $2,500
No data

Source: *World Factbook*, CIA, 2001

Electricity Use

Kuwait 14,377
United Arab Emirates 14,177
United States 12,407
Japan 7,470
Israel 5,372
China 851
India 442
Laos 31

KWh (kilowatt hours) per person per year

Source: *World Factbook*, CIA, 2001

griculture is the predominant land use in Asia, though only one-sixth of the land is
able. Wet grains, such as rice, are the principal crops of China and Southeast Asian
untries. Dry grains, such as wheat, are grown in limited areas of Russia and
hina. A lack of modern farming methods, except in Japan, Russia, and Israel,
s historically limited food production. However, pro-
ction is increasing in some countries as govern-
ents supply the needed technology. The rugged
nd and climate in Northern, Central and
uthwest Asia limits land use to nomadic
rding. Here, animals supply food, shel-
, clothing, and transportation.

Land Use and Resources

Predominant land use

Commercial agriculture
Nomadic herding
Subsistence agriculture
Primarily forestland
Limited agricultural activity

Major resources

Coal
Natural gas
Oil
Forest products
Au Gold
Ag Silver
Fe Iron ore
U   Uranium
Al Bauxite
Diamonds
Other minerals
Fishing
Major manufacturing and trade centers

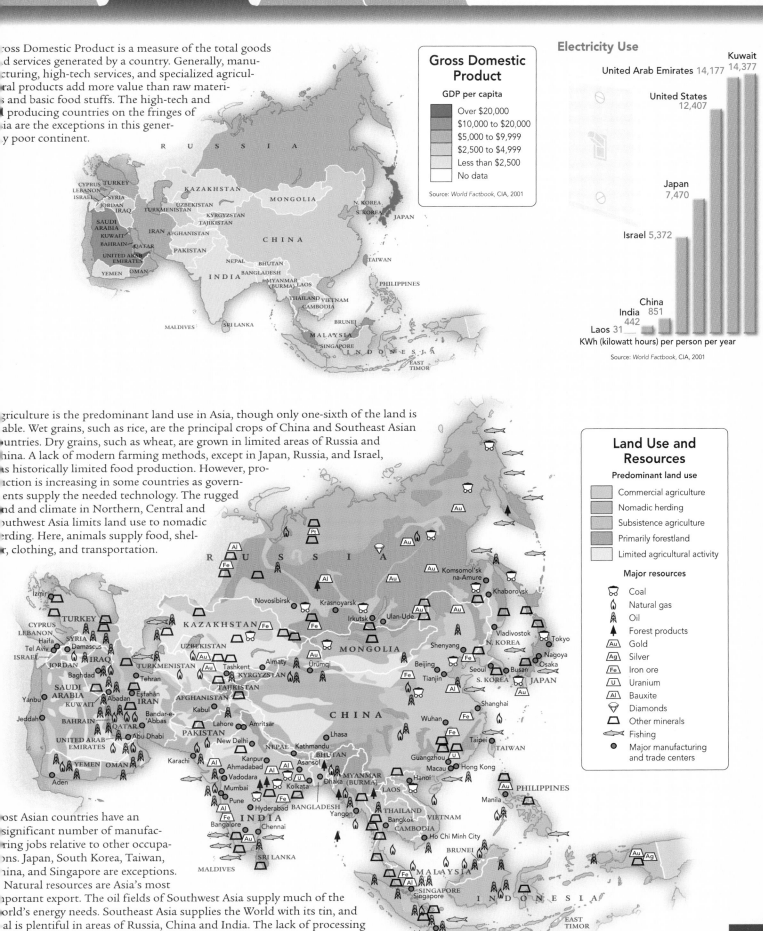

ost Asian countries have an
significant number of manufac-
ring jobs relative to other occupa-
ns. Japan, South Korea, Taiwan,
ina, and Singapore are exceptions.
Natural resources are Asia's most
portant export. The oil fields of Southwest Asia supply much of the
rld's energy needs. Southeast Asia supplies the World with its tin, and
al is plentiful in areas of Russia, China and India. The lack of processing
cilities limits many Asian countries in the use of their resources

Asia has many climates. This can be expected on a landmass that covers an area from below the Equator to the Arctic Ocean and from the Mediterranean Sea to the Pacific Ocean. Weather conditions fluctuate from the sub-freezing temperatures and snow of the tundra climate in Northern Russia, through the more temperate humid continental climate, past the arid conditions of Southwest and Central Asia, and finally to the warm and wet zones of South and Southeast Asia.

See photographs taken in different kinds of climates on pages 24–25.

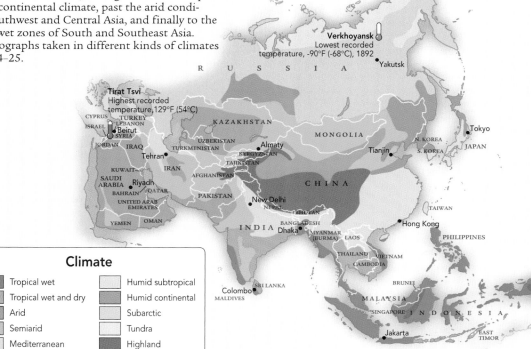

Verkhoyansk
Lowest recorded temperature, -90°F (-68°C), 1892

Tirat Tsvi
Highest recorded temperature,129°F (54°C)

Climate

- Tropical wet
- Tropical wet and dry
- Arid
- Semiarid
- Mediterranean
- Humid subtropical
- Humid continental
- Subarctic
- Tundra
- Highland

Annual Precipitation

Centimeters	Inches
Over 203	Over 80
152 to 203	60 to 80
102 to 152	40 to 60
51 to 102	20 to 40
25 to 51	10 to 20
Under 25	Under 10

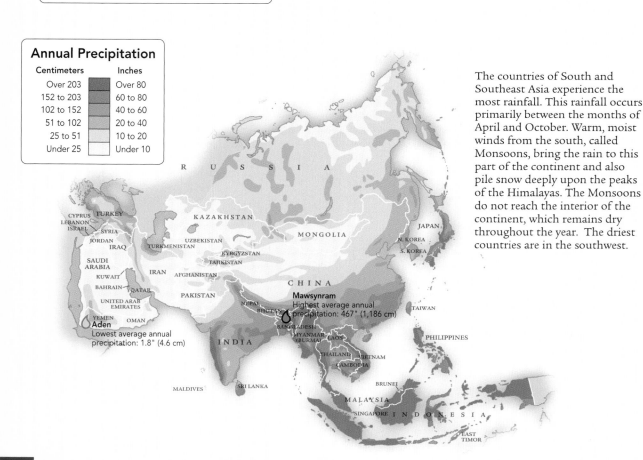

Mawsynram
Highest average annual precipitation: 467" (1,186 cm)

Aden
Lowest average annual precipitation: 1.8" (4.6 cm)

The countries of South and Southeast Asia experience the most rainfall. This rainfall occurs primarily between the months of April and October. Warm, moist winds from the south, called Monsoons, bring the rain to this part of the continent and also pile snow deeply upon the peaks of the Himalayas. The Monsoons do not reach the interior of the continent, which remains dry throughout the year. The driest countries are in the southwest.

Climate Graphs

Average daily temperature range (in °F)
Average monthly precipitation (in inches)
High
Low

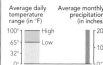

ALMATY, Kazakhstan

BEIRUT, Lebanon
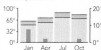

COLOMBO, Sri Lanka
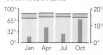

DHAKA, Bangladesh
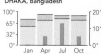

HONG KONG, China
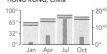

JAKARTA, Indonesia
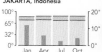

NEW DELHI, India
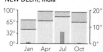

RIYADH, Saudi Arabia
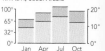

TEHRAN, Iran
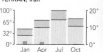

TIANJIN, China
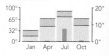

TOKYO, Japan
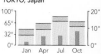

YAKUTSK, Russia
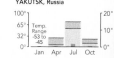

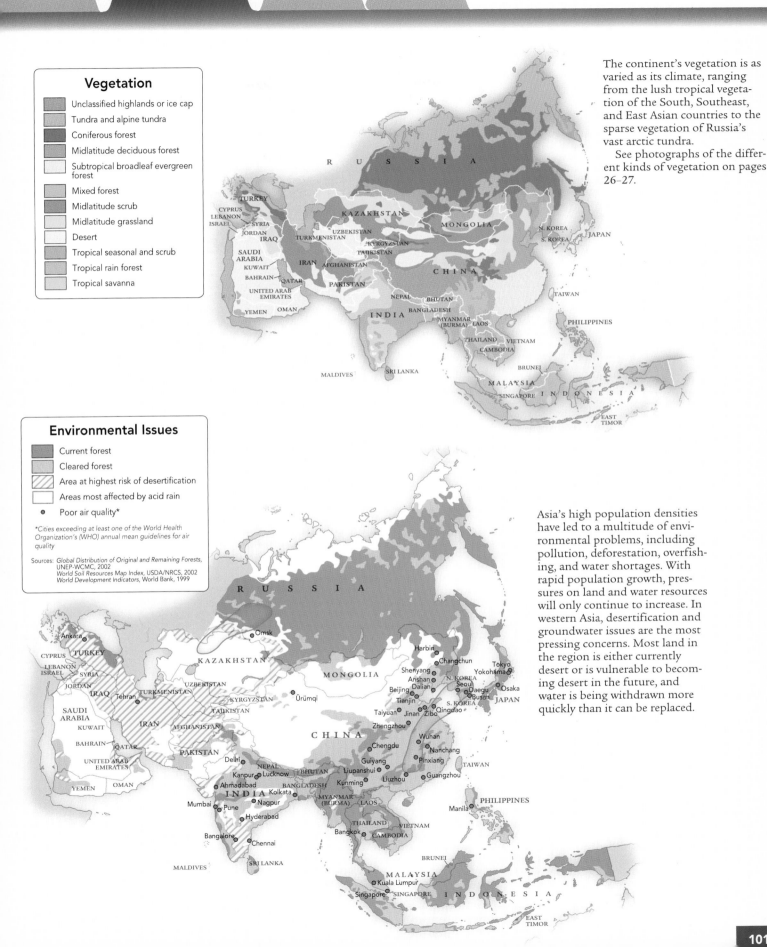

Vegetation

- Unclassified highlands or ice cap
- Tundra and alpine tundra
- Coniferous forest
- Midlatitude deciduous forest
- Subtropical broadleaf evergreen forest
- Mixed forest
- Midlatitude scrub
- Midlatitude grassland
- Desert
- Tropical seasonal and scrub
- Tropical rain forest
- Tropical savanna

The continent's vegetation is as varied as its climate, ranging from the lush tropical vegetation of the South, Southeast, and East Asian countries to the sparse vegetation of Russia's vast arctic tundra.

See photographs of the different kinds of vegetation on pages 26–27.

Environmental Issues

- Current forest
- Cleared forest
- Area at highest risk of desertification
- Areas most affected by acid rain
- • Poor air quality*

*Cities exceeding at least one of the World Health Organization's (WHO) annual mean guidelines for air quality

Sources: *Global Distribution of Original and Remaining Forests*, UNEP-WCMC, 2002
World Soil Resources Map Index, USDA/NRCS, 2002
World Development Indicators, World Bank, 1999

Asia's high population densities have led to a multitude of environmental problems, including pollution, deforestation, overfishing, and water shortages. With rapid population growth, pressures on land and water resources will only continue to increase. In western Asia, desertification and groundwater issues are the most pressing concerns. Most land in the region is either currently desert or is vulnerable to becoming desert in the future, and water is being withdrawn more quickly than it can be replaced.

Australia/ Oceania

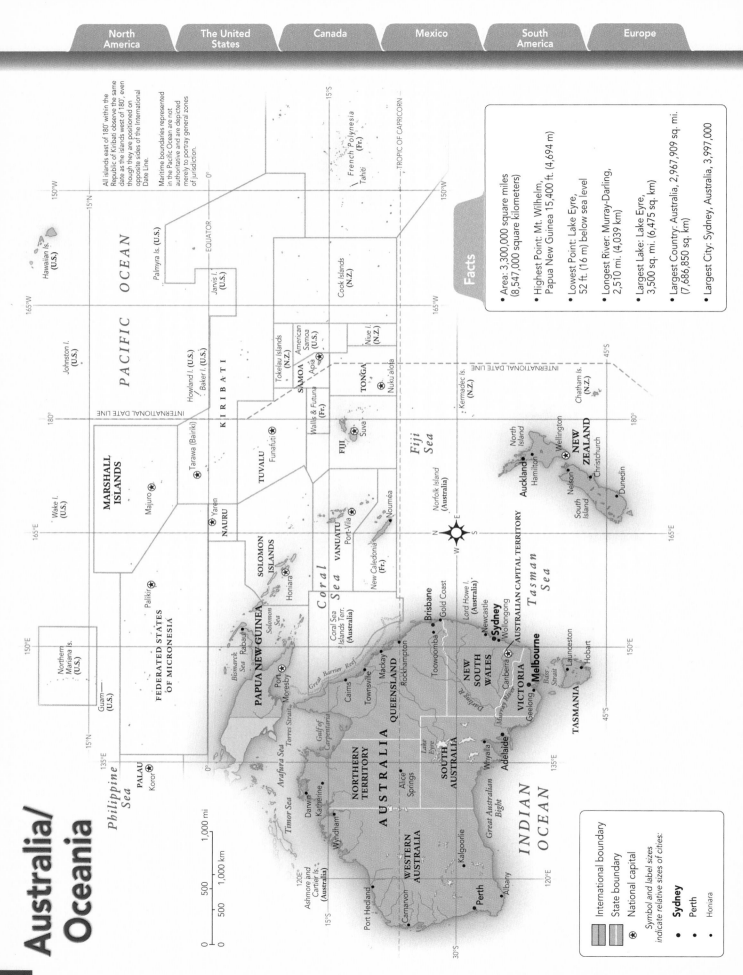

Facts

- Area: 3,300,000 square miles (8,547,000 square kilometers)
- Highest Point: Mt. Wilhelm, Papua New Guinea 15,400 ft. (4,694 m)
- Lowest Point: Lake Eyre, 52 ft. (16 m) below sea level
- Longest River: Murray-Darling, 2,510 mi. (4,039 km)
- Largest Lake: Lake Eyre, 3,500 sq. mi. (6,475 sq. km)
- Largest Country: Australia, 2,967,909 sq. mi. (7,686,850 sq. km)
- Largest City: Sydney, Australia, 3,997,000

All islands east of 180° within the Republic of Kiribati observe the same date as the islands west of 180°, even though they are positioned on opposite sides of the International Date Line.

Maritime boundaries represented in the Pacific Ocean are not authoritative and are depicted merely to portray general zones of jurisdiction.

International boundary
State boundary
National capital

Symbol and label sizes indicate relative sizes of cities:

- **Sydney**
- Perth
- Honiara

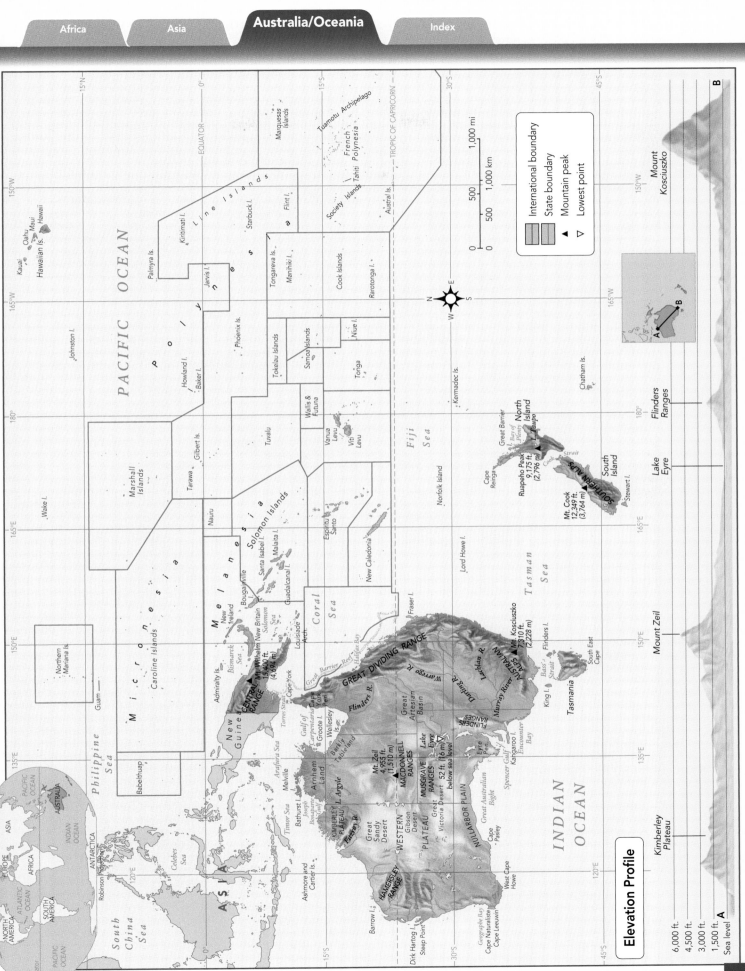

PACIFIC OCEAN

Hawaiian Is.
Kauai
Oahu
Maui
Hawaii

Johnston I.

Line Islands
Kiritimati I.
Starbuck I.
Flint I.
Marquesas Islands
Tuamotu Archipelago
French Polynesia
Society Islands
Tahiti
Austral Is.

TROPIC OF CAPRICORN
EQUATOR

Palmyra Is.
Jarvis I.
Howland I.
Baker I.
Phoenix Is.
Tongareva Is.
Manihiki I.
Cook Islands
Rarotonga I.

Tokelau Islands
Samoa Islands
Niue I.
Tonga

Wallis & Futuna
Vanua Levu
Viti Levu
Fiji Sea

Tuvalu
Gilbert Is.
Tarawa

Marshall Islands

Wake I.

Nauru

Northern Mariana Is.
Guam

Caroline Islands

M i c r o n e s i a

M e l a n e s i a

P o l y n e s i a

Kermadec Is.
Norfolk Island
Lord Howe I.
Chatham Is.

North Island
Bay of Plenty
L. Taupo
Ruapeho Peak 9,175 ft. (2,796 m)
Cape Reinga
Great Barrier I.
Cook Strait
SOUTHERN ALPS
Mt. Cook 12,349 ft. (3,764 m)
South Island
Stewart I.

Tasman Sea

New Guinea
Central Range Mt. Wilhelm 15,400 ft. (4,694 m)
Admiralty Is.
Bismarck Sea
New Ireland
New Britain
Solomon Sea
Bougainville
Santa Isabel I.
Malaita I.
Solomon Islands
Guadalcanal I.
Louisiade Arch.
Espiritu Santo
New Caledonia

Coral Sea

South China Sea
Philippine Sea
Celebes Sea
Arafura Sea
Timor Sea

Babelthuap

Ashmore and Cartier Is.

Timor
Melville
Bathurst
Arnhem Land
Gulf of Carpentaria
Wellesley Is.
Groote I.
Cape York
Torres Strait
Cape York Pen.

Barkly Tableland
Flinders R.

GREAT DIVIDING RANGE
Halifax Bay
Fraser I.

Great Barrier Reef

Mt. Zeil 4,955 ft. (1,510 m)
MACDONNELL RANGES
MUSGRAVE RANGES
Lake Eyre
Great Artesian Basin
Warrego R.
Darling R.
Lachlan R.
Murrumbidgee R.
Murray River
FLINDERS RANGES
Mt. Kosciuszko 7,310 ft. (2,228 m)
AUSTRALIAN ALPS

WESTERN PLATEAU
Great Sandy Desert
Gibson Desert
Great Victoria Desert 52 ft. (16 m) below sea level
NULLARBOR PLAIN
Great Australian Bight

KIMBERLEY PLATEAU
Fitzroy R.
L. Argyle
HAMERSLEY RANGE
Barrow I.

Eyre Pen.
Kangaroo I.
Spencer Gulf
Encounter Bay

King I.
Bass Strait
Flinders I.
Tasmania
South East Cape

Cape Pasley
West Cape Howe
Cape Leeuwin
Cape Naturaliste
Geographe Bay
Dirk Hartog I.
Steep Point

INDIAN OCEAN

A S I A

AUSTRALIA

Legend:
International boundary
State boundary
▲ Mountain peak
▽ Lowest point

1,000 mi
1,000 km
500
0

N E S W

Elevation Profile

6,000 ft.	
4,500 ft.	
3,000 ft.	
1,500 ft.	
Sea level	

Kimberley Plateau
Mount Zeil
Lake Eyre
Flinders Ranges
Mount Kosciuszko

A — B

15°N
EQUATOR
15°S
30°S
45°S

150°E 165°E 180° 165°W 150°W 135°E 120°E

NORTH AMERICA
SOUTH AMERICA
ATLANTIC OCEAN
PACIFIC OCEAN
EUROPE
AFRICA
ASIA
AUSTRALIA
ANTARCTICA
INDIAN OCEAN
Robinson Projection
Equator

Major Metropolitan Areas

Australia
Sydney	3,997,000
Melbourne	3,367,000
Brisbane	1,628,000
Perth	1,340,000
Adelaide	1,073,000
Newcastle	471,000
Gold Coast (Southport)	397,000
Canberra	312,000

Fiji
Suva	167,000
Lautoka	29,000

Kiribati
Tarawa (Bairiki)	25,000

Marshall Islands
Majuro	18,000

Micronesia
Weno	15,000
Colonia	3,000

Nauru
Yaren	4,000

New Zealand
Auckland	1,075,000
Wellington	340,000
Christchurch	334,000

Palau
Koror	13,000

Papua New Guinea
Port Moresby	332,000
Lae	81,000
Madang	27,000
Wewak	23,000

Samoa
Apia	34,000

Solomon Islands
Honiara	61,000

Tonga
Nuku'alofa	30,000

Tuvalu
Funafuti	4,000

Vanuatu
Port-Vila	30,000

International comparability of population data is limited by varying census methods. Where metropolitan population is unavailable, core city population is shown.

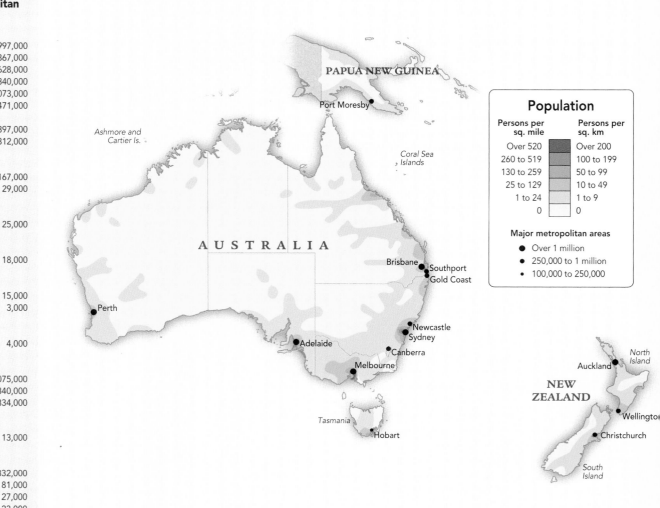

Population

Persons per sq. mile	Persons per sq. km
Over 520	Over 200
260 to 519	100 to 199
130 to 259	50 to 99
25 to 129	10 to 49
1 to 24	1 to 9
0	0

Major metropolitan areas
- ● Over 1 million
- ● 250,000 to 1 million
- · 100,000 to 250,000

Estimated
2002 Population (in millions)
Australia	20
Papua New Guinea	5
New Zealand	4
All other countries	2

Source: U.S. Census Bureau

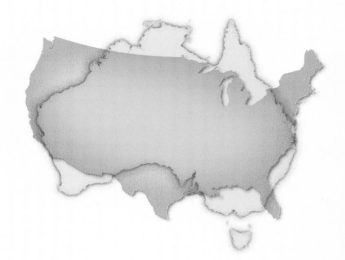

PAPUA NEW GUINEA

AUSTRALIA

GDP of Island Nations

Fiji
Kiribati
Marshall Islands
Micronesia
Nauru
Palau

Samoa
Solomon Islands
Tonga
Tuvalu
Vanuatu

Gross Domestic Product is a measure of the total goods and services generated by a country. Generally, manufacturing, high-tech services, and specialized agricultural products add more value than raw materials and basic food stuffs.

Australia derives its wealth and high standard of living from service industries and mineral extraction and processing. New Zealand's economy is oriented towards the export of animal products. Papua New Guinea's subsistence economy generates little excess wealth.

NEW ZEALAND

Gross Domestic Product

GDP per capita

Over $20,000
$10,000 to $20,000
$5,000 to $9,999
$2,500 to a$4,999
Less than $2,500
No data

Source: *World Factbook*, CIA, 2001

Electricity Use

United States 12,407

Australia 9,211
New Zealand 9,134

Papua New Guinea 353

KWh (kilowatt hours) per person per year

Source: *World Factbook*, CIA, 2001

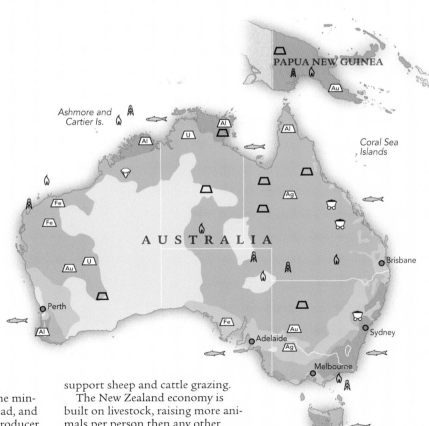

Ashmore and
Cartier Is.

PAPUA NEW GUINEA

Coral Sea
Islands

AUSTRALIA

Brisbane

Perth

Adelaide

Sydney

Melbourne

Tasmania

Land Use and Resources

Predominant land use

Commercial agriculture
Dairying
Livestock ranching
Primarily forestland
Limited agricultural activity

Major resources

Coal
Natural gas
Oil
Forest products
Au — Gold
Ag — Silver
Fe — Iron ore
U — Uranium
Al — Bauxite
Diamonds
Other minerals
Fishing
Major manufacturing and trade centers

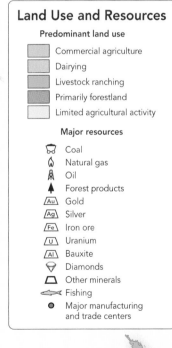

Auckland
North Island

South
Island

NEW
ZEALAND

Australia is rich in mineral resources. It ranks first in the mining of bauxite, diamonds, lead, and zinc while being a leading producer of coal, gold, and iron ore. Its uranium deposits are the largest in the world, though largely undeveloped. Modern methods of farming and irrigation allow a very limited area of commercial agriculture to be highly productive. Despite arid conditions, vast areas of the interior

support sheep and cattle grazing.

The New Zealand economy is built on livestock, raising more animals per person then any other country in the world. Meat and dairy products are important exports.

The economies of Papua New Guinea and the other island nations in the region rely primarily on subsistence agriculture and tourism.

Australia's climate is predominately warm and dry. The northern half of the country lies within the tropics and has very warm conditions year round. The southern half of the country lies below the tropics and experiences a warm summer and a cool winter.

New Zealand's climate is like that of the U.S. Pacific Northwest—mild and moist. Papua New Guinea and other island nations surrounding the equator have climates that are mainly very warm and moist year round.

See photographs taken in different kinds of climates on pages 24–25.

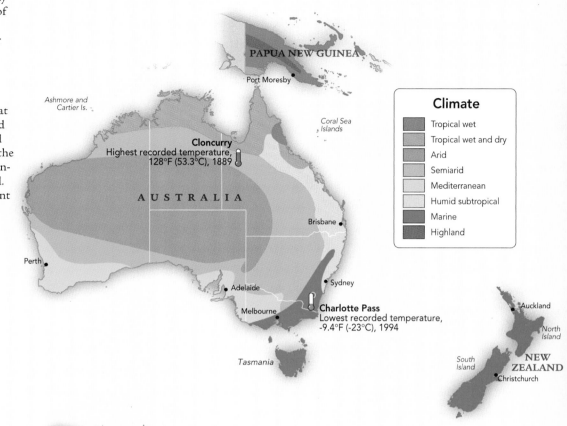

Climate

- Tropical wet
- Tropical wet and dry
- Arid
- Semiarid
- Mediterranean
- Humid subtropical
- Marine
- Highland

Cloncurry
Highest recorded temperature, 128°F (53.3°C), 1889

Charlotte Pass
Lowest recorded temperature, -9.4°F (-23°C), 1994

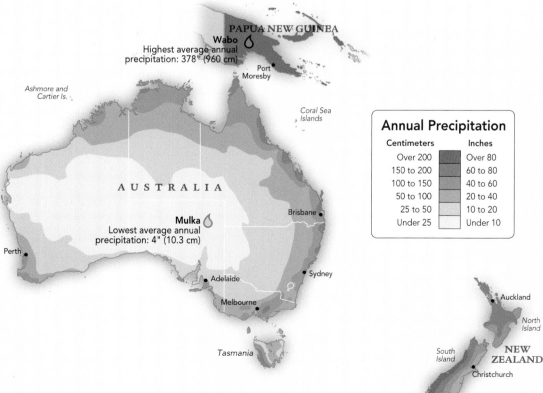

Wabo
Highest average annual precipitation: 378" (960 cm)

Mulka
Lowest average annual precipitation: 4" (10.3 cm)

Annual Precipitation

Centimeters	Inches
Over 200	Over 80
150 to 200	60 to 80
100 to 150	40 to 60
50 to 100	20 to 40
25 to 50	10 to 20
Under 25	Under 10

While Papua New Guinea and other island nations within the tropics receive plentiful and rel able rainfall, rain can be a prob lem in Australia—typically a ca of feast or famine or bad timin Westerly winds off of the Tasman Sea deposit precipita tion on the mountain ranges o New Zealand, often in the form of snow that can be seen on some peaks year round.

Climate Graphs

Average daily temperature range (in °F)   Average monthly precipitation (in inches)

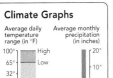
BRISBANE, Australia

PERTH, Australia

AUCKLAND, New Zealand

PORT MORESBY, Papua New Guinea

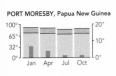
ADELAIDE, Australia

MELBOURNE, Australia

SYDNEY, Australia

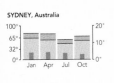
CHRISTCHURCH, New Zealand

Abundant Australian forestlands are limited to relatively narrow coastal regions where moisture, even if seasonal, is adequate. Most of the rest of the continent is covered by species of trees, bush, and grasses adapted to arid conditions. Eucalyptus are the most common trees in Australia.

Papua New Guinea has dense tropical rain forests, and New Zealand has mixed forests and grasslands arising from its temperate climate.

See photographs of different kinds of vegetation on pages 26–27.

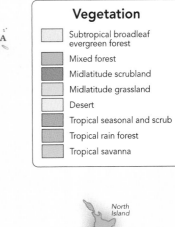

Vegetation
- Subtropical broadleaf evergreen forest
- Mixed forest
- Midlatitude scrubland
- Midlatitude grassland
- Desert
- Tropical seasonal and scrub
- Tropical rain forest
- Tropical savanna

Environmental Issues
- Current forest
- Cleared forest
- Area at highest risk of desertification
- Poor air quality*

*Cities exceeding at least one of the World Health Organization's (WHO) annual mean guidelines for air quality

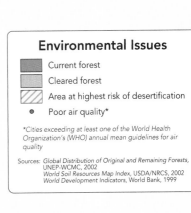

Sources: *Global Distribution of Original and Remaining Forests*, UNEP-WCMC, 2002
World Soil Resources Map Index, USDA/NRCS, 2002
World Development Indicators, World Bank, 1999

Biodiversity loss (a decrease in the variety of life forms and ecosystems) is a leading environmental problem in both Australia and New Zealand. Over the past two hundred years, vast areas have been cleared for settlements and farmland. This land clearing, along with the introduction of non-native plant and animal species, has permanently altered the ecological balance. In New Zealand, it is estimated that eighty-five percent of the original lowland forests and wetlands have been lost due to human influences. Desertification, often brought on by overgrazing, is another serious environmental threat in many parts of Australia.

	Page	Latitude	Longitude
mbia Mts., mountains	75	51°00'N	119°00'W
mbia Plat., plateau	54	45°00'N	118°00'W
mbus, GA	51	32°28'N	84°59'W
mbus, OH	51	39°58'N	83°00'W
itán, Mexico	76	16°15'N	92°07'W
odoro Rivadavia, rgentina	78	45°51'S	67°29'W
orin, C., cape	97	8°00'N	78°00'E
oros, country	90	12°00'S	43°00'E
oros Is., islands	91	11°00'S	43°00'E
akry, Guinea	90	9°31'N	13°42'W
cepción, Chile	78	36°48'S	73°02'W
cepción, Paraguay	78	23°23'S	57°25'W
cepción del Oro, exico	76	24°36'N	101°26'W
ception, Pt., cape	54	34°00'N	120°00'W
chos, river	77	29°00'N	105°00'W
cord, NH	51	43°12'N	71°32'W
go, river	91	2°00'N	22°00'E
go Basin, basin	91	1°00'S	23°00'E
necticut, river	55	42°00'N	73°00'W
necticut, state, U.S.	51	42°00'N	73°00'W
stance, L., lake	85	48°00'N	9°00'E
stanta, Romania	84	44°11'N	28°39'E
stantine, Algeria	90	36°22'N	6°36'E
k Is., dependency, N.Z.	102	20°00'S	158°00'W
k Is., islands	103	20°00'S	158°00'W
k, Mt., peak	103	44°00'S	170°00'E
k Str., strait	103	41°00'S	174°00'E
enhagen, Denmark	84	55°41'N	12°35'E
apó, Chile	78	27°23'S	70°18'W
per Canyon, canyon	77	27°00'N	108°00'W
l Sea, sea	103	15°00'S	155°00'E
l Sea Islands Terr., ependency, Austl.	102	17°00'S	150°00'E
oba, Argentina	78	31°23'S	64°11'W
oba, Spain	84	37°53'N	4°47'W
, Ireland	84	51°54'N	8°28'W
ner Brook, Canada	74	48°57'N	57°57'W
wall, Canada	74	45°02'N	74°45'W
us Christi, TX	50	27°48'N	97°24'W
ientes, Argentina	78	27°30'S	58°49'W
ientes, C., cape	77	20°00'N	106°00'W
ica, island	85	43°00'N	9°00'E
mbá, Brazil	78	19°01'S	57°38'W
a Rica, country	44	10°00'N	85°00'W
d'Ivoire, country	90	5°00'N	5°00'W
umel I., island	77	20°00'N	87°00'W
brook, Canada	74	49°31'N	115°46'W
L., lake	75	57°00'N	108°00'W
e, island	85	35°00'N	25°00'E
e, Sea of, sea	85	36°00'N	25°00'E
ea, peninsula	85	45°00'N	34°00'E
tia, country	84	45°00'N	15°00'E
eiro do Sul, Brazil	78	7°38'S	72°40'W
ndo, river	91	15°00'S	22°00'E
uhtémoc, Mexico	76	28°25'N	106°51'W
a, country	44	22°00'N	80°00'W
a, island	45	22°00'N	80°00'W
ango, river	91	15°00'S	18°00'E
uta, Colombia	78	7°53'N	72°29'W
nca, Ecuador	78	2°54'S	79°01'W
navaca, Mexico	76	18°55'N	99°14'W
bá, Brazil	78	15°35'S	56°07'W
acán, Mexico	76	24°47'N	107°23'W
aná, Venezuela	78	10°27'N	64°11'W
berland, river	55	37°00'N	88°00'W
berland Pen., peninsula	75	66°00'N	65°00'W
berland Plat., plateau	55	35°00'N	85°00'W
berland Sound, bay	75	65°00'N	65°00'W
çao, island	45	12°10'N	69°00'W
iba, Brazil	78	25°27'S	49°16'W
o, Peru	78	13°32'S	71°56'W
ades, islands	85	37°00'N	25°00'E
us, country	96	35°00'N	33°00'E
us, island	97	35°00'N	33°00'E
naica, region	91	25°00'N	24°00'E
ch Rep., country	84	49°00'N	15°00'E
D			
ar, Senegal	90	14°42'N	17°27'W
as, TX	50	32°47'N	96°48'W
natia, region	85	44°00'N	16°00'E
araland, region	91	21°00'S	19°00'E
ascus, Syria	96	33°31'N	36°18'E
nbre, Cap, cape	91	12°00'S	48°00'E
Nang, Vietnam	96	16°03'N	108°12'E
ube, river	85	49°00'N	10°00'E
ube Delta, delta	85	45°00'N	29°00'E
danelles, strait	85	40°00'N	27°00'E
es Salaam, Tanzania	90	6°49'S	39°17'E
ing, river	103	31°00'S	144°00'E
win, Australia	102	12°25'S	130°53'E
ht-e-Kavir, desert	97	35°00'N	54°00'E
gavpils, Latvia	84	55°53'N	26°32'E
phin, Canada	74	51°10'N	100°04'W
ao, Philippines	96	7°04'N	125°36'E
enport, IA	51	41°31'N	90°35'W
s Sea, sea	15	65°00'S	95°00'E
s Str., strait	45	66°00'N	58°00'W
son, Canada	74	64°04'N	139°24'W
son Creek, Canada	74	55°45'N	120°15'W
on, OH	51	39°46'N	84°12'W
d Sea, depression	97	31°00'N	35°00'E
h Val., depression	54	36°00'N	117°00'W
recen, Hungary	84	47°32'N	21°39'E
atur, IL	51	39°50'N	88°57'W
can Plat., plateau	97	23°00'N	79°00'E
ware, river	55	42°00'N	75°00'W
ware, state, U.S.	51	39°00'N	74°00'W
ware Bay, bay	55	39°00'N	75°00'W
ado, C., cape	91	10°00'S	41°00'E
i, India	96	28°41'N	77°12'E
cias, Mexico	76	28°12'N	105°28'W
ne, Canada	74	65°12'N	123°27'W
ocratic Rep. the Congo, country	90	1°00'S	21°00'E
Denakil, region	91	13°00'N	41°00'E
Denmark, country	84	56°00'N	10°00'E
Denmark Str., strait	45	65°00'N	31°00'W
Denver, CO	50	39°44'N	104°59'W
Dese, Ethiopia	90	11°10'N	39°37'E
Des Moines, IA	51	41°36'N	93°37'W
Des Moines, river	55	43°00'N	94°00'W
Desna, river	85	52°00'N	32°00'E
Detroit, MI	51	42°20'N	83°03'W
Devon I., island	75	76°00'N	85°00'W
Dhaka, Bangladesh	96	23°43'N	90°26'E
Diefenbaker, L., lake	75	50°00'N	107°00'W
Dijon, France	84	47°20'N	5°02'E
Dili, East Timor	96	8°35'S	125°36'E
Dinaric Alps, mountains	85	44°00'N	17°00'E
Dire Dawa, Ethiopia	90	9°36'N	41°52'E
Dirk Hartog I., island	103	26°00'S	113°00'E
Distrito Federal, fed. dist., Mex.	76	19°00'N	101°00'W
Djibouti, country	90	11°00'N	41°00'E
Djibouti, Djibouti	91	11°34'N	43°08'E
Dnieper, river	85	47°00'N	33°00'E
Dnieper Upland, highlands	85	49°00'N	32°00'E
Dniester, river	85	49°00'N	26°00'E
Dnipropetrovs'k, Ukraine	84	48°27'N	34°59'E
Dodoma, Tanzania	90	6°09'S	35°42'E
Doha, Qatar	96	25°15'N	51°26'E
Dominica, country	44	16°00'N	61°00'W
Dominican Rep., country	44	20°00'N	70°00'W
Don, river	85	48°00'N	40°00'E
Donets, river	85	49°00'N	38°00'E
Donets Basin, basin	85	48°00'N	38°00'E
Donets'k, Ukraine	84	48°01'N	37°48'E
Douala, Cameroon	90	4°03'N	9°43'E
Dourados, Brazil	78	22°14'S	54°48'W
Douro, river	85	43°00'N	7°00'W
Dover, DE	51	39°09'N	75°31'W
Dover, Str. of, strait	85	51°00'N	1°00'E
Drakensberg, mountains	91	30°00'S	30°00'E
Drake Passage, strait	14	60°00'S	70°00'W
Dresden, Germany	84	51°03'N	13°44'E
Dryden, Canada	74	49°47'N	92°49'W
Dubawnt, river	75	63°00'N	104°00'W
Dubawnt L., lake	75	63°00'N	100°00'W
Dublin, Ireland	84	53°21'N	6°16'W
Dubrovnik, Croatia	84	42°39'N	18°05'E
Duluth, MN	51	46°47'N	92°06'W
Dund-Us, Mongolia	96	47°59'N	91°39'E
Dunedin, New Zealand	102	45°52'S	170°28'E
Durango, Mexico	76	24°02'N	104°39'W
Durango, state, Mex.	76	24°00'N	104°00'W
Durban, S. Africa	90	29°50'S	31°01'E
Dushanbe, Tajikistan	96	38°34'N	68°48'E
Dzungarian Basin, basin	97	45°00'N	88°00'E
E			
East China Sea, sea	97	29°00'N	124°00'E
Easter I., dependency	16	27°07'S	109°22'W
Easter I., island	14	27°07'S	109°22'W
Eastern Desert, desert	91	26°00'N	32°00'E
Eastern Ghats, mountains	97	15°00'N	82°00'E
East London, S. Africa	90	33°00'S	27°54'E
East Siberian Sea, sea	97	73°00'N	165°00'E
East Timor, country	96	9°00'S	125°00'E
Ebro, river	85	43°00'N	2°00'W
Ecuador, country	78	2°00'S	80°00'W
Edinburgh, United Kingdom	84	55°57'N	3°11'W
Edmonton, Canada	74	53°35'N	113°31'W
Edwards Plat., plateau	54	31°00'N	101°00'W
Egypt, country	90	26°00'N	29°00'E
Elba, island	85	43°00'N	10°00'E
Elbe, river	85	54°00'N	11°00'E
Elbert, Mt., peak	54	39°00'N	106°00'W
Elbrus, Mt., peak	85	43°00'N	42°00'E
Elburz Mts., mountains	97	36°00'N	53°00'E
Eldoret, Kenya	90	0°32'N	35°16'E
El Fashir, Sudan	90	13°38'N	25°21'E
El Khârga, Egypt	90	25°27'N	30°33'E
Ellesmere I., island	75	83°00'N	76°00'W
Elliot Lake, Canada	74	46°23'N	82°39'W
Ellsworth Land, region	15	76°00'S	90°00'W
Ellsworth Mts., mountains	15	80°00'S	85°00'W
El Obeid, Sudan	90	13°11'N	30°13'E
El Paso, TX	50	31°46'N	106°29'W
El Salvador, country	44	14°00'N	89°00'W
El Tigre, Venezuela	78	8°53'N	64°16'W
Emi Koussi, peak	91	19°00'N	21°00'E
Encarnación, Paraguay	78	27°20'S	55°52'W
Encounter Bay, bay	103	37°00'S	139°00'E
Enderby Land, region	15	70°00'S	40°00'E
England, division, U.K.	84	52°00'N	2°00'W
English Channel, strait	85	50°00'N	4°00'W
Ensenada, Mexico	76	31°52'N	116°37'W
Equatorial Guinea, country	90	2°00'N	11°00'E
Erg Chech, desert	91	24°00'N	3°00'W
Erie, PA	51	42°08'N	80°05'W
Erie, L., lake	45	43°00'N	83°00'W
Eritrea, country	90	18°00'N	38°00'E
Esfahan, Iran	96	32°39'N	51°39'E
Esmeraldas, Ecuador	78	0°57'N	79°40'W
Espiritu Santo, island	103	15°00'S	167°00'E
Esquel, Argentina	78	42°55'S	71°20'W
Essen, Germany	84	51°27'N	7°03'E
Estevan, Canada	74	49°08'N	103°00'W
Estonia, country	84	59°00'N	29°00'E
Ethiopia, country	90	8°00'N	40°00'E
Ethiopian Highlands, plateau	91	9°00'N	39°00'E
Etna, Mt., peak	85	38°00'N	15°00'E
Eugene, OR	50	44°03'N	123°05'W
Eugenia Pt., cape	77	28°00'N	115°00'W
Euphrates, river	97	33°00'N	42°00'E
Europe, continent	15	50°00'N	10°00'E
Evansville, IN	51	37°58'N	87°33'W
Everest, Mt., peak	97	27°59'N	86°56'E
Eyre, L., lake	103	29°00'S	137°00'E
Eyre Pen., peninsula	103	33°00'S	136°00'E
F			
Fairbanks, AK	50	64°50'N	147°43'W
Faisalabad, Pakistan	96	31°24'N	73°04'E
Falcon Res., lake	77	27°00'N	99°00'W
Falkland Is., dependency, U.K.	78	52°00'S	59°00'W
Falkland Is., islands	79	52°00'S	59°00'W
Farewell, C., cape	45	60°00'N	44°00'W
Fargo, ND	50	46°53'N	96°47'W
Faro, Canada	74	62°16'N	133°24'W
Faroe Is., dependency, Den.	84	62°00'N	7°00'W
Faroe Is., islands	85	62°00'N	7°00'W
Faya-Largeau, Chad	90	17°56'N	19°07'E
Fear, C., cape	55	34°00'N	78°00'W
Federated States of Micronesia, country	102	6°00'N	150°00'E
Feira de Santana, Brazil	78	12°15'S	38°58'W
Fès, Morocco	90	34°04'N	4°58'W
Feuilles, R. aux, river	75	58°00'N	73°00'W
Fianarantsoa, Madagascar	90	21°27'S	47°04'E
Fiji, country	102	19°00'S	178°00'E
Fiji Sea, sea	103	27°00'S	177°00'E
Filchner Ice Shelf, ice shelf	15	80°00'S	40°00'W
Fimbul Ice Shelf, ice shelf	15	70°00'S	5°00'W
Finisterre, C., cape	85	43°00'N	9°00'W
Finland, country	84	66°00'N	26°00'E
Finland, G. of, gulf	85	60°00'N	26°00'E
Fitzroy, river	103	18°00'S	125°00'E
Flagstaff, AZ	50	35°12'N	111°39'W
Flattery, C., cape	54	48°00'N	125°00'W
Flinders, river	103	19°00'S	141°00'E
Flinders I., island	103	40°00'S	148°00'E
Flinders Ranges, mountains	103	32°00'S	139°00'E
Flin Flon, Canada	74	54°48'N	101°52'W
Flint, MI	51	43°01'N	83°41'W
Flint, river	55	31°00'N	84°00'W
Flint Hills, hills	55	38°00'N	97°00'W
Flint I., island	103	11°00'S	152°00'W
Florence, Italy	84	43°46'N	11°15'E
Florencia, Colombia	78	1°36'N	75°35'W
Floriano, Brazil	78	6°47'S	43°00'W
Florianópolis, Brazil	78	27°36'S	48°34'W
Florida, state, U.S.	51	29°00'N	82°00'W
Florida Keys, islands	55	25°00'N	82°00'W
Florida, Straits of, strait	45	24°00'N	82°00'W
Former Yugoslav Rep. of Macedonia, country	84	41°00'N	22°00'E
Fortaleza, Brazil	78	3°46'S	38°33'W
Fort Collins, CO	50	40°35'N	105°05'W
Fort Frances, Canada	74	48°38'N	93°23'W
Fort Lauderdale, FL	51	26°07'N	80°09'W
Fort McMurray, Canada	74	56°41'N	111°22'W
Fort McPherson, Canada	74	67°26'N	134°52'W
Fort Nelson, Canada	74	58°47'N	122°42'W
Fort Peck L., lake	54	48°00'N	107°00'W
Fort St. John, Canada	74	56°13'N	120°51'W
Fort Simpson, Canada	74	61°50'N	121°21'W
Fort Smith, AR	51	35°23'N	94°24'W
Fort Smith, Canada	74	60°00'N	111°57'W
Fort Worth, TX	50	32°44'N	97°19'W
Foxe Basin, bay	75	66°00'N	79°00'W
Foxe Pen., peninsula	75	65°00'N	78°00'W
France, country	84	47°00'N	2°00'E
Franceville, Gabon	90	1°39'S	13°34'E
Francistown, Botswana	90	21°12'S	27°32'E
Frankfort, KY	51	38°12'N	84°52'W
Frankfurt, Germany	84	50°07'N	8°41'E
Franz Josef Land, islands	97	81°00'N	55°00'E
Fraser, river	75	52°00'N	123°00'W
Fraser I., island	103	25°00'S	153°00'E
Fredericton, Canada	74	45°57'N	66°40'W
Freetown, Sierra Leone	90	8°27'N	13°13'W
French Guiana, dependency, Fr.	78	4°00'N	52°00'W
French Polynesia, dependency, Fr.	102	15°00'S	140°00'W
French Polynesia, islands	103	15°00'S	140°00'W
Fresnillo, Mexico	76	23°10'N	102°51'W
Fresno, CA	50	36°45'N	119°46'W
Fria, C., cape	91	18°00'S	12°00'E
Frisian Is., islands	85	54°00'N	6°00'E
Frobisher Bay, bay	75	64°00'N	66°00'W
Front Range, mountains	54	40°00'N	105°00'W
Fuerte, river	77	26°00'N	109°00'W
Fuji, Mt., peak	97	35°22'N	138°44'E
Funafuti, Tuvalu	102	8°37'S	179°07'E
Fundy, Bay of, bay	75	45°00'N	67°00'W
Fuzhou, China	96	26°04'N	119°18'E
G			
Gabes, G. of, gulf	91	34°00'N	12°00'E
Gabon, country	90	0°00'	12°00'E
Gaborone, Botswana	90	24°38'S	25°55'E
Galápagos Is., islands	79	1°00'S	91°00'W
Galdhøpiggen, peak	85	62°00'N	8°00'E
Galveston Bay, bay	55	29°00'N	95°00'W
Gambia, country	90	12°00'N	18°00'E
Gander, Canada	74	48°57'N	54°36'W
Ganges, river	97	25°00'N	80°00'E
Gangetic Plain, plain	97	28°00'N	81°00'E
Gao, Mali	90	16°16'N	0°00'E
Garonne, river	85	45°00'N	0°00'
Garoua, Cameroon	90	9°18'N	13°23'E
Garry L., lake	75	66°00'N	100°00'W
Gary, IN	51	41°36'N	87°21'W
Gaspé, Canada	74	48°50'N	64°30'W
Gaspé Pen., peninsula	75	49°00'N	63°00'W
Gdansk, Poland	84	54°22'N	18°38'E
Gedaref, Sudan	90	14°02'N	35°23'E
Geelong, Australia	102	38°11'S	144°23'E
Genesee, river	55	43°00'N	78°00'W
Geneva, Switzerland	84	46°12'N	6°09'E
Geneva, L., lake	85	46°00'N	7°00'E
Genoa, Italy	84	44°25'N	8°56'E
Geographe Bay, bay	103	33°00'S	115°00'E
George, river	75	57°00'N	77°00'W
Georgetown, Guyana	78	6°47'N	58°07'W
Georgia, country	84	43°00'N	43°00'E
Georgia, state, U.S.	51	33°00'N	83°00'W
Germany, country	84	52°00'N	11°00'E
Ghadamis, Libya	90	30°08'N	9°30'E
Ghana, country	90	9°00'N	2°00'W
Ghardaia, Algeria	90	32°30'N	3°40'E
Gibraltar, dependency, U.K.	84	37°00'N	5°00'W
Gibraltar, Str. of, strait	85	36°00'N	6°00'W
Gibson Desert, desert	103	25°00'S	127°00'E
Gijón, Spain	84	43°32'N	5°41'W
Gila, river	54	33°00'N	112°00'W
Gilbert Is., islands	103	0°00'	173°00'E
Giza, Egypt	90	30°01'N	31°13'E
Glåma, river	85	60°00'N	11°00'E
Glasgow, United Kingdom	84	55°51'N	4°16'W
Gobi, desert	97	43°00'N	105°00'E
Godavari, river	97	19°00'N	78°00'E
Goiânia, Brazil	78	16°42'S	49°15'W
Gold Coast, Australia	102	27°57'S	153°23'E
Gold Coast, region	91	5°00'N	1°00'W
Gonder, Ethiopia	90	12°34'N	37°26'E
Good Hope, C. of, cape	91	35°00'S	18°00'E
Göteborg, Sweden	84	57°42'N	11°56'E
Gotland, island	85	57°00'N	18°00'E
Governador Valadares, Brazil	78	18°51'S	41°59'W
Grain Coast, region	91	6°00'N	10°00'W
Granada, Spain	84	37°11'N	3°36'W
Gran Chaco, plain	79	23°00'S	62°00'W
Grand, river	55	43°00'N	86°00'W
Grand Canyon, canyon	54	36°00'N	113°00'W
Grande, river	79	20°00'S	48°00'W
Grande Prairie, Canada	74	55°11'N	118°48'W
Grand Erg Occidental, desert	91	31°00'N	2°00'E
Grand Erg Oriental, desert	91	31°00'N	8°00'E
Grand Falls-Windsor, Canada	74	49°00'N	55°35'W
Grand Forks, ND	50	47°56'N	97°02'W
Grand Rapids, MI	51	42°58'N	85°40'W
Granite Peak, peak	54	45°00'N	110°00'W
Graz, Austria	84	47°05'N	15°27'E
Great Artesian Basin, basin	103	22°00'S	141°00'E
Great Australian Bight, bay	103	34°00'S	130°00'E
Great Barrier I., island	103	36°00'S	175°00'E
Great Barrier Reef, reef	103	15°00'S	146°00'E
Great Basin, basin	54	40°00'N	117°00'W
Great Bear L., lake	75	65°00'N	120°00'W
Great Dividing Range, mountains	103	22°00'S	149°00'E
Greater Antilles, islands	45	18°00'N	75°00'W
Greater Khingan Range, mountains	97	45°00'N	118°00'E
Greater Sunda Is., islands	97	5°00'S	110°00'E
Great Falls, MT	50	47°30'N	111°18'W
Great Plains, plain	45	45°00'N	105°00'W
Great Salt L., lake	54	41°00'N	113°00'W
Great Salt Lake Desert, desert	54	41°00'N	114°00'W
Great Sandy Desert, desert	103	21°00'S	125°00'E
Great Slave L., lake	75	63°00'N	115°00'W
Great Victoria Desert, desert	103	28°00'S	128°00'E
Greece, country	84	39°00'N	22°00'E
Green, river	55	38°00'N	87°00'W
Green, river	54	42°00'N	110°00'W
Green Bay, WI	51	44°31'N	88°01'W
Greenland, island	45	75°00'N	40°00'W
Greenland (Kalaallit Nunaat), dependency, Den.	44	75°00'N	40°00'W
Greenland Sea, sea	15	65°00'N	10°00'W
Green Mts., mountains	55	44°00'N	73°00'W
Greensboro, NC	51	36°04'N	79°48'W
Grenada, country	44	12°00'N	62°00'W
Grijalva, river	77	17°00'N	93°00'W
Groote I., island	103	14°00'S	137°00'E
Groznyy, Russia	84	43°24'N	45°47'E
Guadalajara, Mexico	76	20°40'N	103°21'W
Guadalcanal I., island	103	10°00'S	160°00'E
Guadalupe I., island	77	29°00'N	118°00'W
Guadalupe Peak, peak	54	32°00'N	104°00'W
Guadeloupe, dependency, Fr.	44	18°00'N	62°00'W
Guadiana, river	85	39°00'N	8°00'W
Guajará-Mirim, Brazil	78	10°48'S	65°22'W
Guam, dependency, U.S.	102	13°00'N	145°00'E
Guam, island	103	13°00'N	145°00'E
Guanajuato, Mexico	76	21°00'N	101°17'W
Guanajuato, state, Mex.	76	22°00'N	101°00'W
Guangzhou, China	96	23°08'N	113°18'E
Guaporé, river	79	13°00'S	63°00'W
Guasave, Mexico	76	25°34'N	108°29'W
Guatemala, country	44	16°00'N	91°00'W
Guatemala City, Guatemala	44	14°37'N	90°31'W
Guayaquil, Ecuador	78	2°12'S	79°54'W
Guayaquil, G. of, gulf	79	3°00'S	80°00'W
Guaymas, Mexico	76	27°55'N	110°53'W
Guernsey, island	85	49°00'N	3°00'W
Guerrero, state, Mex.	76	17°00'N	101°00'W
Guerrero Negro, Mexico	76	27°58'N	114°03'W
Guiana Highlands, plateau	79	5°00'N	62°00'W
Guinea, country	90	11°00'N	12°00'W
Guinea-Bissau, country	90	12°00'N	16°00'W
Guinea, G. of, gulf	91	2°00'N	3°00'E
Guiyang, China	96	26°36'N	106°41'E
Gulf Coastal Plain, plain	55	30°00'N	93°00'W
Gurupi, Brazil	78	11°46'S	49°05'W
Guyana, country	78	7°00'N	59°00'W
Gwardafuy, C., cape	91	12°00'N	51°00'E
Gweru, Zimbabwe	90	19°28'S	29°49'E
H			
Hainan, island	97	19°00'N	110°00'E
Haiti, country	44	19°00'N	73°00'W
Halifax, Canada	74	44°38'N	63°36'W
Halifax Bay, bay	103	19°00'S	147°00'E
Hall Pen., peninsula	75	65°00'N	66°00'W
Hamburg, Germany	84	53°33'N	10°01'E
Hamersley Range, mountains	103	23°00'S	118°00'E
Hamilton, Canada	74	43°16'N	79°51'W
Hamilton, New Zealand	102	37°47'S	175°18'E
Hammerfest, Norway	84	70°40'N	23°42'E
Hannover, Germany	84	52°22'N	9°45'E
Hanoi, Vietnam	96	21°02'N	105°49'E
Happy Valley-Goose Bay, Canada	74	53°20'N	60°23'W
Harare, Zimbabwe	90	17°49'S	31°03'E
Harbin, China	96	45°43'N	126°43'E
Hargeysa, Somalia	90	9°31'N	44°03'E
Harrisburg, PA	51	40°16'N	76°53'W
Hartford, CT	51	41°46'N	72°41'W
Hatteras, C., cape	55	35°00'N	75°00'W
Havana, Cuba	44	23°09'N	82°23'W
Havre-St-Pierre, Canada	74	50°15'N	63°36'W
Hawaii, island	54	20°00'N	155°00'W
Hawaii, state, U.S.	50	21°00'N	158°00'W
Hawaiian Is., islands	54	21°00'N	157°00'W
Hay, river	75	58°00'N	118°00'W
Hay River, Canada	74	60°49'N	115°46'W
Hearst, Canada	74	49°42'N	83°40'W
Hecate Str., strait	75	53°00'N	131°00'W
Helena, MT	50	46°36'N	112°02'W
Helsinki, Finland	84	60°11'N	24°56'E
Hermosillo, Mexico	76	29°04'N	110°55'W
Herrero, Pt., cape	77	19°00'N	87°00'W
Hidalgo, state, Mex.	76	21°00'N	99°00'W
Hidalgo del Parral, Mexico	76	26°56'N	105°41'W
Highlands, mountains	85	57°00'N	5°00'W
High Level, Canada	74	58°31'N	117°06'W
Hiiumaa I., island	85	59°00'N	22°00'E
Hilo, HI	50	19°44'N	155°05'W
Himalayas, mountains	97	27°00'N	86°00'E
Hindu Kush, mountains	97	35°00'N	71°00'E
Hispaniola, island	45	18°00'N	69°00'W
Hobart, Australia	102	42°48'S	147°18'E
Ho Chi Minh City, Vietnam	96	10°43'N	106°43'E
Hokkaido, island	97	44°00'N	143°00'E
Holman, Canada	74	70°43'N	117°41'W
Homel', Belarus	84	52°29'N	31°00'E
Honduras, country	44	17°00'N	85°00'W
Hong, river	97	23°00'N	104°00'E
Hong Kong, China	96	22°15'N	114°11'E
Honiara, Solomon Islands	102	9°19'S	159°44'E
Honolulu, HI	50	21°18'N	157°51'W
Honshu, island	97	37°00'N	140°00'E
Hood, Mt., peak	54	45°00'N	122°00'W
Hormuz, Str. of, strait	97	26°00'N	56°00'E
Horn, C., cape	79	56°00'S	68°00'W
Horn of Africa, region	91	9°00'N	47°00'E
Hotan, China	96	37°08'N	79°54'E
Houston, TX	51	29°46'N	95°22'W
Howland I., dependency, U.S.	102	1°00'N	177°00'W
Howland I., island	103	1°00'N	177°00'W
Hrodna, Belarus	84	53°41'N	23°51'E
Huajuapan de León, Mexico	76	17°48'N	97°47'W
Huambo, Angola	90	12°46'S	15°44'E
Huancayo, Peru	78	12°05'S	75°13'W
Huang (Yellow), river	97	37°00'N	111°00'E
Huánuco, Peru	78	9°54'S	76°16'W
Huascarán, Mt., peak	79	9°00'S	78°00'W
Hudson, river	55	42°00'N	74°00'W
Hudson Bay, bay	75	59°00'N	85°00'W
Hudson Str., strait	75	63°00'N	73°00'W
Hull, Canada	74	45°26'N	75°44'W
Humphreys Peak, peak	54	35°00'N	111°00'W
Hungary, country	84	47°00'N	19°00'E
Huntsville, AL	51	34°44'N	86°35'W
Huron, L., lake	45	47°00'N	82°00'W
Hyderabad, India	96	17°20'N	78°31'E
I			
Iasi, Romania	84	47°10'N	27°36'E
Ibadan, Nigeria	90	7°24'N	3°53'E
Ibagué, Colombia	78	4°24'N	75°15'W
Iberian Pen., peninsula	85	41°00'N	4°00'W
Ibiza, island	85	39°00'N	1°00'E
Ica, Peru	78	14°03'S	75°45'W
Iceland, country	84	65°00'N	18°00'W
Iceland, island	85	65°00'N	18°00'W
Idaho, state, U.S.	50	44°00'N	114°00'W
Iguala, Mexico	76	18°21'N	99°32'W
Iguazú Falls, falls	79	26°00'S	55°00'W
Ilebo, Dem. Rep. of Congo	90	4°20'S	20°38'E
Ilhéus, Brazil	78	14°47'S	39°03'W
Illimani, Mt., peak	79	17°00'S	68°00'W
Illinois, river	55	41°00'N	90°00'W
Illinois, state, U.S.	51	41°00'N	89°00'W
Ilorin, Nigeria	90	8°29'N	4°33'E
Imperatriz, Brazil	78	5°29'S	47°30'W
I-n-Amenas, Algeria	90	28°03'N	9°34'E
India, country	96	23°00'N	79°00'E
Indiana, state, U.S.	51	41°00'N	86°00'W
Indianapolis, IN	51	39°46'N	86°09'W
Indian Ocean, ocean	15	10°00'S	80°00'E
Indochina Pen., peninsula	97	16°00'N	105°00'E
Indonesia, country	96	2°00'S	119°00'E
Indus, river	97	31°00'N	71°00'E
Infiernillo Res., lake	77	19°00'N	102°00'W
I-n-Salah, Algeria	90	27°12'N	2°31'E
Inuvik, Canada	74	68°22'N	133°42'W
Ionian Sea, sea	85	37°00'N	19°00'E
Iowa, river	55	43°00'N	93°00'W
Iowa, state, U.S.	51	43°00'N	94°00'W
Iqaluit, Canada	74	63°45'N	68°26'W
Iquique, Chile	78	20°14'S	70°07'W
Iquitos, Peru	78	3°45'S	73°11'W
Iraklio, Greece	84	35°20'N	25°08'E
Iran, country	96	31°00'N	57°00'E
Irapuato, Mexico	76	20°39'N	101°22'W
Iraq, country	96	32°00'N	41°00'E

Place	Page	Latitude	Longitude
Seward Pen., peninsula	54	65°00'N	165°00'W
Seychelles, country	90	9°00'S	52°00'E
Seychelles Is., islands	91	8°00'S	52°00'E
Sfax, Tunisia	90	34°47'N	10°46'E
Shackleton Ice Shelf, ice shelf	15	64°00'S	100°00'E
Shanghai, China	96	31°12'N	121°28'E
Shasta, Mt., peak	54	42°00'N	122°00'W
Shawinigan, Canada	74	46°33'N	72°45'W
Sheffield, United Kingdom	84	53°22'N	1°28'W
Shenyang, China	96	41°49'N	123°30'E
Sherbrooke, Canada	74	45°24'N	71°53'W
Shetland Is., islands	85	60°00'N	1°00'W
Shikoku, island	97	33°00'N	133°00'E
Shilka, river	97	52°00'N	105°00'E
Shiraz, Iran	96	29°37'N	52°32'E
Shreveport, LA	51	32°31'N	93°45'W
Siberia, region	97	64°00'N	98°00'E
Sicily, island	85	37°00'N	14°00'E
Sicily, Str. of, strait	85	37°00'N	12°00'E
Sidra, G. of, gulf	91	32°00'N	19°00'E
Sierra Azul, mountains	77	23°00'N	99°00'W
Sierra Leone, country	90	9°00'N	12°00'W
Sierra Madre de Chiapas, mountains	77	16°00'N	93°00'W
Sierra Madre del Sur, mountains	77	17°00'N	99°00'W
Sierra Madre Occidental, mountains	77	27°00'N	107°00'W
Sierra Madre Oriental, mountains	77	25°00'N	100°00'W
Sierra Morena, mountains	85	38°00'N	5°00'W
Sierra Nevada, mountains	54	38°00'N	120°00'W
Sierra San Pedro Mártir, mountains	77	32°00'N	116°00'W
Simferopol', Ukraine	84	44°58'N	34°06'E
Sinai Pen., peninsula	91	29°00'N	34°00'E
Sinaloa, state, Mex.	76	24°00'N	107°00'W
Sincelejo, Colombia	78	9°18'N	75°24'W
Singapore, country	96	1°00'N	104°00'E
Singapore, Singapore	96	1°18'N	103°51'E
Sioux City, IA	51	42°30'N	96°24'W
Sioux Falls, SD	51	43°33'N	96°42'W
Siple I., island	15	74°00'S	135°00'W
Siwah, Egypt	91	29°11'N	25°31'E
Skagerrak, strait	85	58°00'N	9°00'E
Skeena, river	75	55°00'N	129°00'W
Skeleton Coast, region	91	22°00'S	12°00'E
Skopje, F.Y.R. Macedonia	84	42°00'N	21°25'E
Skovorodino, Russia	96	54°02'N	123°59'E
Slave, river	75	61°00'N	112°00'W
Slave Coast, region	91	6°00'N	2°00'E
Slovakia, country	84	48°00'N	19°00'E
Slovenia, country	84	47°00'N	15°00'E
Smallwood Res., lake	75	55°00'N	64°00'W
Smoky Hill, river	55	39°00'N	99°00'W
Smolensk, Russia	84	54°48'N	32°03'E
Snake, river	54	44°00'N	116°00'W
Snake River Plain, plain	54	43°00'N	115°00'W
Society Is., islands	103	18°00'S	152°00'W
Socotra, island	97	12°30'N	54°00'E
Sofia, Bulgaria	84	42°43'N	23°20'E
Sokoto, Nigeria	90	13°02'N	5°14'E
Solomon Islands, country	102	7°00'S	160°00'E
Solomon Islands, islands	103	9°00'S	165°00'E
Solomon Sea, sea	103	8°00'S	153°00'E
Somalia, country	90	4°00'N	45°00'E
Somali Pen., peninsula	91	10°00'N	49°00'E
Somerset I., island	75	74°00'N	95°00'W
Songea, Tanzania	90	10°41'S	35°39'E
Sonora, river	77	30°00'N	111°00'W
Sonora, state, Mex.	76	29°00'N	111°00'W
Sonoran Desert, desert	54	34°00'N	114°00'W
South Africa, country	90	30°00'S	21°00'E
South America, continent	14	10°00'S	50°00'W
Southampton I., island	75	65°00'N	85°00'W
South Australia, state, Austl.	102	32°00'S	135°00'E
South Bend, IN	51	41°41'N	86°15'W
South Carolina, state, U.S.	51	34°00'N	81°00'W
South China Sea, sea	97	14°00'N	115°00'E
South Dakota, state, U.S.	50	45°00'N	101°00'W
South East C., cape	103	44°00'S	147°00'E
Southern Alps, mountains	103	44°00'S	171°00'E
Southern Indian L., lake	75	57°00'N	98°00'W
South Georgia, island	79	54°00'S	37°00'W
South I., island	103	44°00'S	171°00'E
South Korea, country	96	35°00'N	128°00'E
South Orkney Is., islands	15	61°00'S	45°00'W
South Platte, river	54	40°00'N	104°00'W
South Pole, pole	15	90°00'S	0°00'
South Saskatchewan, river	75	51°00'N	110°00'W
South Shetland Is., islands	15	62°00'S	60°00'W
Spain, country	84	41°00'N	5°00'E
Spencer G., gulf	103	35°00'S	137°00'E
Split, Croatia	84	43°31'N	16°27'E
Spokane, WA	50	47°40'N	117°25'W
Springbok, S. Africa	90	29°40'S	17°54'E
Springfield, IL	51	39°48'N	89°39'W
Springfield, MO	51	37°13'N	93°18'W
Sri Lanka, country	96	7°00'N	81°00'E
Sri Lanka, island	97	7°00'N	81°00'E
Srinagar, India	96	34°11'N	74°48'E
Stanley, Falkland Is.	78	51°43'S	57°51'W
Stanovoy Range, mountains	97	56°00'N	130°00'E
Starbuck I., island	103	6°00'S	156°00'W
Stavanger, Norway	84	58°57'N	5°45'E
Steep Pt., cape	103	26°00'S	113°00'E
Stewart I., island	103	47°00'S	168°00'E
Stockholm, Sweden	84	59°20'N	18°02'E
Strasbourg, France	84	48°35'N	7°46'E
Stuttgart, Germany	84	48°48'N	9°11'E
Sucre, Bolivia	78	19°03'S	65°15'W
Sudan, country	90	11°00'N	29°00'E
Sudbury, Canada	74	46°29'N	81°00'W
Sudd, swamp	91	9°00'N	29°00'E
Sudeten Mts., mountains	85	51°00'N	16°00'E
Suez Canal, canal	91	31°00'N	34°00'E
Suez, G. of, gulf	91	28°00'N	33°00'E
Sukhona, river	85	60°00'N	42°00'E
Sulawesi (Celebes), island	97	2°00'S	121°00'E
Sumatra, island	97	0°00'	101°00'E
Sunda Str., strait	97	6°00'S	105°00'E
Sundsvall, Sweden	84	62°22'N	17°17'E
Superior, L., lake	45	47°00'N	86°00'W
Surabaya, Indonesia	96	7°13'S	112°44'E
Surgut, Russia	96	61°08'N	73°27'E
Suriname, country	78	4°00'N	57°00'W
Susquehanna, river	55	41°00'N	76°00'W
Sutlej, river	97	31°00'N	73°00'E
Suva, Fiji	102	17°48'S	178°32'E
Svalbard, islands	15	78°00'N	18°00'E
Swaziland, country	90	28°00'S	29°00'E
Sweden, country	84	60°00'N	15°00'E
Swift Current, Canada	74	50°17'N	107°47'W
Switzerland, country	84	46°00'N	8°00'E
Sydney, Australia	102	33°54'S	151°12'E
Sydney, Canada	74	46°09'N	60°12'W
Syktyvkar, Russia	84	61°47'N	51°02'E
Syracuse, NY	51	43°03'N	76°09'W
Syr Darya, river	97	44°00'N	68°00'E
Syria, country	96	35°00'N	38°00'E
Syrian Desert, desert	97	32°00'N	40°00'E
Szczecin, Poland	84	53°26'N	14°33'E

T

Place	Page	Latitude	Longitude
Tabasco, state, Mex.	76	18°00'N	98°00'W
Tabora, Tanzania	90	5°01'S	32°49'E
Tabriz, Iran	96	38°05'N	46°15'E
Tacna, Peru	78	18°02'S	70°15'W
Tacoma, WA	50	47°15'N	122°27'W
Tademait Plat., plateau	91	28°00'N	5°00'E
Tagus, river	85	40°00'N	8°00'E
Tahat, peak	91	24°00'N	5°00'E
Tahiti, island	103	18°00'S	149°00'W
Tahoe, L., lake	54	39°00'N	120°00'W
Taipei, Taiwan	96	25°04'N	121°33'E
Taiwan, country	96	24°00'N	121°00'E
Taiwan, island	97	24°00'N	121°00'E
Taiyuan, China	96	37°55'N	112°36'E
Tajikistan, country	96	39°00'N	71°00'E
Taklimakan Desert, desert	97	39°00'N	81°00'E
Talca, Chile	78	35°26'S	71°38'W
Tallahassee, FL	51	30°26'N	84°17'W
Tallinn, Estonia	84	59°24'N	24°44'E
Tamale, Ghana	90	9°24'N	0°50'W
Tamanrasset, Algeria	90	22°46'N	5°32'E
Tamaulipas, state, Mex.	76	24°00'N	99°00'W
Tambov, Russia	84	52°43'N	41°26'E
Tamiahua Lagoon, bay	77	22°00'N	97°00'W
Tampa, FL	51	27°57'N	82°28'W
Tampa Bay, bay	55	28°00'N	83°00'W
Tampere, Finland	84	61°29'N	23°47'E
Tampico, Mexico	76	22°12'N	97°51'W
Tana, L., lake	91	12°00'N	38°00'E
Tanga, Tanzania	90	5°04'S	39°06'E
Tanganyika, L., lake	91	8°00'S	30°00'E
Tangier, Morocco	90	35°47'N	5°48'W
Tanzania, country	90	5°00'S	32°00'E
Tapachula, Mexico	76	14°54'N	92°15'W
Tapajós, river	79	5°00'S	57°00'W
Taranto, Italy	84	40°28'N	17°15'E
Taranto, G. of, gulf	85	39°00'N	19°00'E
Tarawa, island	103	1°00'N	173°00'E
Tarawa (Bairiki), Kiribati	102	1°19'N	172°58'E
Tarija, Bolivia	78	21°33'S	64°43'W
Tarim Basin, basin	97	40°00'N	83°00'E
Tartu, Estonia	84	58°22'N	26°42'E
Tashkent, Uzbekistan	96	41°14'N	69°16'E
Tasmania, island	103	42°00'S	147°00'E
Tasmania, state, Austl.	102	42°00'S	147°00'E
Tasman Sea, sea	103	38°00'S	159°00'E
Tatnam, C., cape	75	58°00'N	89°00'W
Taupo, L., lake	103	39°00'S	176°00'E
Taxco, Mexico	76	18°32'N	99°36'W
Taymyr Pen., peninsula	97	74°00'N	96°00'E
Tbilisi, Georgia	84	41°41'N	44°47'E
Tegucigalpa, Honduras	44	14°06'N	87°12'W
Tehran, Iran	96	35°41'N	51°26'E
Tehuacán, Mexico	76	18°28'N	97°24'W
Tehuantepec, G. of, gulf	77	15°00'N	95°00'W
Tehuantepec, Isth. of, isthmus	77	17°00'N	95°00'W
Tejupan, Pt., cape	77	18°00'N	104°00'W
Teles Pires, river	79	10°00'S	56°00'W
Temuco, Chile	78	38°44'S	72°36'W
Ténéré, region	91	19°00'N	12°00'E
Tennessee, river	55	35°00'N	86°00'W
Tennessee, state, U.S.	51	36°00'N	87°00'W
Tepic, Mexico	76	21°28'N	104°52'W
Teresina, Brazil	78	5°03'S	42°47'W
Términos Lagoon, bay	77	19°00'N	92°00'W
Tete, Mozambique	90	16°11'S	33°35'E
Texas, state, U.S.	50	31°00'N	99°00'W
Thabana Ntlenyana, peak	91	29°00'S	29°00'E
Thailand, country	96	16°00'N	102°00'E
Thailand, G. of, gulf	97	8°00'N	103°00'E
Thar Desert, desert	97	25°00'N	71°00'E
Thelon, river	75	64°00'N	104°00'W
The Pas, Canada	74	53°47'N	101°16'W
Thessaloniki, Greece	84	40°39'N	22°57'E
Thimphu, Bhutan	96	27°27'N	89°39'E
Thohoyandou, S. Africa	90	22°55'S	30°28'E
Thompson, Canada	74	55°44'N	97°51'W
Thunder Bay, Canada	74	48°26'N	89°14'W
Thurston I., island	15	72°00'S	100°00'W
Tianjin, China	96	39°07'N	117°10'E
Tian Shan, mountains	97	42°00'N	80°00'E
Tibesti Mts., mountains	91	21°00'N	19°00'E
Tibet, Plat. of, plateau	97	34°00'N	90°00'E
Tiburón I., island	77	29°00'N	113°00'W
Tierra del Fuego, island	79	54°00'S	68°00'W
Tigris, river	97	37°00'N	44°00'E
Tijuana, Mexico	76	32°31'N	117°03'W
Timan Ridge, highlands	85	66°00'N	50°00'E
Timisoara, Romania	84	45°46'N	21°14'E
Timmins, Canada	74	48°28'N	81°19'W
Timor, island	97	9°00'S	125°00'E
Timor Sea, sea	97	13°00'S	127°00'E
Tirana, Albania	84	41°20'N	19°49'E
Tisza, river	85	46°00'N	20°00'E
Titicaca, L., lake	79	16°00'S	69°00'W
Tizimín, Mexico	76	21°09'N	88°09'W
Tlaxcala, Mexico	76	19°19'N	98°14'W
Tlaxcala, state, Mex.	76	19°00'N	98°00'W
Toamasina, Madagascar	90	18°10'S	49°22'E
Tobruk, Libya	90	32°05'N	23°57'E
Tocantins, river	79	10°00'S	49°00'W
Togo, country	90	9°00'N	1°00'E
Tokelau Is., dependency, N.Z.	102	9°00'S	172°00'W
Tokelau Is., islands	103	9°00'S	172°00'W
Tokyo, Japan	96	35°40'N	139°45'E
Tolanaro, Madagascar	90	25°02'S	46°59'E
Toledo, OH	51	41°40'N	83°33'W
Toliara, Madagascar	90	23°21'S	43°39'E
Toluca, Mexico	76	19°18'N	99°39'W
Tombigbee, river	55	34°00'N	89°00'W
Tombouctou, Mali	90	16°45'N	3°02'W
Tomsk, Russia	96	56°28'N	84°59'E
Tonalá, Mexico	76	16°03'N	93°44'W
Tonga, country	102	20°00'S	175°00'W
Tonga, islands	103	20°00'S	175°00'W
Tongareva Is., islands	103	10°00'S	158°00'W
Toowoomba, Australia	102	27°34'S	151°59'E
Topeka, KS	51	39°03'N	95°41'W
Tornio, river	85	68°00'N	21°00'E
Toronto, Canada	74	43°39'N	79°23'W
Torreón, Mexico	76	25°32'N	103°27'W
Torres Str., strait	103	10°00'S	142°00'E
Touggourt, Algeria	90	33°07'N	6°04'E
Toulon, France	84	43°08'N	5°57'E
Toulouse, France	84	43°36'N	1°28'E
Tours, France	84	47°24'N	0°41'E
Townsville, Australia	102	19°17'S	146°48'E
Trail, Canada	74	49°06'N	117°44'W
Transantarctic Mts., mountains	15	86°00'S	180°00'
Transcaucasia, region	85	42°00'N	45°00'E
Transylvanian Alps, mountains	85	46°00'N	23°00'E
Trenton, NJ	51	40°13'N	74°45'W
Trinidad, Bolivia	78	14°50'S	64°54'W
Trinidad, island	45	11°00'N	61°00'W
Trinidad and Tobago, country	44	11°00'N	61°00'W
Trinity, river	55	32°00'N	96°00'W
Tripoli, Libya	90	32°53'N	13°11'E
Tripolitania, region	91	30°00'N	14°00'E
Trois-Rivières, Canada	74	46°21'N	72°33'W
Tromsø, Norway	84	69°39'N	18°55'E
Trondheim, Norway	84	63°25'N	10°26'E
Trujillo, Peru	78	8°08'S	79°01'W
Truro, Canada	74	45°21'N	63°16'W
Tshikapa, Dem. Rep. of Congo	90	6°23'S	20°52'E
Tsimlyansk Res., lake	85	48°00'N	43°00'E
Tsumeb, Namibia	90	19°15'S	17°41'E
Tuamotu Arch., islands	103	17°00'S	141°00'W
Tucson, AZ	50	32°13'N	110°56'W
Tula, Russia	84	54°15'N	37°36'E
Tulsa, OK	51	36°09'N	96°00'W
Tumbes, Peru	78	3°35'S	80°26'W
Tunis, Tunisia	90	36°49'N	10°11'E
Tunisia, country	90	34°00'N	9°00'E
Turin, Italy	84	45°05'N	7°41'E
Turkana, L., lake	91	4°00'N	36°00'E
Turkey, country	96	38°00'N	36°00'E
Turkey, country	84	41°00'N	20°00'E
Turkmenistan, country	96	39°00'N	55°00'E
Turks and Caicos Is., dependency, (U.K.)	44	21°44'N	71°35'W
Turku, Finland	84	60°28'N	22°16'E
Tuvalu, country	102	8°00'S	178°00'E
Tuvalu, islands	103	8°00'S	178°00'E
Tuxpan, Mexico	76	20°57'N	97°26'W
Tuxtepec, Mexico	76	18°06'N	96°07'W
Tuxtla Gutiérrez, Mexico	76	16°45'N	93°05'W
Tver', Russia	84	56°54'N	35°53'E
Tyrrhenian Sea, sea	85	41°00'N	12°00'E

U

Place	Page	Latitude	Longitude
Ubangi, river	91	4°00'N	18°00'E
Uberlândia, Brazil	78	18°55'S	48°13'W
Ucayali, river	79	6°00'S	75°00'W
Uganda, country	90	2°00'N	31°00'E
Ukhta, Russia	84	63°36'N	53°51'E
Ukraine, country	84	49°00'N	29°00'E
Ulaanbaatar, Mongolia	96	47°56'N	106°53'E
Ulan-Ude, Russia	96	51°49'N	107°36'E
Ul'yanovsk, Russia	84	54°18'N	48°17'E
Umeå, Sweden	84	63°50'N	20°15'E
Umtata, S. Africa	90	31°33'S	28°42'E
Ungava Bay, bay	75	59°00'N	69°00'W
Ungava Pen., peninsula	75	60°00'N	74°00'W
United Arab Emirates, country	96	24°00'N	53°00'E
United Kingdom, country	84	54°00'N	0°00'
United States, country	44	39°00'N	98°00'W
Upper Pen., peninsula	55	46°00'N	87°00'W
Uppsala, Sweden	84	59°52'N	17°39'E
Ural, river	97	54°00'N	59°00'E
Ural Mts., mountains	85	54°00'N	59°00'E
Uruapan, Mexico	76	19°25'N	102°04'W
Uruguay, country	78	33°00'S	55°00'W
Uruguay, river	79	29°00'S	55°00'W
Ürümqi, China	96	43°47'N	87°37'E
Ushuaia, Argentina	78	54°47'S	68°15'W
Ustyurt Plat., plateau	97	44°00'N	56°00'E
Usumacinta, river	77	18°00'N	92°00'W
Utah, state, U.S.	50	39°00'N	112°00'W
Uzbekistan, country	96	42°00'N	69°00'E

V

Place	Page	Latitude	Longitude
Vaal, river	91	25°00'S	27°00'E
Vaasa, Finland	84	63°06'N	21°39'E
Valdai Hills, highlands	85	57°00'N	32°00'E
Valdés Pen., peninsula	79	43°00'S	64°00'W
Valdivia, Chile	78	39°47'S	73°13'W
Val-d'Or, Canada	74	48°07'N	77°47'W
Valencia, Spain	84	39°29'N	0°21'W
Valencia, Venezuela	78	10°11'N	67°58'W
Valera, Venezuela	78	9°19'N	70°38'W
Valladolid, Mexico	76	20°41'N	88°12'W
Valladolid, Spain	84	41°39'N	4°43'W
Valletta, Malta	84	35°54'N	14°31'E
Valparaíso, Chile	78	33°02'S	71°38'W
Vancouver, Canada	74	49°15'N	123°07'W
Vancouver I., island	75	49°00'N	127°00'W
Vänern, lake	85	59°00'N	13°00'E
Vanua Levu, island	103	16°00'S	179°00'E
Vanuatu, country	102	17°00'S	167°00'E
Varna, Bulgaria	84	43°12'N	27°55'E
Vatican City, country	84	42°00'N	12°00'E
Vatnajökull, glacier	85	67°00'N	16°00'W
Vättern, lake	85	58°00'N	14°00'E
Velikiy Novgorod, Russia	84	58°32'N	31°14'E
Venezuela, country	78	8°00'N	66°00'W
Venice, Italy	84	45°26'N	12°20'E
Veracruz, Mexico	76	19°09'N	96°08'W
Veracruz, state, Mex.	76	18°00'N	96°00'W
Verde, river	54	35°00'N	112°00'W
Verde, river	77	20°00'N	98°00'W
Verkhoyansk Range, mountains	97	65°00'N	130°00'E
Vermont, state, U.S.	51	44°00'N	73°00'W
Verona, Italy	84	45°26'N	11°00'E
Vert, Cap, cape	91	14°00'N	17°00'W
Vicebsk, Belarus	84	55°13'N	30°13'E
Victoria, Canada	74	48°26'N	123°22'W
Victoria, Seychelles	90	4°37'S	55°27'E
Victoria, state, Austl.	102	37°00'S	145°00'E
Victoria Falls, falls	91	19°00'S	26°00'E
Victoria I., island	75	72°00'N	109°00'W
Victoria L., lake	91	1°00'S	33°00'E
Viedma, Argentina	78	40°51'S	62°59'W
Vienna, Austria	84	48°13'N	16°22'E
Vientiane, Laos	96	17°58'N	102°38'E
Vietnam, country	96	14°00'N	109°00'E
Vigo, Spain	84	42°13'N	8°44'W
Villa Ahumada, Mexico	76	30°37'N	106°30'W
Villahermosa, Mexico	76	17°59'N	92°55'W
Vilnius, Lithuania	84	54°41'N	25°16'E
Vinson Massif, mountains	15	78°00'S	88°00'W
Virginia, state, U.S.	51	38°00'N	77°00'W
Virginia Beach, VA	51	36°51'N	75°59'W
Virgin Is., dependency, U.S./U.K.	44	18°00'N	65°00'W
Viscount Melville Sound, strait	75	75°00'N	108°00'W
Vistula, river	85	53°00'N	19°00'E
Viti Levu, island	103	18°00'S	178°00'E
Vitória, Brazil	78	20°18'S	40°19'W
Vitória da Conquista, Brazil	78	14°51'S	40°50'W
Vizcaíno Desert, desert	77	27°00'N	114°00'W
Vladivostok, Russia	96	43°08'N	131°55'E
Volcán Misti, peak	79	16°00'S	72°00'W
Volga, river	85	57°00'N	35°00'E
Volga Delta, delta	85	46°00'N	48°00'E
Volga-Don Canal, canal	85	48°00'N	43°00'E
Volga Upland, highlands	85	52°00'N	46°00'E
Volgograd, Russia	84	48°45'N	44°30'E
Volgograd Res., lake	85	52°00'N	46°00'E
Volta, L., lake	91	8°00'N	0°00'
Volta Redonda, Brazil	78	22°28'S	44°04'W
Voronezh, Russia	84	51°36'N	39°24'E
Vychegda, river	85	62°00'N	47°00'E

W

Place	Page	Latitude	Longitude
Wabash, river	55	39°00'N	88°00'W
Waco, TX	50	31°33'N	97°09'W
Waddington, Mt., peak	75	52°00'N	126°00'W
Wake I., dependency, U.S.	102	19°00'N	167°00'E
Wake I., island	103	19°00'N	167°00'E
Wales, division, U.K.	84	52°00'N	3°00'W
Wallachia, region	85	45°00'N	24°00'E
Wallis and Futuna, dependency, Fr.	102	13°00'S	176°00'W
Wallis and Futuna, islands	103	13°00'S	176°00'W
Walvis Bay, Namibia	90	22°57'S	14°32'E
Warrego, river	103	27°00'S	145°00'E
Warsaw, Poland	84	52°15'N	20°59'E
Wasatch Range, mountains	54	40°00'N	111°00'W
Washington, DC	51	38°54'N	77°02'W
Washington, state, U.S.	50	46°00'N	121°00'W
Washington, Mt., peak	55	44°00'N	71°00'W
Watson Lake, Canada	74	60°09'N	128°46'W
Wau, Sudan	90	7°42'N	28°00'E
Wawa, Canada	74	47°59'N	84°45'W
Webi Jubba, river	91	5°00'N	42°00'E
Weddell Sea, sea	15	73°00'S	45°00'W
Wellesley Is., islands	103	16°00'S	140°00'E
Wellington, New Zealand	102	41°16'S	174°47'E
Weser, river	85	52°00'N	9°00'E
West Cape Howe, cape	103	35°00'S	118°00'E
West Dvina, river	85	55°00'N	25°00'E
Western Australia, state, Austl.	102	24°00'S	119°00'E
Western Ghats, mountains	97	13°00'N	75°00'E
Western Plat., plateau	103	25°00'S	125°00'E
Western Sahara, disputed territory, Mor.	90	25°00'N	15°00'W
West Ice Shelf, ice shelf	15	66°00'S	83°00'E
West Indies, islands	14	19°00'N	79°00'W
West Palm Beach, FL	51	26°43'N	80°03'W
West Siberian Plain, plateau	97	61°00'N	79°00'E
West Virginia, state, U.S.	51	39°00'N	105...
Wheeler Peak, peak	54	37°00'N	105...
Wheeling, WV	51	40°04'N	80...
White, river	55	35°00'N	91...
White, river	55	39°00'N	87...
White, river	54	44°00'N	101...
Whitecourt, Canada	74	54°07'N	115...
Whitehorse, Canada	74	60°44'N	135...
White Mts., mountains	55	45°00'N	71...
White Nile, river	91	12°00'N	32...
White Sea, sea	85	66°00'N	36...
Whitney, Mt., peak	54	37°00'N	119...
Wholdaia L., lake	75	62°00'N	105...
Whyalla, Australia	102	33°01'S	137...
Wichita, KS	50	37°42'N	97...
Wilhelm, Mt., peak	103	6°00'S	145...
Wilkes Land, region	15	70°00'S	120...
Williams Lake, Canada	74	52°09'N	122...
Williston L., lake	75	56°00'N	125...
Wilmington, DE	51	39°45'N	75...
Windhoek, Namibia	90	22°33'S	17...
Windsor, Canada	74	42°18'N	83...
Windward Is., islands	45	14°00'N	61...
Winisk, river	75	55°00'N	88...
Winnipeg, Canada	74	49°54'N	97...
Winnipeg, L., lake	75	53°00'N	98...
Winnipegosis, L., lake	75	53°00'N	100...
Winston-Salem, NC	51	36°06'N	80...
Wisconsin, river	55	45°00'N	90...
Wisconsin, state, U.S.	51	44°00'N	89...
Wollaston L., lake	75	58°00'N	104...
Wollongong, Australia	102	34°24'S	150...
Woods, L. of the, lake	55	49°00'N	95...
Worcester, MA	51	42°16'N	71...
Wrangel I., island	97	71°00'N	18...
Wrath, C., cape	85	58°00'N	5...
Wrocław, Poland	84	51°06'N	17...
Wuhan, China	96	30°32'N	114...
Wyndham, Australia	102	15°29'S	128...
Wyoming, state, U.S.	50	43°00'N	10...

X

Place	Page	Latitude	Longitude
Xai-Xai, Mozambique	90	25°03'S	33...
Xalapa, Mexico	76	19°32'N	96...
Xi, river	97	24°00'N	110...
Xi'an, China	96	34°17'N	108...
Xingu, river	79	7°00'S	52...

Y

Place	Page	Latitude	Longitude
Yablonovyy Range, mountains	97	53°00'N	115...
Yakutsk, Russia	96	62°04'N	129...
Yamoussoukro, Côte d'Ivoire	90	6°45'N	5...
Yangon (Rangoon), Myanmar	96	16°49'N	96...
Yaoundé, Cameroon	90	3°52'N	11...
Yaqui, river	77	28°00'N	110...
Yaren, Nauru	102	0°31'S	166...
Yarmouth, Canada	74	43°48'N	66...
Yaroslavl', Russia	84	57°36'N	39...
Yazoo, river	55	33°00'N	90...
Yekaterinburg, Russia	96	56°51'N	60...
Yellowknife, Canada	74	62°29'N	114...
Yellow Sea, sea	97	34°00'N	123...
Yellowstone, river	54	46°00'N	108...
Yellowstone L., lake	54	44°00'N	110...
Yemen, country	96	15°00'N	49...
Yenisey, river	97	67°00'N	88...
Yerevan, Armenia	84	40°04'N	44...
Yokohama, Japan	96	35°27'N	139...
York, C., cape	103	11°00'S	142...
Yorkton, Canada	74	51°12'N	102...
Yucatán, state, Mex.	76	21°00'N	89...
Yucatán Channel, strait	77	22°00'N	86...
Yucatán Pen., peninsula	77	19°00'N	89...
Yukon, river	45	65°00'N	150...
Yukon Terr., territory, Can.	74	65°00'N	135...
Yuma, AZ	50	32°44'N	114...
Yumen, China	96	39°52'N	97...

Z

Place	Page	Latitude	Longitude
Zacatecas, Mexico	76	22°46'N	102...
Zacatecas, state, Mex.	76	24°00'N	103...
Zagreb, Croatia	84	45°49'N	15...
Zagros Mts., mountains	97	30°00'S	53...
Zambezi, river	91	16°00'S	32...
Zambia, country	90	15°00'S	25...
Zanzibar, Tanzania	90	6°10'S	39...
Zanzibar I., island	91	6°00'S	39...
Zaporizhzhia, Ukraine	84	47°44'N	35...
Zapotitlán, Pt., cape	77	19°00'N	95...
Zaragoza, Spain	84	41°39'N	0...
Zaria, Nigeria	90	11°06'N	7...
Zeil, Mt., peak	103	23°00'S	133...
Zhengzhou, China	96	34°47'N	113...
Zimbabwe, country	90	19°00'S	29...
Zinder, Niger	90	13°48'N	9...
Zürich, Switzerland	84	47°23'N	8...

Abbreviations

Arch.	Archipelago	Den.	Denmark	Gr.	Greece	N. Korea	North Korea	S. Africa	South A...
Austl.	Australia	Dominican Rep.	Dominican Republic	I.	Island	N.Z.	New Zealand	S. Korea	South K...
Bos. & Her.	Bosnia & Herzegovina	fed. dist.	Federal District	Is.	Islands	Pen.	Peninsula	Sp.	Sp...
C.	Cape	Fed.	Federated States of Micronesia	Isth.	Isthmus	Plat.	Plateau	St., St-	S...
Cen. African Rep.	Central African Republic	Fr.	France	It.	Italy	Pt.	Point	Ste., Ste-	
Czech Rep.	Czech Republic	Ft.	Fort	L.	Lake	R.	River	Str.	
Dem. Rep. of Congo	Democratic Republic of Congo	F.Y.R. Macedonia	Former Yugoslav Republic of Macedonia	Liecht.	Liechtenstein	Rep.	Republic	Terr.	Terr...
				Mex.	Mexico	Rep. of the Congo	Republic of the Congo	U.K.	United Kingd...
		G.	Gulf	Mor.	Morocco	Res.	Reservoir	U.S.	United S...
				Mt.	Mount	Russ.	Russia	Val.	
				Mts.	Mountains	Serb. & Mont.	Serbia and Montenegro		
				Mtn.	Mountain				
				Neth.	Netherlands				

For U.S. two-letter state abbreviations, see pages 52–53.